Learn at Home
Grade K

From the Editors of American Education Publishing

Table of Contents

Welcome!

Congratulations on your decision to educate at home! Perhaps you are a bit nervous or overwhelmed by the task ahead of you. *Learn at Home* will give you the guidance you need to provide your child with the best kindergarten education possible. However, this book is only a guide. You are encouraged to supplement your child's kindergarten curriculum with other books, activities and resources that suit your situation and your child's interests.

Create an inviting learning environment for your child. It should be comfortable and attractive, yet a place in which your child can work without distractions. Your child's work area should include a desk or table for your child, a chalkboard or dry-erase board, an easel, appropriate writing and art materials, a cozy area for reading (perhaps with pillows or a bean bag chair), a bulletin board for displaying work and shelves for books and storage. Collect blocks or other building toys, old magazines and a variety of small manipulatives for various activities. Hang a clock and a calendar in the room as well.

The Learn at Home Series

The Learn at Home series is an easy-to-use resource guide for parents who have chosen to teach their children at home. It includes an introductory section called **Background Information and Supporting Activities** with general information and activity ideas. This section is followed by 36 weeks of instruction in six curricular areas: Reading, Language, Math, Science, Social Studies and Gross/Fine Motor Skills. Each week is then further divided into three sections: **Lesson Plans, Teaching Suggestions and Activities** and **Activity Sheets**.

Each week's **Lesson Plan** includes lesson and activity suggestions for all six curricular areas. The lesson plans are brief, but further explanation is provided in the **Teaching Suggestions and Activities** section.

The **Teaching Suggestions and Activities** section provides helpful background information in each curricular area and lists the materials, supplies and books needed for the week's lessons and activities. This section also provides more detailed directions for activities listed in the **Lesson Plans**, as well as a variety of related activities.

Activity Sheets immediately follow each week's lesson plan. The sheets are grouped by subject and in the order in which they appear in the lesson plans. Activity Sheets are highlighted by bold print in the **Lesson Plans** and **Teaching Suggestions and Activities** sections.

Background Information and Supporting Activities

LANGUAGE

Language skills are largely an extension of reading skills used in everyday situations. Your child takes what he/she has learned from reading and applies that knowledge to other areas of life. As a teacher and parent, there are many ways you can foster that transfer of skills. Some suggestions are listed below.

▶ POETRY AND MUSIC

Introduce your child to the world of poetry—to the rhythms and words of poetic language. Teach your child to listen for and name the rhyming words in a poem or even to complete a poem with a word that rhymes. Guide him/her to not only complete poems but to write simple poetry as well. Instill in your child an appreciation for this literary art form.

Music is closely related to poetry. Try to make music a regular part of your child's day. Create songs and movements to help your child learn something new or to help him/her recall something already learned. Use music as a signal for changing activities or to indicate that it is time for a rest or a snack. Check out audio tapes and CD's from your local library for the enjoyment of the whole family.

▶ LISTENING/CONVERSING

Teach your child to maintain good eye contact. By paying careful attention to what is being said, your child will not only learn more but will develop the skill of being a good conversationalist as well. Teach your child that it is proper etiquette to listen carefully when another person is talking. Explain that it is poor etiquette to talk with one's mouth full, to interrupt and to finish other people's sentences for them. Listen to your child, and in family or other settings, provide your child with ample opportunity for conversation.

▶ FOLLOWING DIRECTIONS

Give your child short two- or three-step directions. After he/she successfully completes these, give him/her four-step directions. Following directions requires good listening skills, so if your child is unable to follow even simple directions, make sure that you have his/her attention first. You know your child best; adapt the skills presented in this book to his/her level. You may want to write multi-step directions in picture form or create a jingle, incorporating key words in the directions.

▶THINKING

Children love riddles, jokes and tongue twisters. Use these word games to develop your child's thinking skills. Have your child make up his/her own story and tell it while being videotaped. Further foster your child's creativity by asking him/her to tell a story while you write it down. Then, have him/her illustrate each page and make a book.

READING

The information presented below will help you guide your child in forming a sound basis in reading. At this level, your child is developing reading readiness skills. Reading readiness includes recognizing the letters of the alphabet, knowing the sounds the letters make, listening to and following a story that is read aloud and comprehending the meaning of words.

▶ALPHABET

As you work through this book with your child, you will notice that he/she is asked to recognize the letters of the alphabet—both upper- and lower-case—and to discriminate the letter in the current lesson from letters previously learned. Your child will practice writing the letters correctly and be asked to match corresponding upper- and lower-case letters of the alphabet.

▶PHONICS

An important skill developed in this book is recognizing and discriminating between the different sounds represented by the letters of the alphabet. Consonant sounds are introduced, reviewed and covered in a variety of ways. Vowel sounds are also introduced but will be covered with more emphasis at a higher grade level.

▶READING ALOUD

Reading aloud to your child will foster his/her desire to learn and read. As you read to your child, you nurture the following important skills: listening, appreciation of good literature, comprehension and critical thinking.

LISTENING

Provide an appropriate environment that will enable your child to develop good listening skills. Minimize distractions. This may mean providing quiet background music to cover distracting noises. Don't expect your child to sit and be attentive for long periods of time. Some telltale signs of distraction are squirming and loss of eye contact. When your child appears distracted, try switching to a new activity.

APPRECIATION

Read chapter books by authors of classic literature to your child. These books will provide good models of literature and should heighten your child's appreciation for a well-written story.

CRITICAL THINKING

Critical thinking can be encouraged in a number of ways: ask your child to create a new ending to a common story or have him/her be the "teacher" and ask you questions about what was read.

COMPREHENSION

Before reading an informative book, tell your child what to listen for. This helps focus your child's listening and will help him/her recall important details. It is very important to begin with this preparation, or introduction, each time a new story is presented. Follow the story with some basic questions to check your child's comprehension. Use these questions to determine if your child understands the vocabulary from the story and is able to follow the storyline. If your child is unable to recall important details from the story, you may need to reread a paragraph or page from the selection.

Explore the differences between fantasy and reality. After listening to a story, your child should be able to tell whether the events really could have happened or if they were "pretend" or imaginary. Your child will have a better grasp of the concept if you ask him/her to give examples of how he/she knew it was fantasy *(Dogs don't drive cars)* or reality *(We go to the grocery store, too)*.

Sequencing story events or simple events in his/her daily life is a good indication of whether or not your child is comprehending. After reading a book, have your child look back through the pictures and retell the story.

MATH

Math is an integral part of a young child's world. In the math lessons presented, you will teach your child math topics ranging from very basic concepts to higher-level skills. A wide range of activities is presented, much of which may serve only as an introduction for your child. Once again, let your child's interests and abilities guide your lesson planning.

SHAPES

Your child will learn to recognize five basic shapes: circle, square, rectangle, triangle and star. Children see shapes in the world around them. Capitalize on this by pointing out different shapes in your home or in the world at large. Your child will see how these five basic shapes are associated with real objects. He/she will practice making these shapes in a variety of ways.

▶NUMBERS

Skills presented in this section range from recognizing and counting numbers from 1–100 to counting by tens. Your child will also learn the correct formation of numerals and learn to see the relationship between a numeral and that same number of objects. Help your child learn the concept of "sets" by asking him/her to use manipulatives to form a specified set. Your child will also learn the concept of ordinal numbers. The ordinal numbers are introduced, as well as the ordinal number words *first* through *tenth*.

▶ADDITION/SUBTRACTION

Lessons are provided throughout this book to introduce your child to addition and subtraction using manipulatives, number lines and a variety of resource books. The suggestions given will help you reinforce these concepts. As with any skill, you may find it necessary at times to provide additional activities for further practice and/or reinforcement.

▶SEQUENCE

Each day has a logical sequence. Sequence is introduced and reinforced through activities which may be familiar to your child. Talk with your child about things that happen during the day, in the order that they normally occur. Help him/her understand this concept by associating it with something he/she has experienced.

▶BASIC CONCEPTS

While the concepts of *beside, behind, between, above* and *below* may seem clear to an adult, children need to build these spatial concepts. Help your child grasp these concepts by providing manipulatives for him/her to place in various positions. Provide further practice by asking your child to place him/herself beside or behind something or to describe where he/she is in relation to other objects.

Spatial concepts are based in language, but quantitative concepts, such as *full, empty, less* or *more*, are based in mathematics. Your child may understand these terms as they relate to him/her, but the mathematical ideas may be harder to grasp.

▶MEASURING/ESTIMATING/MONEY

Your child probably understands the idea of *more/less*, the concept of an *approximate number* and the concept of *full*. This book provides lessons to introduce and reinforce these concepts, but you can also do this by walking through a grocery store or by looking at the fruit in a bowl on your table. Simple fractions are introduced, then applied to your child's world. Graphs are presented as a way of organizing information. The concept of money is not new but using it may be. Your child will learn to recognize a penny and to count pennies to "buy" things.

SCIENCE

While all the skills presented in this book are important life skills, those taught in science provide a way for your child to understand the physical world around him/her. Your child will learn to look at things critically and to build on those observations.

▶ VISUAL DISCRIMINATION/OBSERVATION

Your child will learn to not only notice things in the world but to look for changes in given objects and to observe and describe differences among objects.

▶ COMPARING/CONTRASTING AND CLASSIFYING

Help foster your child's ability to observe similarities and differences among objects—first, obvious differences and similarities, then more subtle differences and similarities. Organizing objects into groups with similar properties (classifying) can be done in many ways. For example, have your child group a set of objects by color, then by size, or ask him/her to list similarities and differences between two pets or two friends.

▶ QUESTIONING/PREDICTING

When your child asks questions, help him/her find the answers by guiding him/her to appropriate reference materials or by asking related questions. Help your child make a connection between inventors/scientists and their accomplishments. How did they impact human culture? Use the activities in this book as a springboard to more investigations, guiding your child to become a thinker.

▶ ANALYZING

As your child analyzes the results of simple experiments, help guide him/her to basic conclusions. If the results of an experiment cause your child to ask more questions, help him/her design a second experiment to help answer those questions.

▶ CHARTING

In this book, your child will be introduced to charts. This form of record-keeping presents an interesting and very practical way of analyzing information. Your child may enjoy charting the weather each day or comparing the results of experiments. While you may be the one writing the information on some of the charts, allow your child to provide you with the information or to create pictorial charts him/herself.

SOCIAL STUDIES

A child's perceptions of him/herself and the surrounding world are influenced by Social Studies skills. These skills are an important part of your child's education—not only for your child but for others in his/her community as well. How a child sees and interprets his/her social environment can greatly enhance or detract from his/her behavior. The Social Studies lessons in this book focus on helping your child learn about people in his/her immediate surroundings, as well as studying children and families in other parts of the world.

▶TAKING CARE OF ME

Your child will be introduced to personal safety issues that affect him/her in the home as well as in the neighborhood. Introduce or reinforce your child's knowledge of good nutrition and, at the same time, help your child make wise choices in his/her diet. Teach good health habits so that your child sees the importance of keeping his/her body healthy. Convey to your child that he/she is special.

▶DEVELOPING FRIENDSHIPS

Teach your child by example how to interact with others, whether in the family or in the surrounding community (teams, clubs, church and play groups). Your child should learn—then practice—courtesy. If he/she is taught to treat others the way he/she would like to be treated, your child will build many friendships. Encourage your child to invite friends over to your home. This is a great opportunity to practice courtesy and to teach your child to share. You will have the chance to evaluate, then reteach, if necessary, any of those skills.

▶MANNERS/RESPONSIBILITY

Help build your child's character by teaching (again, by example) good manners. Take time at the dinner table to practice and reinforce manners; an unprompted please or thank you will be your reward. Help your child realize that we all have responsibilities, both to ourselves and to others.

▶CARING FOR MY WORLD

Teach your child to be environmentally responsible. Encourage him/her to participate in community activities that focus on taking care of the world. Discuss ways in which he/she can make a difference, such as recycling, conserving resources, picking up litter, etc.

▶CHILDREN OF THE WORLD

Help your child develop an attitude of acceptance of others. Read about and discuss people from other parts of the United States and the world and learn about foreign customs and traditions. Help your child realize that people are to be respected though they may look or sound different or do things in a different way.

▶GREAT AMERICANS

Help your child develop an appreciation for important leaders, such as George Washington, Abraham Lincoln and Martin Luther King, Jr. Help your child realize that problems and adversity do not necessarily mean failure.

GROSS/FINE MOTOR SKILLS

Developing gross and fine motor skills is important to your child's physical development and reading/writing skills. Many people—both adults and children—learn by doing, so what may seem like "play" may help your child internalize a lesson or skill.

▶DEVELOPING GROSS MOTOR SKILLS

The movement of the large muscle groups is considered gross motor activity. Activities such as jogging, swimming, dancing, a variety of sports and exercise use the body's large muscles. Your child will develop gross motor skills as he/she learns to skip or act out a poem. Simply taking a walk not only allows your child to observe the world but also provides healthy exercise as well.

▶DEVELOPING FINE MOTOR SKILLS

Many activities in this book require your child to use the body's small muscle groups to accomplish tasks such as tracing, cutting, writing, folding and using building blocks. These are fine motor skills. Encourage your child to keep working on these skills even though they may be difficult at first. As these small muscles develop, both of you will see improvement in your child's skill level.

	Reading	**Language**	**Math**
Monday	**B, b** Sing the alphabet song. Stress the letter *b* so your child will notice where it comes in the alphabet. Then, spray shaving cream on a tray or tabletop and spread it out evenly. Using your finger, make upper- and lower-case letter *b*'s. Have your child trace over your letters, then make his/her own. *See* Reading, Week 1, number 1.	Begin a discussion with your child about what makes him/her special. Explain that he/she will make an *All About Me* book to tell all about the things that make him/her special. Let your child choose a sheet of colored construction paper for the cover, and help him/her write *All About Me* at the top. At the bottom, he/she should write *by (your child's name)* and the year. Let your child decorate the cover in any way he/she chooses.	**Shapes: Circles and Squares** Set out several circular objects, such as plates and lids, for your child to trace on a sheet of paper. Ask your child to name the shape as he/she traces. Have your child find as many circle shapes in your home as he/she can. Ask if there are any points or sides on them. Then, have your child find circle shapes outside your home. Keep a list of all the circle shapes your child finds on a chart labeled *Circles*.
Tuesday	Have your child glue beads to pieces of paper cut in the shape of an upper- and lower-case *b*. Read *The Shapes Game* by Paul Rogers. *See* Reading, Week 1, number 2. Have your child complete **Letter B, b** (p. 16).	Have your child create page 1 of his/her *All About Me* book. Ask your child to look in a mirror and describe what he/she sees—his/her eye color, hair color, freckles, glasses, etc. Then, have your child draw a self-portrait for page 1 of his/her *All About Me* book. For additional activities *see* Language, Week 1, number 1–4 Have your child complete **This Is Me** (p. 18).	Have your child look through magazines for circle shapes. Let him/her cut them out and lay them on a table. Discuss the kinds of things your child found. Add any circle shapes he/she found that are not already on the *Circles* chart. Then, let your child use the magazine pictures to create a circles collage.
Wednesday	Have your child blow up a balloon. While he/she is blowing, tell him/her the sound that the letter *b* makes. Tie the balloon. Have your child say the *b* sound along with you several times. Then, have your child look through magazines or coloring books to find letter *b* words. Have him/her cut these out and glue them to the letter *b* balloon. *See* Reading, Week 1, number 3.	Use a tape measure to show your child how to measure his/her height. Then, weigh your child. Help him/her record his/her height and weight on page 2 of the *All About Me* book. Have your child complete **Watch Me Grow** (p. 19).	Look at a TV together. Explain that it is a square. Count the four sides with your child, and help him/her discover that all four sides are the same length by measuring them with a tape measure. Have your child find five other square-shaped objects in the house. Have your child trace around them with his/her finger. Ask how many points or corners there are. *See* Math, Week 1, numbers 1–3.
Thursday	Play a *b* bubble game with your child. As you blow bubbles, challenge your child to name a *b* word before they pop. Then, let your child blow bubbles while you think of *b* words. *See* Reading, Week 1, number 4. Have your child complete **Book Bonanza** (p. 17).	*Food, food, food.* *I love grapes and peas and pears.* *Food, food, food.* *What different shapes are there?* Recite this rhyme with your child. Showing your child different foods, have him/her name each shape. Then, for page 3 of the *All About Me* book, have him/her draw his/her favorite foods. Have your child complete **My Favorite Foods** (p. 20).	Help your child create riddles using shape clues. **Example**: *I am a circle on the wall. I tell you what time it is. What am I?* (Answer: a clock) *See* Math, Week 1, numbers 4 and 5. Have your child complete **Circle and Square** (p. 22).
Friday	Have a letter *b* scavenger hunt. Give your child ten minutes to find as many letter *b* objects around the house as possible. *See* Reading, Week, 1, number 5.	For page 4 of the *All About Me* book, have your child draw a picture of his/her friends. Have your child complete **My Friends** (p. 21).	Place several round and square items in a bag. Have your child close his/her eyes and reach into the bag, pulling out an object. With his/her eyes still closed, he/she must name the shape of the object. Repeat until no more objects remain in the bag. Then, help your child make a construction paper mobile of circle- and square-shaped objects he/she has discovered throughout the week.

Science	Social Studies	Gross/Fine Motor
Autumn Read *Discover the Seasons* by Diane Iverson. As you read, discuss the pictures with your child. Ask him/her to describe different aspects of the pictures. What parts are his/her favorites? Ask what the scene would sound or smell like. *See* Science, Week 1, numbers 1–5 for additional activities. Have your child complete **The Four Seasons** (p. 23).	**All About Me** Help your child learn more about him/herself by creating a life-sized "body portrait." Have your child lie on a large sheet of butcher paper. Trace around his/her body, then cut out the outline. Have your child look in a full-length mirror and describe what he/she sees. Provide wallpaper scraps, wrapping paper, fabric, yarn, crayons and markers for your child to decorate his/her paper image. Review and label the parts of his/her body.	Teach your child how to make circles with his/her hands, arms and body while reciting this finger play: *Here is a circle,* *All smooth and round.* *Where are the sides?* *There are none to be found!* *See* Gross/Fine Motor Skills, Week 1, numbers 1–6 for additional activities.
Discuss the signs of autumn. Chant this poem: *Autumn is here; autumn is here!* *The little gray squirrels tell us that* *Autumn is here.* *Autumn is here; Autumn is here!* *The golden leaves tell us that* *Autumn is here!* *Autumn is here; Autumn is here!* *The cool breezes tell us that* *Autumn is here!*	Read *Faces* by Barbara Brenner. Discuss how all people's faces are the same in many ways, yet each person's face is unique. Give your child a rice cake on which to create an edible self-portrait. Provide cream cheese, peanut butter, carrot curls, raisins, coconut and other healthful goodies for your child to use to create his/her "face"! *See* Social Studies, Week 1, numbers 1–3. Have your child complete **All About Me** (p. 24).	Provide your child with glue, paper and toothpicks. Have your child glue toothpicks in square shapes on the paper to create a picture. When he/she has finished, ask your child to think of a title for the picture. Write the title across the top of the page.
Take a walk with your child. Discuss the signs of autumn that you see on your walk. When you return home, make a list of the signs that you saw. Challenge your child to use what you noticed on your walk to add verses to the poem "Autumn Is Here."	Show your child pictures of him/her as a baby. To show your child how he/she has changed, cut two strings—one to your child's birth length and one to his/her current length (height). Have him/her compare the two. Ask your child: *How much have you grown? How many "baby lengths" of string does it take to equal your current height?* Have your child complete **When I Was Small** (p. 25).	Have your child bounce up and down while saying: *Bouncing babies, bumblebees,* *Balloons and bubbles,* *B-B-B.* Challenge your child to say this, as many in a row as he/she can, while bouncing.
Read *Fall* by Ron Hirschi. Afterwards, go back through the story and have your child retell it.	Discuss your child's favorite foods. Ask your child: *What main dishes, snacks, drinks and desserts do you like best? Why do you like these foods?* Help your child make one of his/her favorite foods. Share memories of working together on recipes with your family while you were growing up.	Help your child create motions to go along with "Seasons Song": *Summer sizzle,* *Hot, hot, hot!* *Fall so breezy,* *Leaves that drop.* *Winter snowing,* *Brr…brr…brr!* *Springtime growing,* *Green a blur!*
Read *The Tiny Seed* by Eric Carle. Explain that new plants grow from seeds. Collect pine cones, maple wings (helicopters), acorns, and thistles. Explain how these seeds travel. Some are winged (maple wings) to help them flutter down, others are sticky or prickly (burdocks) and attach to people or animals and still others are plumed (dandelions) so the wind carries them. Open the protective cases of your seeds to see the actual seeds inside.	Ask your child to tell you about his/her special friends. Ask: *Who is your best friend? Why do you like this person? What do you and your friend(s) most like to do when you are together?* (*See* today's Language lesson.)	Make fall ornaments using seeds. Cut shapes out of poster board. Spread glue on each shape, then add seeds. Shake off any excess seeds. Use hot glue to attach a piece of jute around the edge for a hanger.

TEACHING SUGGESTIONS AND ACTIVITIES

READING (B, b)

▶ 1. Emphasize the letter of the week by including a special snack or treat that starts with *b*. Buy a pack of your child's favorite bubblegum or treat him/her to a bagel or brownie (or some other *b* food) on the first day of *B* Week.

▶ 2. Have your child glue dried beans onto a sheet of construction paper in the shape of an upper- and lower-case letter *b*.

▶ 3. Ask your child to search for pictures of objects beginning with the letter *b* in magazines and coloring books. Have your child cut out the pictures and keep them in an old billfold.

▶ 4. Read books with your child in which the main character's name starts with *B*, such as the Babar books by Jean de Brunhoff. Show your child the *b* word and help him/her sound it out. Whenever he/she sees your finger get to that word, he/she can read it by him/herself.

▶ 5. Go to the bakery with your child to buy the best treats for a "Blazing *B* Day!"

LANGUAGE

▶ 1. Obtain a copy of *Alpha-Bakery Children's Cookbook* by Gold Medal. The address is: Gold Medal Alpha-Bakery Cookbook, P.O. Box 5119, Minneapolis, MN 55460-5119. The cost is $2.00. The cookbook includes recipes, along with pictures, for each letter of the alphabet.

▶ 2. Brainstorm a list of words related to autumn. Help your child write a poem about fall, using some of the words you listed.

▶ 3. Help your child make a tongue twister using the letter *b*.

▶ 4. Read *Trees* by Peter Mellett.

MATH (Shapes: Circles and Squares)

▶ 1. Use round and square cookie cutters to cut four slices of bread. Have your child match the shapes to make a circle sandwich and a square sandwich. Fill them with your child's favorite sandwich spread and enjoy.

▶ 2. Pre-cut various sizes of circles and squares from construction paper. Have your child glue the shapes together to form a picture, such as a truck, clown or bicycle.

▶ 3. Make a shape bingo game. Cut a piece of poster board into a 9" x 9" square. Divide this square into nine 3" squares. Draw different shapes in different colors on the squares. You may use a shape or color more than once. Cut out a circle of poster board to use as the spinner. Cut out a poster board arrow and attach it to the center of the circle with a paper fastener. Divide the circle into pie segments to represent every shape and color used.

▶ 4. Play "I Spy a Shape." Choose a shape in your surroundings and give your child clues about it. Say, for example, *I spy a triangle. It is brown and filled with ice cream.* Your child will respond, *It is an ice-cream cone!*

▶ 5. Read *Bears on Wheels* by Stan and Jan Berenstain. Discuss the shape of a wheel. Ask your child to name the objects in the story that have wheels. Can he/she think of anything else that has wheels?

SCIENCE (Autumn)

1. Go to a local nursery and talk to a knowledgeable consultant about trees. Have your child prepare questions ahead of time to ask the specialist, such as *Why do leaves change color in the autumn?*

2. Visit a wildlife preserve or bird sanctuary. Enjoy autumn in a quiet, natural environment.

3. Go to the library and research the term *autumn*. What does the word *autumn* mean? Can your child guess why autumn is also called fall?

4. Start a simple leaf collection by ironing a leaf between two sheets of wax paper. Use a tree identification book to help your child identify and label the leaf. Do the same with other leaves. Keep the leaves together in a portfolio.

5. Enjoy the fun fall activities in *Get Set . . . Go! Autumn* by Ruth Thomson.

SOCIAL STUDIES (All About Me)

1. Take your child to visit the hospital where he/she was born. Look at babies together in the nursery. Talk about how you felt when your child was born.

2. Discuss how you chose your child's name. What does his/her name mean? If you don't know, look it up together in a baby book. What would your child have been named had he/she been born the opposite sex?

3. Have your child make a nameplate using play dough. It is best if he/she makes "snakes" (long coils) first, then turns them into letters. Connect the letters by overlapping them slightly and squeezing them gently together. Bake the letters at 250° until hard, then paint.

GROSS/FINE MOTOR SKILLS

1. Have your child do exercises that involve circles, such as making arm circles or jogging in a circle. How many exercises can you think of? Enjoy doing them together.

2. Play badminton, basketball, baseball or ride a bike during *B* Week.

3. Have your child think of a special way to decorate his/her bedroom for *B* Week.

4. Go to a beach during *B* Week. Take along a warm coat and enjoy the beauty of fall.

5. Weave a basket for *B* Week. You can purchase reeds for weaving at large craft stores. Basket weaving is a simple skill which your child can learn quite easily.

6. Go bird watching for *B* Week. Take your binoculars and enjoy a close look at nature.

Letter B, b

UPPER-CASE

lower-case

These pictures begin with the letter B, b. **Color** the pictures.

Learn at Home, Grade K

Book Bonanza

Color each picture which begins with the sound of B, b. **Cut out** and **glue** the B, b pictures on the book.

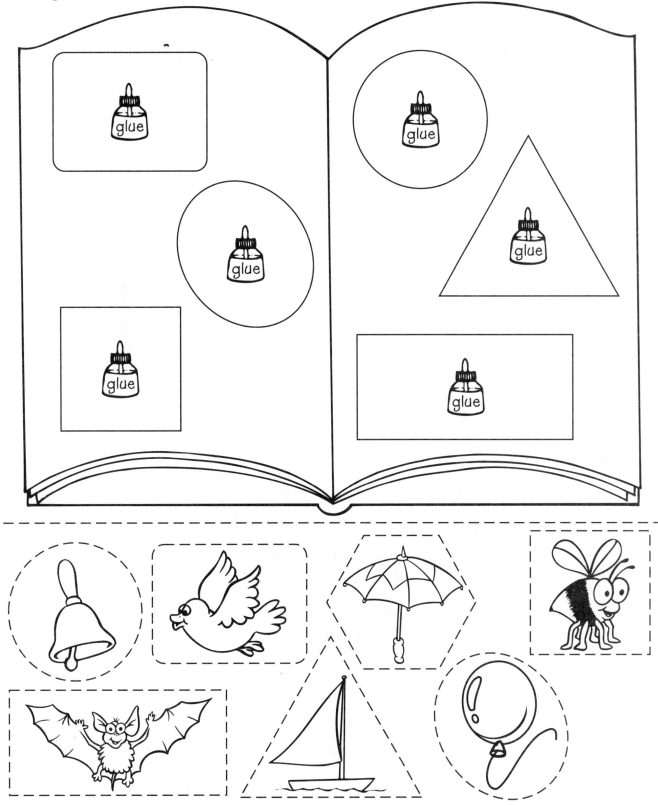

Learn at Home, Grade K

Watch Me Grow

I am growing each day!

_____

_____

I am _____ inches tall.

_____

_____

I weigh _____ pounds.

Learn at Home, Grade K

My Favorite Foods

These are my favorite foods.

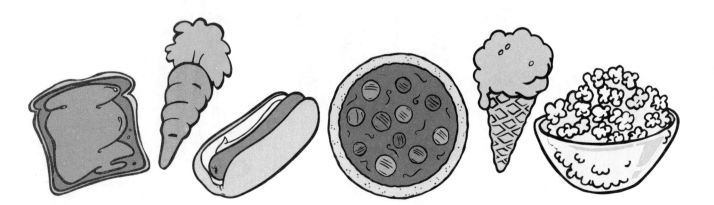

My Friends

These are my friends.

Circle and Square

Color the circle and square. **Cut out** each one and **glue** it on the matching shape.

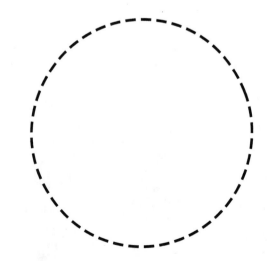

The Four Seasons

1. **Draw** a rake in the picture of fall.

2. **Draw** a sled in the picture of winter.

3. **Draw** a butterfly in the picture of spring.

4. **Draw** a swimming pool in the picture of summer.

All About Me

I have _____ hair.
(color)

I am a _____ .
(girl or boy)

My eyes are _____ .
(color)

I am _____ -handed.
(right or left)

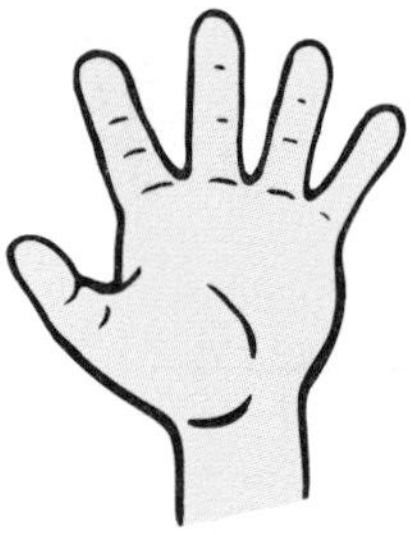

I have lost _____ teeth.
(number)

24

When I Was Small

When I was only one year old . . .

I could . . .

1.

2.

I couldn't . . .

1.

2.

I looked like this.

	Reading	Language	Math
Monday	**T, t** Roll up two towels (one large and one small) into "lines" and show your child how to form an upper- and lower-case *t*. Have your child trace the fuzzy *t*'s. Then, unroll the towels and see if your child can make his/her own towel *t*'s. *See* Reading, Week 2, numbers 1–6 for additional activities.	Sing this song to the tune of "Frère Jacques": *I am special!* *I am special!* *Can't you see?* *Can't you see?* *Everything about me* *Everything about me* *Is special as can be!*	**0 — Zero** Set out two bowls. Pour some cereal into just one of the bowls. Have your child count the number of cereal pieces in that bowl. Then, ask your child how much is in the other bowl. Explain that *nothing* or an *empty* bowl is the same as zero. *See* Math, Week 2, number 1. Have your child complete **Hungry Kittens** (p. 33).
Tuesday	Make a cup of very strong tea. Using a paintbrush dipped in the tea, let your child "paint" an upper- and lower-case letter *t* on construction paper. Explain the sound a letter *t* makes. Help your child make a list of words that begin with the letter *t*.	Teach your child the song "I'm a Little Teapot." *I'm a little teapot,* *Short and stout.* *Here is my handle,* *And here is my spout...* Sing the song several times with your child. Then, show him/her the actions that go with the song and do them together. Next, print out the words to the rhyme. Have your child circle every *t* that he/she sees. *See* Language, Week 2, number 1.	Using chocolate pudding as finger paint, write the word *zero* on a sheet of paper. Read it to your child, pointing to each letter as you sound out the word. Then, draw a big zero around the word. Have your child do the same. Let your child practice making zeros and writing the word *zero* with the pudding.
Wednesday	Set a timer for 5 minutes. Give your child clues for the following *t* words and see how many he/she can guess in 5 minutes: *tiger, tickle, tiptoe, tent, tepee, turtle, top, treat, tiny* and *tray*. Then, switch roles: have your child think of *t* words and give you hints. Have your child complete **Letter T, t** (p. 30).	For the final page of your child's *All About Me* book, have him/her draw a picture of your family. Encourage him/her to write each family member's name below his/her picture. Ask your child if he/she would like to add anything else to the *All About Me* book. Then, staple the pages of the book along the left-hand side. Let your child "read" the book to you. Have your child complete **My Family** (p. 32).	Go outside with your child. Ask him/her to bring you a specific number of objects, such as leaves, twigs or acorns. Be sure to use the number 0 frequently. **Example:** *Please bring me zero leaves.* Save the accumulated objects for tomorrow's lesson.
Thursday	Make large t-shirts out of construction paper. Using magazines and coloring books, have your child find *t* words and pictures to tape on each shirt. Have your child tell family members about each letter *t* t-shirt. Have your child complete **Tiger's T-Shirts** (p. 31).	Have your child arrange pictures from each year of his/her life in chronological order (*see* today's Social Studies lesson). Help him/her glue the pictures onto a long strip of cardboard or construction paper. Have your child write his/her age and a brief sentence under each picture. He/she can then write the caption *Watch me grow!* along the bottom of the strip.	Using the objects gathered from nature yesterday, show your child how to create simple patterns, such as *leaf, acorn, leaf, acorn. . . .* Have him/her practice creating and continuing a variety of different patterns. Save these objects for tomorrow's science activity. Have your child complete **Fall Patterns** (p. 34).
Friday	Make a construction paper tepee. Have your child trace and cut a large circle from a sheet of construction paper. Cut a slit from the center to an edge and form a cone shape. Before taping the tepee together, let your child draw or glue *t* objects on it.	Teach your child the poem "Three Little Oak Leaves." *See* Language, Week 2, number 2. Read the poem several times with your child. Then, have him/her draw pictures to go along with the poem.	Help your child make hot chocolate for a treat after a walk in the brisk autumn air. Help him/her measure 1 teaspoon of cocoa powder and 2 tablespoons of sugar into a mug. Add milk until full. Microwave for a minute and a half and top with whipped cream. Write out the recipe, emphasizing the numbers and *t*'s.

Science	Social Studies	Gross/Fine Motor
Autumn Read *Sky Tree* by Thomas Locker. Discuss the questions at the bottom of each page. Have your child complete **Dress for the Weather** (p. 35).	**All About Me** Continue your discussion about what makes your child unique. Help your child trace his/her hands onto **My Fingerprints** (p. 36). Using a stamp pad, help your child place each of his/her fingerprints at the end of each finger outline. Help him/her examine each fingerprint with a magnifying glass. Explain to your child that no one else has fingerprints exactly like his/hers!	Using chocolate and pistachio pudding as finger paints, have your child make his/her own Sky Tree.
Take a walk and observe the trees in your neighborhood. Point out the basic parts of a tree: trunk, branches, bark, leaves and roots. Explain that roots carry water and nutrients to the rest of the tree. As you move on and observe other trees, have your child name the parts. Ask your child which trees he/she likes best. Ask: *Do any of them remind you of the Sky Tree? Why?*	Share with your child any record you may have of his/her baby footprints. Ask your child how his/her baby footprints differ from his/her footprints now. Trace each of your child's feet for a page in his/her *All About Me* book. *See* Social Studies, Week 2, number 1.	Encourage your child to make up actions to accompany this poem: *Leaves flutter, trickling down.* *Squirrels scamper all around.* *Children run and jump and yell:* *Fall, fall, we love you well!* For extra fun, give your child strips of crepe paper in fall colors to use in acting out the poem.
Read the first part of *Squirrels* by Emilie U. Lepthien. Discuss the illustrations and highlights from the first half of the book.	Encourage your child to describe the special qualities of each member of your family. Have your child draw a picture of your family for the final page of his/her *All About Me* book. *See* Social Studies, Week 2, number 2.	Collect a variety of leaves to make leaf rubbings. Have your child put a thin sheet of white paper over the leaves. Using the side of a crayon, have him/her gently rub over the leaves.
Read and discuss the rest of *Squirrels*. Then, go outside on a squirrel search. Ask: *What kinds of squirrels did you see? What were they doing? Did the squirrels' activities remind you of anything you read about in the squirrel book?*	Look through old photo albums with your child, and let him/her select a favorite picture from each year of his/her life. Share stories with your child about each year of his/her life. *See* Social Studies, Week 2, number 3.	Teach your child the "Busy Squirrel" fall finger play. *See* Gross/Fine Motor Skills, Week 2, number 1.
Create an autumn collage wreath with your child. Have your child cut the center out of a paper plate. Use the leaves, acorns and twigs gathered from Wednesday's Math lesson. Ask your child to glue these objects onto the plate, covering it completely. Help your child use hot glue to attach a fall ribbon, tied in a bow, on the bottom. Hang up the finished wreath and celebrate fall!	For the final lesson in the *All About Me* unit, help your child make a paper bag puppet of him/herself. *See* Social Studies, Week 2, number 4. Have your child use **A "Me" Bag Puppet** (p. 37).	Have you child chant this rhyme as you rake leaves: *Leaves, leaves,* *Crunchy and bold!* *Raking and jumping* *Out here in the cold!* *See* Gross/Fine Motor Skills, Week 2, numbers 2–6 for additional activities.

TEACHING SUGGESTIONS AND ACTIVITIES

READING (T, t)

▶ 1. Have your child dictate as many *t* words as he/she can for you to write.

▶ 2. Spin a top and challenge your child to say as many *t* words as he/she can before it stops.

▶ 3. Let your child type *t* words on a computer or typewriter. Spell for your child the *t* words he/she suggests, and let him/her type them.

▶ 4. Make a letter *t* centerpiece for your table. Use *t* objects and arrange them creatively.

▶ 5. Let your child practice making the letter *t* with toothpaste.

▶ 6. Help your child find as many *t* objects as possible and form a letter *t* with them.

LANGUAGE

▶ 1. Look at picture books about trains, such as *Trains* by Donald Crews. Have your child name the shapes and colors he/she sees. Talk about what trains carry.

▶ 2. Teach your child the poem "Three Little Oak Leaves":

> *Three little oak leaves: red, yellow, gold,*
> *Were happy when the weather turned cold.*
> *One said, "I'll make a coat for an elf*
> *So that he'll be able to warm himself."*
> *One said, "I'll make a home for a bug*
> *So that she'll be as snug as a bug in a rug."*
> *One said, "I'll cover a seed in the ground*
> *'Til spring, it will be very safe and very sound."*
> *Three little oak leaves: red, yellow, gold,*
> *Were happy when the weather turned cold.*

MATH (0 — Zero)

▶ 1. Show your child a ruler or tape measure. Point out where the zero is located or where it would be if it is not marked. Explain that this is a starting point for counting and for measuring things.

SOCIAL STUDIES (All About Me)

► 1. Let your child make an audio- or videotape about him/herself. Have him/her tell a joke, sing a favorite song or just be him/herself.

► 2. Help your child learn more about his/her roots or heritage by completing a family tree together. Look through old photographs and share interesting facts and memories about your relatives.

► 3. Give your child a photo album or scrapbook for saving special pictures and mementos.

► 4. To help your child understand how special he/she is to you, read *Love You Forever* by Robert N. Munsch.

GROSS/FINE MOTOR SKILLS

► 1. Teach your child the "Busy Squirrel" finger play:

The little gray squirrel makes a scampering sound	**(Wiggle fingers.)**
As she gathers the nuts that fall to the ground.	**(Hold fingers high, then touch the ground.)**
She buries the nuts in a secret, dark place,	**(Hold one hand over the other.)**
And covers them over with hardly a trace.	**(Make a covering-up motion with hands.)**
Little gray squirrels always seem to know	**(Point to head.)**
That the robins have gone, and it's time for snow.	**(Wiggle fingers, moving them down.)**

► 2. Play the game "Twister" by Milton Bradley.

► 3. Let your child show off his/her talents for *T* Week. Help him/her plan a special talent demonstration for the family.

► 4. Go to a theater this weekend to celebrate *T* Week.

► 5. Let your child build a tower of *t* objects.

► 6. Help your child make thumbprint creatures. Have him/her dip his/her thumb in paint or on a stamp pad and press it down on paper. Using markers and crayons, let your child explore the different kinds of creatures or objects he/she can make.

Letter T, t

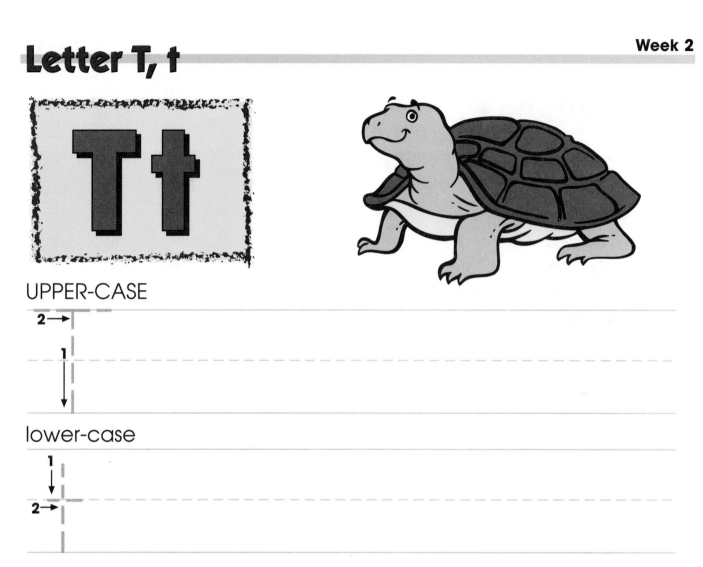

UPPER-CASE

lower-case

These pictures begin with the letter T, t. **Color** the pictures.

Learn at Home, Grade K

Tiger's T-Shirts

Help Tad Tiger decide which T-shirts to buy. **Color** only the T-shirts with pictures that begin with the sound of T, t.

Learn at Home, Grade K

My Family

This is my family.

Hungry Kittens

The hungry kittens ate all the food in some bowls. **Color** the food bowls that have **0** food in them.

Practice **writing** the number 0.

0

Fall Patterns

Color and **cut out** the pictures at the bottom of this page. **Glue** the pictures to continue the pattern in each row.

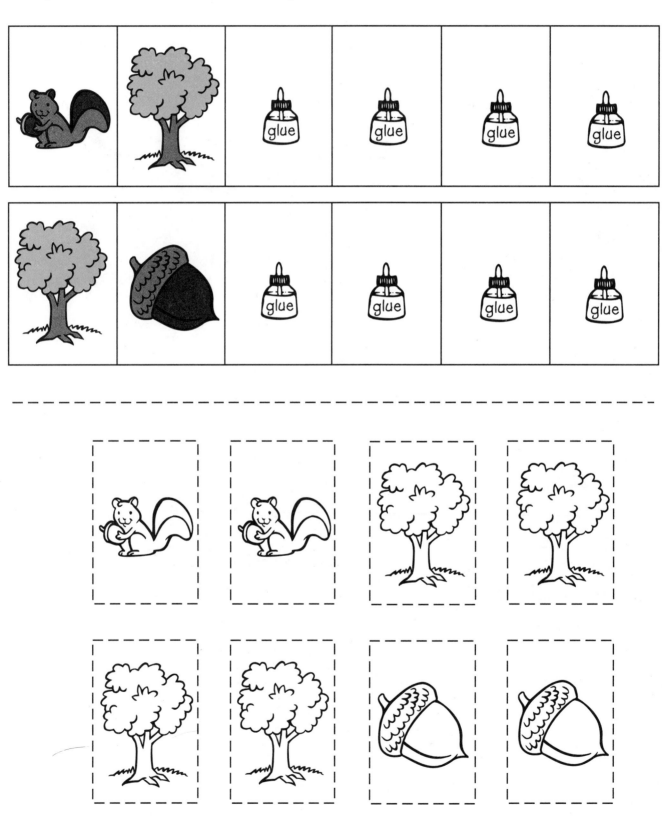

Learn at Home, Grade K

Dress for the Weather

Draw an **X** on the children who are wearing the wrong clothes.
Color the children who are wearing the correct clothes.

Learn at Home, Grade K

My Fingerprints

Trace your hands. Put your fingerprints at the end of each finger.

Left hand   **Right hand**

A "Me" Bag Puppet

Make a paper bag puppet of yourself. **Draw** and **color** your face and hair on the head below. **Draw** and **color** the clothes you most like to wear on the body. **Cut out** the pieces. **Glue** the head to the bottom of the paper bag. **Glue** the body to the bag below the head. Use the puppet to tell your family about you.

Learn at Home, Grade K

	Reading	**Language**	**Math**
Monday	**Consonant Review** Challenge your child to sing "Old MacDonald Had a Farm," naming only animals and objects that begin with the letters *b* or *t*. Have your child sing the beginning letter of that word in the "with a ____, _____" spot. **For example:** *And on his farm,* *he had a turtle, E-I-E-I-O.* *With a t, t here and a t, t there.* *Here a t, there a t, everywhere a t, t.*	Share this rhyme with your child: *This is my family.* *We share love, a home and time,* *But what I like best is* *It's all mine.* *See* Language, Week 3, numbers 1–2.	**1 — One** Take a tour of the house, pointing out those objects you only have one of. As you point them out, say *one*. *See* Math, Week 3, number 1. Have your child complete **Number 1** (p. 43).
Tuesday	Sing the alphabet song together. Then, read *The ABC Book* by Dr. Seuss. When you get to the *b* and *t* pages, ask your child for other words that would fit in those blanks. Sing "Old MacDonald Had a Farm" again. Write out the words on chart paper. Point to the words as you sing the song together. *See* Reading, Week 3, numbers 1–3 for additional activities.	Make paper dolls together. Fold a sheet of paper accordion-style, then cut out the shape of a person, being careful to keep the folded side intact. Ask: *Are the people in our family exactly the same, like these paper dolls? Is there any other family in the world just like ours? How are other families like ours? How are other families different from ours?*	Make cookies using pre-made refrigerated sugar cookie dough. Write the letter *O*, *N* or *E* in the center of each cookie with chocolate chips. Explain that *one* is the word for the number 1. Bake the cookies at 250° until done. Have your child arrange the cookies to spell *one* as many times as possible. Eat any extra letters right away! *See* Math, Week 3, numbers 2 and 3 for additional activities.
Wednesday	Cut out giant construction paper upper- and lower-case letters *b* and *t*. Have your child cut pictures out of magazines that begin with those letters and glue them on.	Read and discuss *The Keeping Quilt* by Patricia Polacco. Talk about the quilt that was passed down through the family in the story. Share family heirlooms or traditions that have been passed down through your family. *See* Language, Week 3, number 3.	Have your child make two small play dough "nests." Put one egg in one nest and leave the other empty. Have your child tell you how many eggs are in each one. Then, keep adding eggs to see how high your child can count. Let your child practice making the numeral 1 with the play dough. Have your child complete **One Fun** (p. 44).
Thursday	Using a tube of frosting, have your child write upper- and lower-case letters *b* and *t* on round cookies or crackers. Let your child match upper- and lower-case letter crackers, put them together and eat them! Have your child complete **Letters B, b and T, t** (p. 42).	Model farm animal riddles for your child. **For example:** *I walk like this. When you eat eggs, think of me. I eat grain. I say "cluck, cluck, cluck." Who am I?* (Answer: a chicken) Then, let your child practice giving clues about a farm animal he/she is pretending to be.	Play "Simon Says" with your child, using the number 1. Give instructions, such as *Simon says hold up one hand* or *Write the number 1 on a sheet of paper.* Make sure to use some *zero* commands as well.
Friday	Using play dough, have your child shape an upper- and lower-case letter *b* and *t*. Then, let your child place *b* and *t* pictures and objects under the matching play dough letter.	Sing about each family member's job. Create a new stanza for each person and sing to the tune of "The Mulberry Bush." **Example:** *This is the way I clean my room,* *Clean my room,* *Clean my room.* *This is the way I clean my room* *Every single morning!* Add motions to go along with the song.	Using a bag of small candies or raisins, ask your child to give you six pieces. Have him/her count them out into your hand. Then, ask for *one more*. See if your child understands the concept. If not, explain it and demonstrate. Let your child eat the six candies, and ask for *one more* for yourself. Once again, be sure he/she understands what you mean. You can also practice the concept of "one more" with blocks, books or other manipulatives.

Science	Social Studies	Gross/Fine Motor
Farm Animals Read *The Big Red Barn* by Margaret Wise Brown. Provide your child with a toy farm set or farm animal stickers, and let him/her retell the story using the farm animals. *See* Science, Week 3, numbers 1–4 for additional activities.	**My Family** Ask your child what he/she thinks a family is. After your child shares his/her ideas, discuss that a family is a group of people who love each other and help each other. Have your child list the members of your family. Help your child name each family member's relation to him/her—i.e., aunt, cousin, brother, mother, etc.	Use play dough to create any farm animals mentioned in *The Big Red Barn* that your toy farm set doesn't include. *See* Gross/Fine Motor Skills, Week 3, numbers 1–3 for additional activities.
Read *The Usborne Book of Farm Animals* by Felicity Everett. Looking at the pictures on the left of each page, have your child describe the similarities and differences between the different animals.	Read *Families Are Different* by Nina Pellegrini. Discuss different families you know. Have your child compare your family to a friend's family. Ask: *How are the families alike? How are they different?* Lead your child to understand that families come in all colors, sizes and shapes and that everyone's family is special. *See* Social Studies, Week 3, numbers 1 and 2.	Trace and cut simple farm animals from tagboard for your child to finger paint. Give your child a variety of colored tempera paint. Add other ingredients to the paint to add texture and interest. For example, add soap flakes to white paint for the sheep or coffee grounds to brown paint for the horses or cows.
Read *Seasons on the Farm* by Jane Miller and discuss the words *male* and *female*. Then, discuss the different names for baby animals. Use **Farm Animals Patterns** (p. 45) to make a memory game. Cut out the cards and place them facedown. Let your child try to match them. When he/she gets a match, he/she must give the correct baby animal name to keep the cards.	After you have read *The Keeping Quilt* by Patricia Polacco (see today's Language lesson), help your child make a *My Family Is Special* keeping quilt. Ask your child what he/she thinks makes your family special. **Example:** *Our family helps each other.* On a fabric square, write his/her words. Then, he/she can illustrate it. Complete several more squares in this way until you have enough to sew together to make a quilt.	Using sidewalk chalk, draw a hopscotch game. Have your child draw pictures of farm animals in each box, starting with the smallest animals at the top and ending with the largest. When there are two hopscotch squares side by side, draw a mother and a baby of the same animal. Play regular hopscotch, only have your child say the appropriate animal sounds as he/she jumps on the squares.
Talk about chickens—their appearance, sound, movement and usefulness to people. Teach your child how an egg hatches into a baby chick. Read *Egg to Chick* by Millicent Selsam, and discuss with your child the changes that occur inside the egg over a period of 21 days.	Talk about ways in which your family has grown and changed since your child was a baby. Ask your child: *Is our family bigger or smaller? Have we moved from one place to another?* Then, have your child create a "family time line" on a long sheet of butcher paper. Have him/her draw pictures to show the family's changes. Ask how he/she feels about these changes. Ask your child how he/she thinks your family will change in the future.	Ask your child to act out this rhyme: *Strut like a chicken, cluck, cluck, cluck.* *Wallow like a piggy in oozy muck.* *Waddle like a duckie, quack, quack, quack.* *Gallop like a pony, giddy-up back.*
Watch the video adaptation of *Charlotte's Web*. Discuss the ways the different animals worked together in the barnyard.	Discuss ways in which your family works together. Ask your child to list family rules and how each family member helps the rest of the family. What is each person's job? What happens if one person doesn't do his/her part? Suggest that you and your child create a *Family Job Chart*, listing each family member's responsibilities. Set a family goal and plan a special family outing if everyone does his/her job for 1 week.	Let your child jump rope while chanting the following rhyme: *Father, mother, sister, brother,* *All live happily together* *When each one tries* *To be wise* *And do their jobs* *With happy eyes!*

39

TEACHING SUGGESTIONS AND ACTIVITIES

READING (Consonant Review)

▶ 1. Have your child bounce a ball around the house while looking for *b* objects.

▶ 2. Have a scavenger hunt. Hide notes with *b* and *t* pictures on them. For example, give your child a picture of a table. When your child looks around the table, he/she will find another note with a picture of a ball. Continue in this manner. Have the hunt lead to a *t* and *b* snack. Each time your child finds a note, he/she must say the first letter of the picture.

▶ 3. Make a list of all the letter *b* and *t* names your child can think of. As he/she names them, write them down. **Example:** *Tammy, Tom, Beth, Bill,* etc.

LANGUAGE

▶ 1. Read *The Berenstain Bears Are a Family* by Stan and Jan Berenstain.

▶ 2. Discuss with your child his/her favorite storybook family. Ask: *What do you like about that family? How are the Berenstain Bears like your family? How are they different?*

▶ 3. Talk about your child's favorite family activities. What does he/she like about those activities? Discuss how family members help one another and share household chores. Talk about some of the problems that you sometimes have as a family. Discuss ways to handle and resolve conflict, such as identifying a problem, discussing possible solutions and compromising.

MATH (1 — One)

▶ 1. Have your child write the numeral *1* and the word *one* with one pen.

▶ 2. Make your child a shopping list using only pictures and numbers. Hand your child a grocery bag. He/she must pick the appropriate number of each object to put in the bag. **Example:** 1 🍎, 3 ▭, etc.

▶ 3. Give everyone in your family "just one" kiss.

SCIENCE (Farm Animals)

▶ 1. Contact your local county extension office to find a person who spins wool. See if he/she would allow your child to observe and ask questions.

▶ 2. Visit a turkey farm. Encourage your child to make observations about the farm and the turkeys.

▶ 3. Visit a dairy farm and give your child the opportunity to milk a cow.

▶ 4. Drive around the countryside with your child. Have him/her make observations about the different barns and farms you see. What animals does he/she see? What do the barns look like? About how many animals are on each farm?

SOCIAL STUDIES (My Family)

▶ 1. Look through old photo albums to begin a discussion about your family. Ask your child questions about his/her family: *How many people are in your family? What makes your family so special? How has the family grown and changed?*

▶ 2. Help your child write a short poem that describes why your family is so special.

GROSS/FINE MOTOR SKILLS

▶ 1. Let your child dictate to you the things he/she can do. Create a poster-sized chart with the heading *I Can Do It!* As your child learns to do new things, add them to the chart.

▶ 2. Choose a project your family can work on together, such as making a meal or painting a room in the house.

▶ 3. Make a large farm mural and create "tactile" farm animals to glue onto it. Use cotton balls for sheep, pink felt for pigs, brown burlap for horses, etc.

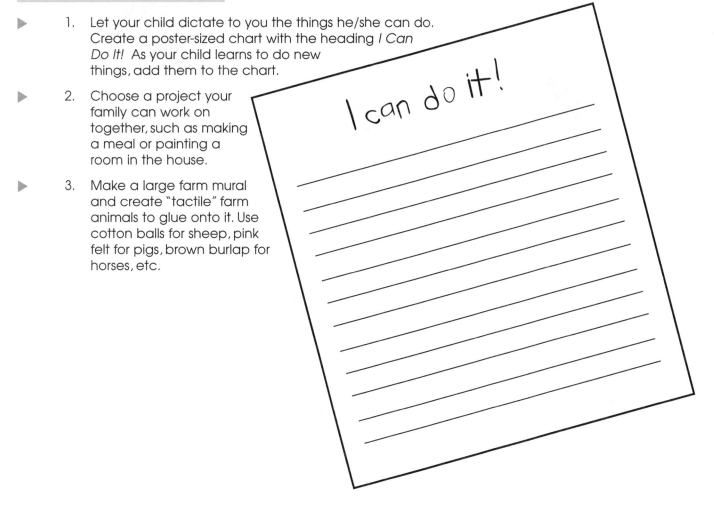

Letters B, b and T, t

Circle the beginning sound for each picture.

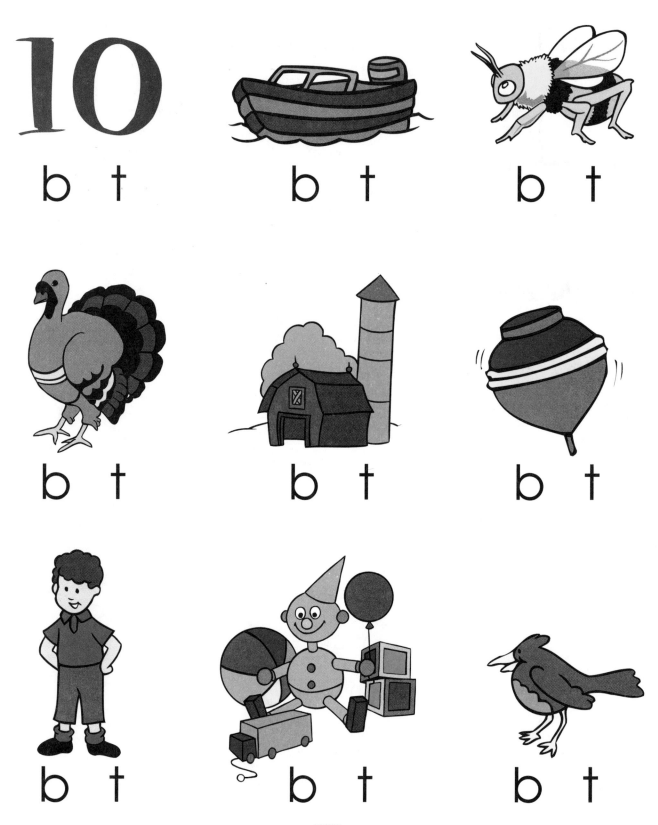

10   b t

b t

b t

b t

b t

b t

b t

b t

b t

42

Number 1

This is the number 1. **Color** the picture.

How many things are in this picture? _____

Trace the 1's.

1 ↓

Write your own 1's.

One Fun

Circle 1 thing in each group. **Color** the pictures you circled.

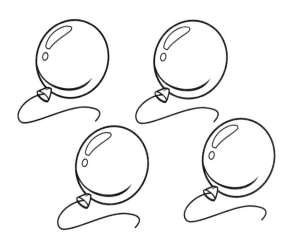

Practice **writing** the number 1.

Farm Animal Patterns

Make a memory game. **Cut out** the cards and place them facedown. Play the game with a partner. Take turns turning the cards over to **match** mother and baby animals.

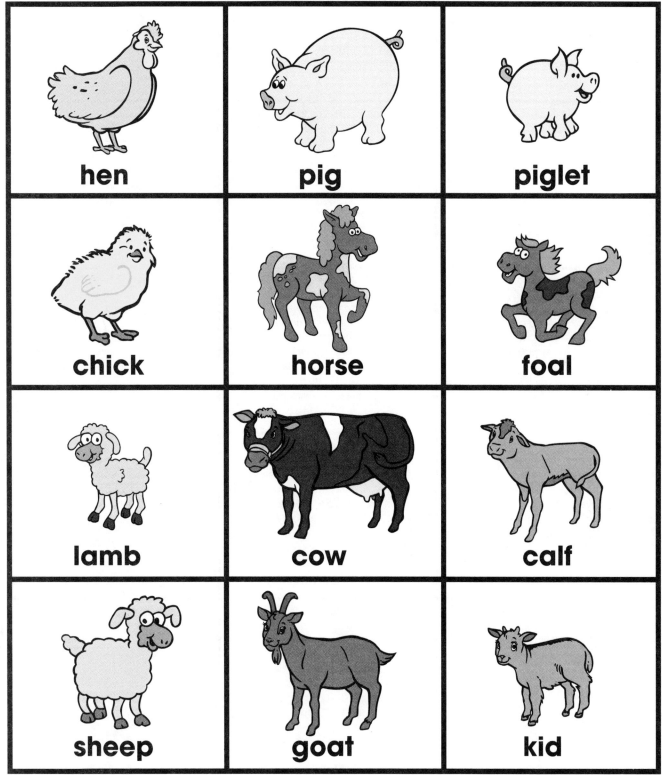

hen	**pig**	**piglet**
chick	**horse**	**foal**
lamb	**cow**	**calf**
sheep	**goat**	**kid**

	Reading	Language	Math
Monday	**C, c** Show your child how elbow macaroni forms the letter c. Explain that an upper-case C looks just like a lower-case c, only bigger. Have your child draw a large upper- and lower-case letter C on a sheet of paper. Have him/her trace the letters with glue, then cover the glue with elbow macaroni. Have your child complete **Letter C, c** (p. 50).	Plan a trip to a working farm. Have your child dictate a list of questions he/she has about the farm and the animals on it. **Example:** *What do the different animals eat?* Bring your child's questions along on your visit, and encourage your child to ask the farmer the questions he/she has prepared. *See* Language, Week 4, numbers 1–4 for additional activities.	**Basic Concepts** To help your child practice his/her visual discrimination skills, set out two similar objects, such as a dish towel and a hot pad. Have your child describe the similarities and differences between them. *See* Math, Week 4, numbers 1–3 for additional activities. Have your child complete **Same and Different** (p. 54).
Tuesday	Cut off the end of a carrot. Have your child dip the tip into paint and paint upper- and lower-case letter c's on a piece of cloth. *See* Reading, Week 4, numbers 1–4 for additional activities.	Use the **Farm Puppets** patterns (p. 51–52) to help your child create farm animal puppets. *See* Language, Week 4, number 4. Use the puppets to sing the traditional song, **"Down on Grandpa's Farm"** (p. 53). Sing the verses provided, then help your child add additional verses to the song. Call your child's attention to the describing word, color word and animal word that each new verse will need.	Set out a variety of coins. Let your child sort them into piles, noting the similarities and differences among them. Then, provide your child with an assortment of buttons. Let him/her sort the buttons according to color, size, shape and number of holes.
Wednesday	Read *C Is for Clown* by Stan and Jan Berenstain. Tell your child the sound letter c makes. Make the sound several times with your child for reinforcement. Then, let your child dictate as many c words as he/she can for you to write. Read *Rosie's Walk* by Pat Hutchins with your child. (*See* today's Language lesson for a related activity.)	After you have read *Rosie's Walk* with your child (*see* today's Reading lesson), make word cards for the positional words that describe where Rosie went on her walk—*across, around, over, through* and *under*. To build your child's understanding of these concepts, go on a walk outside and find things for your child to go across, around, over, through and under—just like Rosie!	Using the coins from yesterday's lesson, let your child practice making simple patterns, such as *penny, penny, nickel, penny, penny, nickel....* Have your child color and cut out the pictures on **Farm Patterns** (p. 55–56). Let him/her create farm animal patterns, such as *cow, cow, duck, cow, cow, duck....*
Thursday	Play "I Spy a C Word" in which you give hints for c words. **Example:** *I spy something that starts with c. It is an animal that is covered with fur. It chases mice and sleeps on your bed at night. What is it?* (Answer: a cat) Play several times, then let your child do the "spying" and describing.	Read *Cuckoo: A Mexican Folktale* by Lois Ehlert. As you read the story, have your child follow along and point to every c he/she sees. This book also provides your child with exposure to another culture and language as each page is also written in Spanish.	Set out three different-sized toys. Have your child put them in order from largest to smallest. Add more toys for your child to sort and order by size. Have your child complete **Growing Up** (p. 57).
Friday	Create a tongue twister full of letter c words, and challenge your child to repeat it after you. Then, help your child create a letter c tongue twister of his/her own!	Have your child make a place mat for each family member using a large piece of construction paper and markers. Ask your child to draw a picture of a different family member in the center of each sheet. At the top of each sheet, have your child write *I love you because....* Cover the completed placemat with contact paper.	Set out a bowl of fruit. Ask your child if the bowl is empty or full. Remove the fruit. Ask again if the bowl is empty or full. Give your child further practice with the concepts of empty and full. Say, for example, *I want a full bowl of fruit* or *I want an empty bowl.* Then, let your child decide what to give you.

Learn at Home, Grade K

Science	Social Studies	Gross/Fine Motor
Farm Animals Visit a farm during chore time. (*See* today's Language lesson.) Allow your child to participate as much as possible. Ask him/her to use all five senses to describe the experience. What does it smell like? What does each animal feel like? What sounds do they make? *See* Science, Week 4, numbers 1–4 for additional activities.	**My Family** Read *Me and My Family Tree* by Joan Sweeney to your child. Make a list of family members for your child's family tree. Sketch a large tree on brown paper for your child to cut out. Give your child a photograph of each family member to place on the tree. Help your child write each family member's name under his/her picture. *See* Social Studies, Week 4, numbers 1–3 .	After your visit to a farm, help your child create a large farm mural. Using a large sheet of butcher paper, paint the ground area brown. Add a barn, silo and field. Then, have your child paint the farm animals he/she observed on the visit. *See* Gross/Fine Motor Skills, Week 4, numbers 1 and 2 for additional activities.
Help your child make up a farm version of "Here We Go 'Round the Mulberry Bush." List some of the farm activities you observed on your farm visit, and make up actions to go with the new verses: *This is the way we feed the pigs,* *Feed the pigs,* *Feed the pigs.* *This is the way we feed the pigs* *So early every morning!*	Read *The Patchwork Quilt* by Valerie Flournoy aloud to your child. Discuss Tanya's discovery about the "secret ingredient" in her Grandma's special quilt of memories. In the story, Mama and Grandma teach Tanya to sew. Discuss with your child the many things family members learn from each other. Have your child draw some examples of things he/she has learned from different members of your family.	Make a gingerbread farm. Frost a toilet paper roll and a large gelatin box for the silo and barn. Add graham cracker doors to the barn, then use licorice to make an X on each door. Decorate the barn with candies. Use animal crackers for your animals and coconut mixed with yellow food coloring for straw.
Read *All About Farm Animals* by Brenda Cook. Discuss what each of the farm animals eats. Have your child compare what happened in the story to his/her own visit to a farm. What was the same? What was different?	Families have special favorite foods. Plan a dinner for your family that includes everyone's favorites. For instance, let Mom choose the appetizer, Dad the salad, Sister the main course and Brother the dessert. *See* Social Studies, Week 4, number 4.	Help your child make a simple farm food chain using strips of cardboard and pictures from coloring books and magazines. Start with grass → cow → person. Glue or draw a picture of each organism on cardboard and draw arrows between to show the direction of the chain. Help your child see that cows eat grass and people eat cows. Lead your child through other simple food chains, and let him/her cut out or draw pictures to illustrate them.
Set milk, eggs, hamburger, steak, cheese, bacon, ham and a wool sweater on the table. Ask your child what they all have in common. Discuss all the things farm animals give us. Ask your child to draw pictures of different farm animals with arrows pointing to the things that come from them.	Define the word *tradition*. Describe your family's traditions as you were growing up, and why these are important to you. Ask your child: *What traditions do we have as a family? Which of these are important to you? Why? What new tradition would you like to start?* Together, decide on a new tradition for your family, such as celebrating half-birthdays with a milk shake or designating a particular night as "Family Night," complete with pizza and a movie.	Make a french bread pizza for lunch. Use frozen garlic bread, thawed. Top with spaghetti sauce and your child's favorite toppings, then bake. Talk about which of the pizza ingredients come from farm animals.
Make homemade butter. Pour a pint of heavy cream into a jar and cover tightly. Let your child shake the jar while chanting this rhyme: *Shake, shake, shake,* *Our cows we thank,* *Shake, shake, shake,* *For butter we make.* As the cream thickens, have your child describe the changes taking place. As the butter forms, pour off the milk and add a little salt.	Plan a special activity to celebrate your family. Write each family member's name on a slip of paper, fold and place it in a basket. Have each person draw a name. Then, each person plans something special for the family member whose name he/she has chosen. Encourage your child to make a gift, a picture or write a special note or poem for the family member. Share the surprises at your next "Family Night."	Make a rhyme to the tune of "Shortening Bread" using your child's name: *Mommy loves Katie, Katie, Katie,* *Mommy loves Katie, baby Kate.* *Katie loves Mommy, Mommy, Mommy,* *Katie loves Mommy,* *She's the best!* Ask your child to make up rhymes about other family members to use with the tune.

TEACHING SUGGESTIONS AND ACTIVITIES

READING (C, c)

▶ 1. Celebrate *C* Week by using colored chalk to draw *c* objects all over your sidewalks or on a large piece of poster board.

▶ 2. Help your child tape different-sized boxes together to create a castle. Then, brush on glue and sprinkle sand over the glue.

▶ 3. Toss *c* objects to your child and see how many he/she can catch.

▶ 4. Have your child cut out *c* pictures from old magazines and catalogs. Then, help him/her create a letter *c* paper chain, using one *c* picture per link.

LANGUAGE

▶ 1. Read *Clifford, the Small Red Puppy* by Norman Bridwell. Clifford books are great for letter *C* Week.

▶ 2. Take a trip to the library. Make a special effort to find books whose titles or main characters' names begin with the letter *c*.

▶ 3. Visit a petting zoo (*see* Science). After you return home, help your child write down words to describe how each of the animals felt.

▶ 4. Duplicate the farm animal puppet patterns on pages 51–52 and have your child make stick puppets. Have your child color the animals first, then cut them out. Glue a craft stick to the back of each puppet. Use the puppets to act out the song, "Down on Grandpa's Farm."

MATH (Basic Concepts)

▶ 1. Set out several *c* objects, such as cookies, containers and toy cars. Ask your child to tell you the shape of each object.

▶ 2. The day before you buy groceries, open your cupboards and refrigerator and talk about the concept of *empty*. After buying groceries, talk about the concept of *full*.

▶ 3. Have your child point in the appropriate directions while saying this rhyme:

Look up, look down,
Look all around.
Look under, over
Your little dog, Rover.
Look far, look near,
Look right over here.
Look in, look out,
Then shout, shout, shout!

SCIENCE (Farm Animals)

▶ 1. Visit a place where food products that come from animals, such as cheese, are made. Take a tour and enjoy a sample.

▶ 2. Go to a petting farm or zoo, and encourage your child to pet the baby animals. What sound does each baby animal make? What do the animals eat? How does each animal's fur feel?

▶ 3. Take a field trip to a grocery store and point out some of the different foods that come from animals, such as milk, cheese and eggs.

▶ 4. Go to a mall or clothes store. Browse through the different fabrics and materials. Encourage your child to feel the different textures. Point out a wool sweater to your child. Explain that wool comes from sheep. Then, look for clothing and/or shoes made from leather. Tell your child that these items are made from animal skin.

SOCIAL STUDIES (My Family)

▶ 1. Make a family tree with your child. As you work together, tell your child a little about each of the relatives you are including.

▶ 2. While looking through old photographs, tell your child stories about different relatives.

▶ 3. Watch old home movies together.

▶ 4. Try some favorite family recipes together.

GROSS/FINE MOTOR SKILLS

▶ 1. Plan an obstacle course full of letter *c* commands. **Example:** *Crawl under the table to the bedroom, then eat a cracker.* Let your child help you plan the activities. Then, race against each other to see who can finish first.

▶ 2. Play this letter *c* game: Throw a cap in the air, and challenge your child to try and catch it on his/her *cabeza* (Spanish for head)!

Letter C, c

Cc

UPPER-CASE

lower-case

These pictures begin with the letter C, c. **Color** the pictures.

Learn at Home, Grade K

Farm Animal Puppets

Learn at Home, Grade K

Farm Animal Puppets

Down on Grandpa's Farm

Oh, we're on our way, we're on our way, on our way to Grand-pa's farm. We're on our way, we're on our way, on our way to Grand-pa's

1. to 4. To Verses 5.

farm. _____ farm. 1. Down on Grand-pa's farm, there is a

big brown cow. Down on Grand-pa's farm, there is a big brown

cow. The cow, she makes a sound like this: Moo! Moo! The

cow, she makes a sound like this: Moo! Moo!

2. Down on Grandpa's farm, there is a little yellow chick.
3. Down on Grandpa's farm, there is a shaggy gray goat.
4. Down on Grandpa's farm, there is a fuzzy white duck.
5. Down on Grandpa's farm, there is a big pink pig.

Learn at Home, Grade K

Same and Different

Color the two pictures in each row that are the same.

Farm Patterns

Learn at Home, Grade K

Growing Up

Color and **cut out** the people below. **Glue** them in a row from small to large.

	Reading	Language	Math
Monday	**S, s** Sing the alphabet song. Cook spaghetti and shape the strands into an upper- and lower-case letter *s*. Have your child trace each letter with his/her finger. Give him/her several spaghetti strands to shape into *s* shapes, also. *See* Reading, Week 5, numbers 1–4 for additional activities. Have your child complete **Letter S, s** (p. 62).	**Poetry** Copy this poem onto chart paper and read it with your child: *Colors* *Colors, colors, everywhere,* *Red, yellow, blue and pink.* *Tomatoes, lilies, seas and bows,* *They're all my favorites, I think.* *See* Language, Week 5, numbers 1–5 for additional activities.	**2 — Two** Have your child name his/her body parts that come in pairs. As he/she names them, point to the body parts and count *one, two. See* Math, Week 5, numbers 1–4 for additional activities. Have your child complete **Number 2** (p. 65).
Tuesday	Using a bar of soap, have your child write an upper- and lower-case *s* on a sheet of paper. Have him/her color over the *s*'s with the side of a crayon, revealing the letters. Have your child complete **Soap Suds** (p. 63).	Use ketchup to spell out the word *red* for your child. Then, let him/her try to spell it with ketchup. Sound out the word with your child. Then, have your child go on a "red" scavenger hunt, searching for red objects throughout the house.	Use glue to write the word *two* on a sheet of construction paper. Sprinkle glitter on the glue and gently shake off the excess. Have your child use glue to draw two objects and the number 2. Have him/her add glitter and shake off any excess.
Wednesday	*Sammy's going to San Diego, and in his suitcase, he'll pack a sandwich.* Ask your child to repeat this sentence, adding another *s* word after *sandwich*. **Example:** *Sammy's going to San Diego, and in his suitcase, he'll pack a sandwich and a suit.* Continue taking turns, repeating the sentence and adding letter *s* words, until one of you makes a mistake.	Use mustard to write out the word *yellow*. Allow your child to try, also. Sound out the word *yellow* together. Then, have your child name yellow objects.	Write directions, using only pictures and number words, for your child to get from one hidden note to the next. Have the last note lead to a treasure of candy. Have your child complete **Blowing Bubbles** (p. 66).
Thursday	Set several objects on the kitchen table, including some that begin with the letter *s*. Your child must put all the *s* objects on one side of the table and the rest of the objects on the other.	Write the following words on a sheet of paper and see if your child recognizes them: *red, yellow, orange, zero, one* and *two*. Have your child complete **Red and Yellow** (p. 64).	Arrange a pattern of twos, using apples and lemons. Place two apples, then two lemons, side by side. Have your child complete this pattern by adding the next four pieces of fruit. Then, encourage your child to try other patterns.
Friday	Read a short book with your child. Whenever he/she hears an *s* sound, your child must clap his/her hands.	Chant the following in singsong fashion with your child: *Roy G. Biv, Roy G. Biv* *Our rainbow's made by Roy G. Biv.* Explain to your child that each letter in *Roy G. Biv* stands for a color of the rainbow in the correct order of colors. The colors of the rainbow, in order, are *red, orange, yellow, green, blue, indigo* and *violet*.	Read and enjoy *The M&M's Counting Book* by Barbara Barbieri McGrath. Then, use M&M's to do several of the activities together.

Learn at Home, Grade K

Science	Social Studies	Gross/Fine Motor
Color Drop food coloring into glasses of water. Ask your child to name each color. After making red, yellow and blue (the primary colors), have your child experiment to see how to make orange, purple and green (the secondary colors). *See* Science, Week 5, numbers 1–4 for additional activities.	**My Address and Phone Number** Unplug your phone and have your child practice punching in your telephone number. Have your child tell you why it is a good idea to know his/her phone number.	Play "Red Light, Green Light." Have your child stand at one end of the room, while you stand at the other end, with your back to your child. When you say *green light*, your child should start to move towards you. After a few moments, call out *red light* while turning around. If your child is moving, he/she must go back to the wall. If he/she is not moving, you turn back around and call *green light*. The game is over when your child touches you.
Read *Color* by Ruth Heller. Ask your child what three colors make all the other colors. Explain that these colors—red, yellow and blue—are called the primary colors.	Help your child learn his/her phone number. Sing it in a catchy rhythm to help him/her remember it. *See* Social Studies, Week 5, number 1. Have your child complete **My Telephone Number** (p. 67).	Teach your child this color finger play: *See, see, see!* *What colors do I see?* *Purple plums,* (point to thumb) *Red tomatoes,* (point to second finger) *Yellow corn,* (point to middle finger) *Brown potatoes,* (point to fourth finger) *Green lettuce!* (point to fifth finger) *Yum, yum, yum, good!* *I learn so many colors when I eat my food!*
Colors can inspire different feelings and moods. Ask your child what he/she thinks or feels about certain colors.	Discuss with your child what to do if he/she becomes lost. Help your child practice saying his/her full name and phone number.	Using mustard as yellow finger paint, have your child paint a scene with a cheery sun. **Note:** Your child's fingers will be stained yellow for a short time after this activity. *See* Gross/Fine Motor Skills, Week 5, numbers 1–3 for additional activities.
Have your child mix ketchup and mustard together. What color do they make? Scoop this mixture into a pastry bag and write the word *orange*. Save the leftover mixture for later (*see* today's Gross/Fine Motor lesson).	Go outside and show your child your house number and street sign. Talk about why it is important to know your own address. Help your child say your street name and number. *See* Social Studies, Week 5, number 2.	Using your homemade orange ketchup and mustard paint from today's Science lesson, have your child paint a big pumpkin on a sheet of butcher paper.
If today is sunny, make a rainbow by turning on your garden hose and spraying it for a few minutes. A rainbow will appear just above the water spray. Have your child name the colors he/she sees in the rainbow.	Role-play with your child. Set up a scenario in which your child is lost. What would he/she do? Then, have him/her act it out. Make sure your child includes telling his/her phone number and street address as part of the scenario. *See* Social Studies, Week 5, number 3.	Use play dough to make two slithering snakes, shaped like an upper- and lower-case *s*. Bake at 250° for several hours until hardened. Let the letters cool, then have your child paint them in the colors of the rainbow.

TEACHING SUGGESTIONS AND ACTIVITIES

READING (S, s)

▷ 1. In honor of letter *s*, teach your child how to sew with yarn. Cut out the shape of a shirt from a piece of poster board. Punch holes all around the edge. Tape a piece of yarn to the back. Wrap a piece of tape around the loose end of the yarn so it doesn't fray. Then, let your child pull the yarn through the holes. When he/she is finished, have your child write a big *s* in the center of the shirt.

▷ 2. Fill a shallow pan half-full with sand. Let your child make letter *s* shapes in the sand.

▷ 3. Invent several new sandwiches in honor of *S* Week. Think of a creative name for each one.

▷ 4. Recite the following poem. Have your child name an *s* word at the end of the rhyme.

> *Letter s, letter s,*
> *Speak, speak, speak.*
> *Say a word that rhymes with _____. (box)*
> *Yes! You guessed! My word is _____. (socks)*

LANGUAGE

▷ 1. Have your child look through the book *Of Colors and Things* by Tana Hoban. Have him/her create a story using the objects on each page.

▷ 2. Read *Caps for Sale* by Esphyr Slobodkina. Have your child name the color of each cap the peddler wore, in order.

▷ 3. Declare each day of this week a color day, such as *Blue Tuesday* or *Red Friday*, and encourage your child to dress in that particular color.

▷ 4. Talk about scarecrows and their purpose in gardens. Make a scarecrow using as many colors as possible.

▷ 5. Read *Green Eggs and Ham* by Dr. Seuss.

MATH (2 — Two)

▷ 1. Have your child go on a scavenger hunt for pairs. Give him/her 10 minutes to bring back as many pairs of things as he/she can find.

▷ 2. Talk about a special friend your child has. Ask why your child sometimes has more fun when his/her friend is around. Talk about the benefits of doing things in pairs.

▷ 3. Introduce your child to the number line. Ask him/her to show you specific numbers, focusing on the number 2.

▷ 4. Place a slip of paper with the numeral 2 inside of a shoe. In the other shoe, place the word *two*. Say the following rhyme:

> *Two, two,*
> *How are you?*
> *You look so comfy*
> *In my shoe!*

Then, try making other "number rhymes" with your child.

SCIENCE (Color)

▶   1.   Give your child 5 minutes to name as many red objects as he/she can, another 5 minutes to name yellow items and still another 5 minutes to name orange ones. Ask: *Which color objects were the easiest for you to name? Why?*

▶   2.   Look through a jumbo box of crayons. Have your child sort the crayons into eight different categories: red, orange, yellow, green, blue, purple, brown and black. Ask: *Which color has the most different shades? Which colors were the most difficult to sort?*

▶   3.   Write the words *yellow*, *red* and *orange* down the left side of a sheet of paper. Draw a red, orange and yellow box (one of each color) down the right side. Have your child draw a line matching each color word to the correct color box.

▶   4.   Make a "rainbow cake." Make a cake, then frost a rainbow on top. Let your child mix the colors for the frosting.

SOCIAL STUDIES (My Address and Phone Number)

▶   1.   Help your child find a friend's phone number, then call the friend. Let your child dial the number him/herself.

▶   2.   Help your child make a list of what is special about his/her house. Then, read *The Little House*, a book about another special house, written by Virginia Lee Burton. What is that house's address?

▶   3.   Have your child make a pictorial directory. Gather pictures of your child's special friends and relatives. Have your child tape each picture to a small sheet of paper with the person's phone number listed beneath. With just a few pages of phone numbers (one number per page), your child will have his/her own miniature phone directory.

GROSS/FINE MOTOR SKILLS

▶   1.   Let your child make interesting glue designs on a paper plate. Then, have him/her drop food coloring into sand. Let your child sprinkle the colored sand over the plate, then shake off any excess. He/she may continue until he/she has used several colors.

▶   2.   Play "tag" with "base" as any object or location of a particular color.

▶   3.   Make color collages. For example, have your child glue green objects onto poster board and write the word *green* in the center with a green marker.

Letter S, s

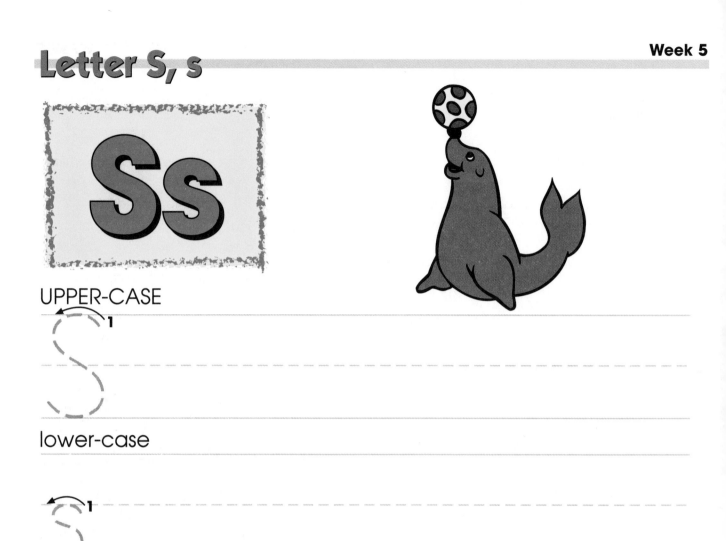

UPPER-CASE

lower-case

These pictures begin with the letter S, s. **Color** the pictures.

Learn at Home, Grade K

Soap Suds

Trace each S in yellow. **Trace** each s in purple.

Learn at Home, Grade K

Red and Yellow

Use red and yellow crayons to **color** the picture.

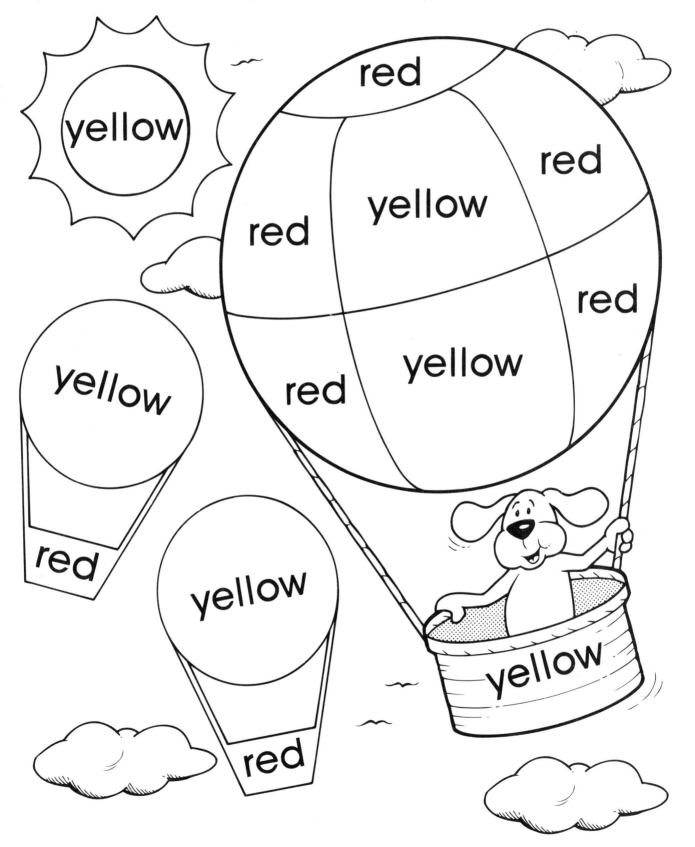

Learn at Home, Grade K

Number 2

This is the number 2. **Color** the pictures.

How many things are in this picture? _____

Trace the 2's.

Write your own 2's.

Blowing Bubbles

Color 2 bubbles blue, 2 bubbles green and 2 bubbles yellow.

Practice **writing** the number 2.

2 2

Learn at Home, Grade K

My Telephone Number

Write your telephone number on the line below the telephone. Practice dialing your telephone number. **Color** in the numbers you use.

	Reading	**Language**	**Math**
Monday	**Consonant Review** Give your child a page from a newspaper. Then, dictate the following directions: *Draw a circle around every c you find.* (Pause for a few minutes.) *Draw a square around each s.* (Another pause.) *Underline every b and cross out each t. See* Reading, Week 6, numbers 1-4 for additional activities.	Write the word *purple* with permanent marker on your dried purple cloth (*see* today's Science lesson). Have your child do the same. Sound out the word *purple* together several times. *See* Language, Week 6, numbers 1–5 for additional activities.	**3 — Three** Make several sets of three objects on a table. Ask your child if the sets have anything in common. Guide your child to see that each group has three objects in it. Discuss other common properties of the objects. Then, have your child count each set aloud. Have your child complete **Number 3** (p. 74).
Tuesday	Thaw frozen bread dough. Have your child create one simple dough object beginning with each review letter: *b, t, c* and *s.* Bake for about 15 minutes in a 350° oven.	Sing the nursery rhyme "Three Blind Mice" with your child: *Three blind mice, three blind mice,* *See how they run, see how they run!* *They all ran after the farmer's wife,* *Who cut off their tails with a carving knife.* *Did you ever see such a sight in your life* *As three blind mice?*	Have your child draw a large 3 on a sheet of paper. Then, have him/her trace the number with glue and add sets of three objects, such as cereal, dried beans or macaroni noodles until the glue is covered. Have your child complete **Seashore Numbers** (p. 75).
Wednesday	Have your child fill in each blank with a word that starts with the same beginning sound as the other words in the sentence. Have him/her state the beginning letter. *Billy believes* _____. *Tigers tickle* _____. *Carol cleans* _____. *Sarah sees* _____. Then, make up your own sentences together.	Using pistachio pudding, let your child finger paint several green objects on a sheet of paper. To get different shades of green, tint the pistachio pudding with vanilla or chocolate pudding. In the center of the paper, have him/her write the word *green.*	Give your child a variety of directions using jelly beans. **Example:** *Count out three red jelly beans, eat two yellow jelly beans, give me one orange jelly bean…. See* Math, Week 6, number 1. Have your child complete **Jolly Jelly Beans** (p. 76).
Thursday	Have a scavenger hunt in your home. Plant various objects around the house. Instruct your child to find a *b* word on the bed, a *t* word in the tub, a *c* word in the cupboard and an *s* word in the sink. Have your child complete **Letters C, c and S, s** (p. 72).	Write out the word *blue* on a sheet of paper. Have your child do the same. Then, have your child glue magazine pictures of blue objects all around the word.	Give your child a slip of paper with directions on it, such as *Count the number of TVs we have and write the answer on your paper.* Plan four or five assignments like this, incorporating the numbers 0–3. *See* Math, Week 6, numbers 2 and 3. Have your child complete **Beary Good!** (p. 77).
Friday	Set objects beginning with the letters *b, t, c* and *s* on a table. Using yarn or tape, divide the tabletop into quarters. Have your child make four sets based on beginning letters. Then, ask him/her to write each beginning letter on a note card and place it in the correct section of the table.	Review the color words by using the helium balloons from Wednesday's Science lesson. Have your child complete **Color Garden** (p. 73).	Draw a triangular tree shape with a trunk at the bottom. Point out how *tree* and *three* are spelled similarly. Write both words on a sheet of paper and have your child tell you the differences between the words. Then, show your child that the basic shape of a pine tree has three sides. In the center of the tree, write *tree,* and on each side of it, write out the number words *one, two* and *three.*

Science	Social Studies	Gross/Fine Motor
Color Make your own colors or dyes. Boil beets in water until the water turns a deep purple. Soak a piece of white cloth in the water. Ask your child what color it is now. Brainstorm other plants or foods that can be used as dyes. *See* Science, Week 6, numbers 1–4 for additional activities.	**My Address and Phone Number** Get out a map of your state. Have your child trace his/her finger around the edge of the state. Show your child the location of your town. Emphasize its name. Point out other cities of relevance to him/her. Ask your child if he/she can find your town on the map.	Supervise your child as he/she cuts out purple objects from the purple cloth made in today's Science lesson. Ask your child to name each object, then label the objects for him/her. *See* Gross/Fine Motor Skills, Week 6, numbers 1–4 for additional activities.
Buy one sheet each of red, yellow and blue cellophane. Let your child explore overlapping colors to create new ones. Read *Little Blue and Little Yellow* by Leo Lionni.	Show your child a map of the United States. Ask if he/she can remember the name of your state. Can he/she find the state on the map, based on its shape? If not, then show your child. Point out other relevant states as well.	Introduce your child to pastel colors. Explain that pastels are simply colors that have white added to them. Dip colored chalk in water and create a beautiful, pastel picture. Or let your child make his/her own pastel paint by adding white paint to a primary color.
Purchase helium balloons in the following colors: red, orange, yellow, green, purple and blue. On the outside of each balloon, have your child use markers to carefully write the correct color word.	Show your child a globe. Help him/her find the United States. Explain that the U.S. is located on the continent of North America. Help your child find your state on the globe.	Let your child finger paint with different colors while chanting this rhyme: *Red, green, yellow, brown and blue,* *Orange, purple and black, too!* *One bright color in each dish,* *With your fingers, dip and swish!*
Using a set of watercolor paints, allow your child to mix and match as he/she dabs a brush in different colors. As your child works, ask him/her to identify the primary colors.	Use the recipe for shredded wheat compound. *See* Social Studies, Week 6, number 1. Have your child make a model of your state with the wheat mixture. Review your address and phone number with your child.	Use a box mix to make blueberry muffins. Let your child follow the directions, which are often in picture form.
Experiment with colors by splatter-painting a large piece of poster board. Have your child write his/her name in the center with his/her handprints on each side.	Have your child draw a picture of your house on a sheet of paper. At the bottom of the page, ask your child to write your street address and phone number. *See* Social Studies, Week 6, numbers 2–5 for additional activities.	Take a walk around the block. Give your child directions, such as *Stop if you see red* or *Jog if you see yellow.*

TEACHING SUGGESTIONS AND ACTIVITIES

READING (Consonant Review)

▶ 1. Make a spinner using a circle cut out of construction paper. Use a paper fastener to attach an arrow to the center of it. Divide the circle into four pie shapes. Write one of the following in each pie segment: *foods, places, names, stores.* To review each letter, spin the spinner. Your child will then need to think of objects that fit in that particular category and begin with the review letter. Set a timer and see how many he/she can think of in 3 minutes.

▶ 2. Cook alphabet soup and challenge your child to find at least one of the review letters in each spoonful of soup.

▶ 3. Have your child draw a picture in which each of the review letters is represented twice.

▶ 4. Give your child a sheet of paper. Say a word that begins with one of the review letters, and have your child write down the beginning letter sound. Repeat with other words.

LANGUAGE

▶ 1. Have your child write a short poem or nursery rhyme about his/her house. You may need to help your child get started. **Example:** *Sparkle, sparkle, our white house....*

▶ 2. Design a color matching game using note cards. Have your child color on one side of each card. On another set of note cards, have him/her write the corresponding color words. When all of the cards are made, turn them facedown. Ask your child to try to match them.

▶ 3. Plan a menu with your child around a particular color.

▶ 4. Make matching family sweatshirts, using fabric paint. Have each family member dip a hand in paint and stamp it on. In the center write *The _____ Family.*

▶ 5. Read "What Is Purple?" from *Hailstones and Halibut Bones* by Mary O'Neill.

MATH (3 — Three)

▶ 1. Dictate a picture for your child to draw. Include specific numbers of objects. **Example:** *Draw three pumpkins on a fence. Draw two girls standing next to them. Write the number 1 on each girl's shirt.*

▶ 2. Give your child a list of chores to do in picture, word or number form.

▶ 3. Cut a sheet of white paper into a square. Have your child fold the square twice (once lengthwise and once crosswise) to make four smaller squares. Tell your child to color three of the squares.

SCIENCE (Color)

▶ 1. Ask your child to find three different green-colored textures and do a crayon rubbing of each of them. **Examples:** blade of grass, leaf, pine needle. Do the same for red and yellow.

▶ 2. Buy face paint. Let your child apply color to his/her face, hands, feet, etc. Then, ask him/her to tell you what color different parts of his/her body are. **Example:** *My face is blue and red.*

▶ 3. Buy colored glue. Let your child experiment to see what kinds of crafts he/she can make.

▶ 4. Have your child use different colors of yarn to make designs. He/she can spread glue into different shapes, then fill in the shapes with yarn to create an interesting design or picture.

SOCIAL STUDIES (My Address and Phone Number)

▶ 1. Recipe for colored shredded wheat compound: Mix $\frac{1}{3}$ cup of glue with several drops of food coloring and stir. Break up one shredded wheat biscuit into the glue mixture. Then, stir again. Form it into the shape of your state and place it onto a sheet of wax paper.

▶ 2. Have your child draw several pictures for family members. Help him/her address the envelopes and send a picture to each one of them.

▶ 3. Show your child a phone bill. Talk about the expense of calling long distance. Point out the phone numbers of people your child knows.

▶ 4. Go outside with your child and look at your house. Have your child describe it to you.

▶ 5. Get in the car and drive a short, familiar distance away. See if your child can direct you home again. If he/she can't, discuss again the importance of knowing your address.

GROSS/FINE MOTOR SKILLS

▶ 1. Make a color wheel. See Ruth Heller's *Color* for reference.

▶ 2. Have your child cut sponges into different shapes, dip them into paint and make a sponge painting.

▶ 3. Fill a squirt gun with water, and let your child write and draw with water on the sidewalk.

▶ 4. Let your child use stamps and different colors of ink to create interesting pictures. Encourage your child to find ways to combine the rubber stamps into a picture that is realistic—or into one that is fantastic!

Letters C, c and S, s

Trace the letters. **Color** the picture in each box which begins with the sound of the letter.

Color Garden

Color the petals on each flower. **Color** and **cut out** the circles.
Glue the circles in the middle of each flower.

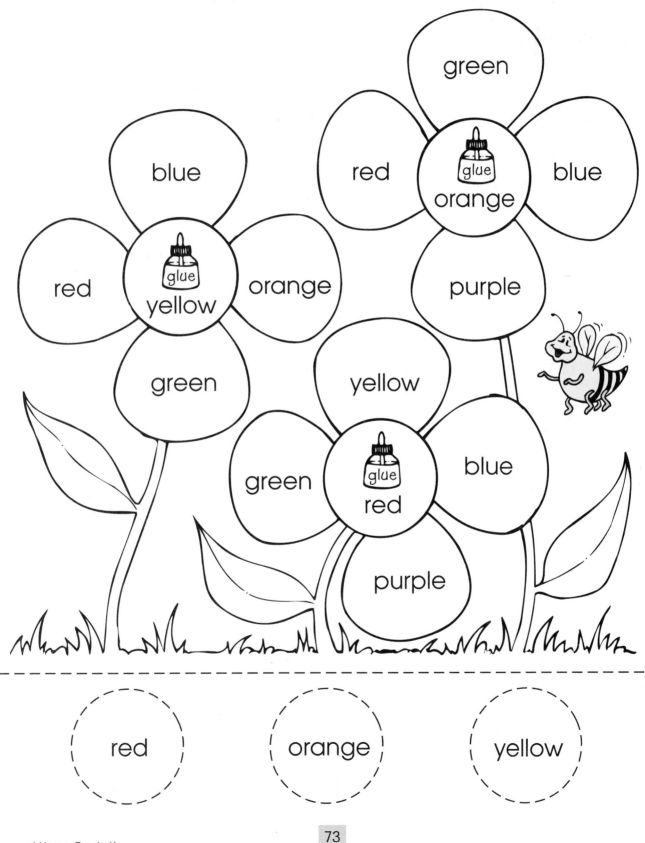

Learn at Home, Grade K

Number 3

This is the number 3. **Color** the pictures.

How many things are in this picture? _____

Trace the 3's.

Write your own 3's.

Learn at Home, Grade K

Seashore Numbers

Circle 3 things in each group. **Color** the pictures you circled.

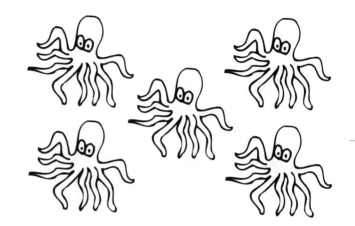

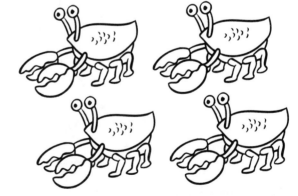

Practice **writing** the number 3.

3 3

Jolly Jelly Beans

Color 3 jelly beans red, 3 jelly beans yellow and 3 jelly beans orange.

Practice **writing** the number 3.

3 3

Beary Good!

How many? **Count**. **Color** 1 blue, 2 red, and 3 yellow.

	Reading	Language	Math
Monday	**D, d** Set out dishes in the shape of an upper- and lower-case *d*. Ask your child if he/she can tell what letter the dishes are forming. Mix them up and have your child arrange them in letter *d*'s. *See* Reading, Week 7, numbers 1 and 2. Have your child complete **Letter D, d** (p. 82).	Explain what a daydream is. Then, encourage your child to use his/her imagination to come up with a crazy *d* dream. A possible daydream might be about a *d*uck *d*ancing in a field of *d*andelions or of a *d*og wearing a *d*ress and playing the *d*rum. Ask your child to think of as many crazy *d* things as he/she can. Then, let him/her choose one picture to draw. Cut out a cloud shape from a piece of white poster board for your child to use for his/her drawing.	**Basic Concepts** Play "Teacher Says" (like "Simon Says"), giving your child directions that use the concepts of up/down, over/under and in/out. **Example:** *Teacher says crawl under the table* or *Go to your bedroom. See* Math, Week 7, numbers 1–4 for additional activities.
Tuesday	Have your child use glue to write an upper- and lower-case letter *d*. Let your child glue either dirt or dimes to the letter *d*'s.	Read *The Very Hungry Caterpillar* by Eric Carle. Have your child match the day of the week to the fruit the caterpillar ate.	Give your child several different scenarios, and have him/her sequence each of the actions. **Example:** Brushing your teeth. What would your child do first? What would he/she do next? What would he/she do last? Your child may need help thinking through the steps in order. Have your child complete **What Comes First?** (p. 84).
Wednesday	Fill a large shallow container with sand. Hide several objects in the sand, including several whose names begin with *d*, such as a dime, toy dog, dinosaur, dice, dish or a doll. Then, let your child try "digging for *d*'s." As he/she uncovers an object, he/she must say whether it is a *d* word or not.	Teach your child the finger play "Five Juicy Apples." *See* Language, Week 7, number 1.	Set out small groups of crayons, each containing one to three crayons. Put a slip of paper beside each group. Have your child count the crayons in each group and write the appropriate number on the slip of paper. Have your child complete **Count 1-2-3!** (p. 85).
Thursday	Help your child make up a *d* tongue twister. Have your child complete **Dudley's Doghouses** (p. 83).	Read and discuss *The Pumpkin Patch* by Elizabeth King. Then, visit a pumpkin patch. Ask your child to describe the pumpkins and to compare the sizes of various pumpkins. Let him/her choose one pumpkin to buy. (*See* today's Science lesson.)	Set out a variety of dishes and have your child sort them into groups by size, shape, pattern or use.
Friday	Make doughnuts using refrigerated biscuit dough. Have your child shape them into upper-case *d*'s. Heat oil in a pan until it sizzles when dough is added to it. Put the *d* doughnuts in the pan and cook them for 5 to 8 minutes, or until golden brown, turning them once. Drain them on paper towels and roll them in cinnamon and sugar or powdered sugar. (Warn your child to stand back when you put the doughnuts in the oil, because there may be some splattering.)	Put several kinds of fruit in a bag. Ask your child to reach in and see if he/she can tell, by touch and smell, what each fruit is.	Turn on a lamp in a dark room. Position yourself so you can make shadows on the wall. Position your child in front of you with instructions not to turn around. Hold up different shapes and objects. Ask your child to guess what they are, based solely on the shadows they create. Have your child complete **Shadow Shapes** (p. 86).

Learn at Home, Grade K

Science	Social Studies	Gross/Fine Motor
Fruits and Vegetables Read *A Book of Fruit* by Barbara Hirsch Lember. You and your child will enjoy this book about how different fruits grow. *See* Science, Week 7, number 1.	**Calendar Skills** Show your child a calendar. Explain how it is organized with the days of the week across the top. Have your child count the number of days in a week. Then, point to the days of the week as you read their names.	Tell your child on what day of the week he/she was born. Using play dough, have him/her design a plate that says *[Tuesday's] Child.* This works best if your child first makes snakes with the dough, then shapes each snake into a letter. Place the letters side by side and gently smooth them together to hold them in place. You may have to use hot glue to attach some pieces after baking. Bake at 250° until the dough hardens. Then, let your child paint it.
Set a variety fruits and vegetables on a table. Ask your child to tell you which are fruits and which are vegetables. Ask him/her what the difference is. Explain that a fruit is the part of a plant that contains the plant's seeds. Usually we think of fruits as being sweet and vegetables as not sweet. However, this is not always the case. The key is to check for seeds. If it has seeds, it is a fruit.	Point to a day on the calendar. Ask your child to find the name of the day of the week. Read it out loud, then have your child repeat it with you. Explain that each day of the week is different. Talk about what your family does on each particular day. Then, review the days of the week.	Draw a hopscotch grid with sidewalk chalk. Have your child draw a fruit or vegetable in each square. If it is a two-square spot, the pictures in both squares must match. As your child hops on each space, he/she must call out *fruit* or *vegetable. See* Gross/Fine Motor Skills, Week 7, numbers 1 and 2 for additional activities.
Encourage your child to examine an apple. Cut it lengthwise. Then, cut a second apple through the center or crosswise. Have your child pull out the seeds and count them. Ask your child if an apple is a fruit or a vegetable. How does he/she know? *See* Science, Week 7, numbers 2–4. Have your child complete **Fruit and Vegetable Puzzles** (p. 87).	Have your child find today's date on the calendar. Ask him/her what day of the week it is. Review the days of the week. Read *Wacky Wednesday* by Dr. Seuss.	Cut apples crosswise. Dip them in paint and use them as stamps. Let your child make patterns or a picture on a large sheet of paper.
Buy a pumpkin (*see* today's Language lesson). Cut out the stem. Have your child explore the inside of the pumpkin. What does it feel and smell like? Have your child clean it out, saving the seeds (*see* today's Gross/Fine Motor lesson). Ask your child if the pumpkin is a fruit or a vegetable. *See* Science, Week 7, number 5.	Have your child find today's date on the calendar. What day of the week is it? Explore the months of the calendar. Flip through the pages and talk about what happens during each month. *See* Social Studies, Week 7, number 1.	Wash the pumpkin seeds from today's Science lesson and soak them in salt water for a few hours. Place the seeds on a cookie sheet and bake them at 300°, turning once. Watch the seeds closely while they bake so they don't scorch.
Blindfold your child. Give him/her a taste of different fruits. See if he/she can tell what they are. This is a good time to introduce your child to a variety of fruits. Purchase some fruits that you do not normally eat. Let your child choose two or three from the produce section.	Have your child find today's date on the calendar. What day of the week is it? Explain that Friday is the last day of the work week for many people. It ushers in the weekend. Explain the concept of the weekend to your child.	Help your child make a fruit salad. Cut up his/her favorite fruits, add a little sugar and toss them together.

READING (D, d)

▶ 1. If you have stairs anywhere in your house, play the "Downstairs Game." Have your child start at the top stair and say *Downstairs, downstairs, D-D-D. I have a word that starts with D.* Your child must say a *d* word before he/she can take a step down. Continue until he/she is standing at the foot of the stairs.

▶ 2. Play tag in the dark. Tell your child that just before someone tags him/her, he/she can be rescued by shouting out a *d* word.

LANGUAGE

▶ 1. "Five Juicy Apples" (finger play)

> *Five juicy apples grew upon a tree.*
> *I looked right at them and they looked back at me.*
> *I picked one apple and I put it in a sack.*
> *I took it to school and I had it for a snack.*
> *Now there are four,*
> *And not one more.*
> *Four juicy apples!*
> *A bird came along and she ate her fill.*
> *She pecked at an apple with her little yellow bill.*
> *Now there are three,*
> *As you can see.*
> *Three juicy apples!*
> *A pony came by and he was very tall.*
> *He picked one apple and he ate it, leaves and all.*
> *Now there are two,*
> *But we're not through.*
> *Two juicy apples!*
> *A bear came along and he climbed up the tree*
> *He said, "Here's an apple for me!"*
> *Now there is one.*
> *We'll soon be done.*
> *One juicy apple!*
> *One red apple decided not to stay.*
> *It fell from the tree and it rolled far away.*
> *Now we are done,*
> *For there are none.*
> *No juicy apples!*

MATH (Basic Concepts)

▷ 1. Cut an apple into different-sized slices. Have your child arrange the apple slices from smallest to largest.

▷ 2. Set out two bowls of grapes. Put only a few grapes in one bowl so the comparison is obvious. Ask your child which bowl has more and which bowl has fewer grapes. Then, fill the bowls with water. Have your child use the terms *more* and *less* to compare the amounts of water. Next, fill the bowls with a nearly equal number of grapes. Have your child count the grapes to determine which has more and which has fewer. Then, fill the bowls with nearly equal amounts of water. Help your child pour them into measuring containers to see which has more.

▷ 3. Cut three lengths of yarn. Have your child put them in order from shortest to longest. Then, have your child put three dolls, three books and three bowls in size order.

▷ 4. Write three numbers on slips of paper. Have your child put the numbers in order. Write three letters of the alphabet on slips of paper. Ask him/her to put those in order, too. If this is easy, add more alphabet letters and numbers to make it more challenging.

SCIENCE (Fruits and Vegetables)

▷ 1. For fruit and vegetable project ideas, consult *Get Growing!* by Lois Walker.

▷ 2. Read *The Life and Times of the Apple* by Charles Micucci.

▷ 3. Read books to help your child learn more about Johnny Appleseed.

▷ 4. Take your child to an apple orchard to pick your own apples. Ask your child questions which encourage him/her to observe the orchard closely.

▷ 5. Read *The Berenstain Bears and the Prize Pumpkin* by Stan and Jan Berenstain.

SOCIAL STUDIES (Calendar Skills)

▷ 1. Find an old calendar. Tell your child specific dates of family members' birthdays. See if your child can find the correct month and day on the calendar. Then, have him/her write the person's name on that day.

GROSS/FINE MOTOR SKILLS

▷ 1. Use face paint and dress up to look like *d* creatures, such as a *d*ragon, *d*warf, *d*og or *d*uck.

▷ 2. Ask your child to gather household *d* objects and place them on his/her *d*esk.

Letter D, d

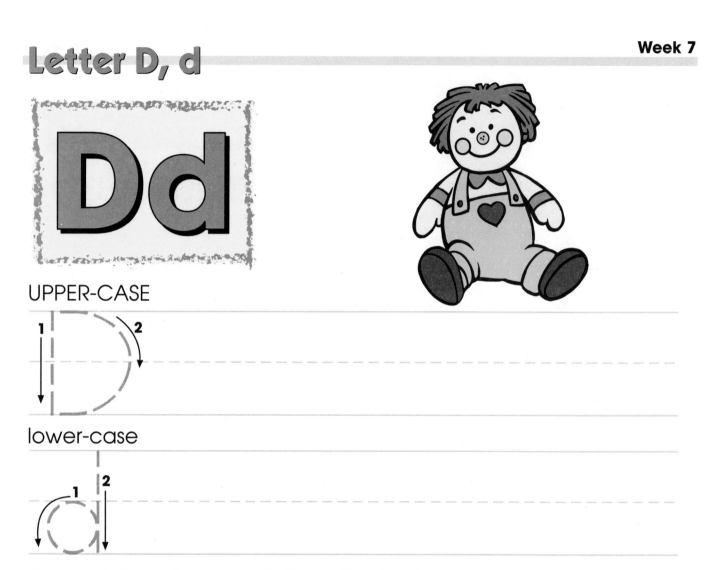

Dd

UPPER-CASE

lower-case

These pictures begin with the letter D, d. **Color** the pictures.

Dudley's Doghouse

Help Dudley find a D, d picture for each doghouse. **Color** and **cut out** each picture which begins with the sound of D, d. **Glue** each picture on a doghouse.

What Comes First?

Color the pictures. **Cut out** the pictures in each row and put them in the order to show what comes first, second and third.

Count 1-2-3!

Trace the number in each row. **Count** and **color** that number of things in each row.

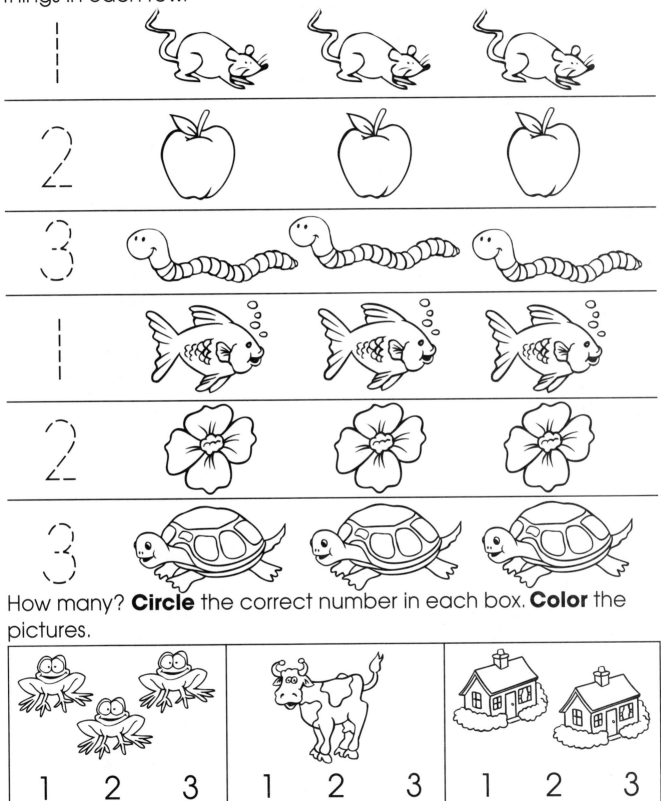

How many? **Circle** the correct number in each box. **Color** the pictures.

1 2 3	1 2 3	1 2 3

Learn at Home, Grade K

Shadow Shapes

Look at the shadow shapes in the first row. **Draw** a line from the shadow to the picture it matches.

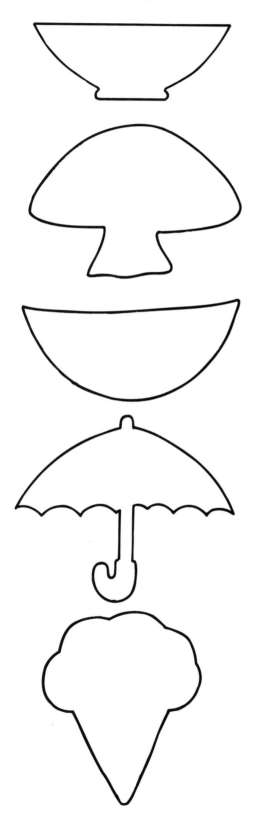

Learn at Home, Grade K

Fruit and Vegetable Puzzles

Color and **cut out** the puzzle pieces below. **Match** each picture with its name.

apple

carrot

pumpkin

grapes

	Reading	**Language**	**Math**

Monday	**M, m**
	Place marbles on a carpet (to prevent rolling) in the shape of an upper- and lower-case *m*. Try tracing the letters lightly with your fingers. Have your child do the same. *See* Reading, Week 8, numbers 1–3 for additional activities.
	Have your child complete **Letter M, m** (p. 92).
		Teach your child this poem:
		  Mushrooms
		  M is for mushrooms in my soup,
		  On my pizza, with my troop.
		  We love to hunt them in the woods,
		  Inspect them, wash them, gobble 'em up.
		
		See Language, Week 8, numbers 1–3.
			4 — Four
			Set out a four from each suit in a deck of playing cards. Ask your child to describe how the cards are similar and how they are different. *See* Math, Week 8, numbers 1–4 for additional activities.
			Have your child complete **Number Four** (p. 94).

Tuesday	Use glue to make an upper- and lower-case *m*. Cover the glue with miniature marshmallows. Have your child complete **Mouse Magic** (p. 93).	Write color words that describe every vegetable you have in your kitchen. See if your child can match each vegetable with the correct color. If not, review color words with him/her.	Give your child four toothpicks or pretzels. Have him/her make the number 4 with them. Cook spaghetti noodles. Give your child four noodles to use to write the word *four*. Sound out the word with your child several times.
Wednesday	Review the *m* sound with your child. Tell him/her that today he/she will be managing mail. Place pictures of *m* words in ten envelopes, one picture per envelope. Help your child make his/her own mailbox and have him/her put the envelopes in your "mailbox." Ask your child to get the mail. Have him/her open each envelope, look at the picture inside and write the beginning letter of the object on the outside of the envelope.	Help your child write a postcard to a grandparent or other relative. Have your child tell all about the words he/she can read, such as color and number words.	Give your child a grocery bag. Let him/her go "grocery shopping" in your refrigerator and cupboards. Tell him/her what to buy and how many of each object you want. Your child should put the correct objects in the grocery bag. Have your child complete **What Belongs?** (p. 95).
Thursday	Think of songs your child knows which have titles that begin with the letter *m*. Choose one, hum the melody and ask your child to guess the song. Repeat with others.	Give your child clues in the form of a riddle that describes a fruit or vegetable. Have him/her guess the food, then tell if it is a fruit or vegetable.	Write the numbers 0 to 4 down the left side of a piece of paper. On the other side, spell out the number words. Have your child match each number to the correct number word on the right. If this is difficult, give your child more practice.
Friday	Make paper mittens. Have your child trace around each hand twice (with his/her fingers close together) on a sheet of construction paper. Have your child cut out the mittens, then write an upper-case *M* on one and a lower-case *m* on the other. Staple two of the mittens together, stuffing them with tissue. Repeat with the second mitten. You may want to staple a piece of yarn between them to keep the mittens together.	Make more construction paper mittens. Cut the right mitten of each pair out of white paper. Write a color word on each one— include all of the color words your child now knows. Cut the left mittens out of colored paper to correspond with each color word. Mix up the mittens and ask your child to match each color word mitten with the correct colored mitten.	Teach your child this pumpkin finger play: *Four Little Pumpkins* *Four little pumpkins sitting by a tree,* *One got squashed and then there were three.* *Three little pumpkins sitting in the dew,* *Grandma came along and then there were two.* *Two little pumpkins searching for the sun,* *Brother pulled one up and then there was one.* *One little pumpkin left on the vine,* *'Til Mom came along and made a pumpkin pie!*

Science	Social Studies	Gross/Fine Motor
Vegetables Read and discuss *Vegetables* by Susan Wake. *See* Science, Week 8, numbers 1–5 for additional activities.	**Calendar Skills** Ask your child to find today's date on a calendar. Review the days of the week, then play calendar games. Ask questions about which day of the week certain dates fall on. Then, have your child ask you questions. *See* Social Studies, Week 8, numbers 1–3 for additional activities.	Slice mushrooms in half. Let your child dip them in paint and use them as stamps. Encourage your child to paint an outdoor scene using the mushroom stamps. *See* Gross/Fine Motor Skills, numbers 1–3 for additional activities.
Set out all the vegetables you have in your home. Have your child tell you their names, colors and sizes.	Have your child find today's date on a calendar. Review the days of the week. Ask your child to locate certain holidays on the calendar, then draw an appropriate picture for each one.	Use a stick to trace letter *m*'s in the mud. Then, write the word *brown* in it. Have your child do the same. Help your child sound out the word and repeat it.
Set out root vegetables, such as carrots, beets and radishes. Explain that they grow underground, because they are roots. To help your child understand the word *root*, go outside and look at tree roots that may be visible. Set out seed vegetables, such as green beans and corn. Explain that a corn kernel is actually a seed and can grow into another corn plant. Open up the bean and show the seeds inside.	Have your child find today's date on a calendar. Review the days of the week. Say *I'm thinking of a month in which*….See if your child can find the correct month based on your description.	Walk around the block counting the number of mailboxes you see. Have your child keep count on his/her fingers.
Set out leaf vegetables, such as lettuce and cabbage. Explain that they grow above ground because they are leaves. Then, set out stem vegetables, such as celery and asparagus. Explain that these are the stem, or stalk, of the plant. Lastly, set out flower bud vegetables, like broccoli and cauliflower.	Have your child find today's date on a calendar. Review the days of the week. Ask your child to count the number of days until Halloween, Thanksgiving and the next birthday in the family.	Play "Vegetable Tag." Tell your child that if he/she drops down on his/her knees and names a vegetable before you tag him/her, he/she is safe.
Visit a large supermarket. Look at and talk about the common as well as the more unusual produce. Review with your child the names of various fruits and vegetables, then have him/her classify each as a fruit or vegetable. Then, let your child choose one unusual fruit and one vegetable to buy.	Have your child find today's date on a calendar. Review the days of the week. Have your child jump rope as he/she recites the days of the week in order.	Scrub the fruit and vegetable you and your child chose at the supermarket (*see* today's Science lesson). Eat the fruit, then decide together how to cook the vegetable.

TEACHING SUGGESTIONS AND ACTIVITIES

READING (M, m)

▶ 1. Describe the following *m* words to your child and challenge him/her to guess as many as he/she can in 1 minute: *monkey, moon, money, mail, me, music, mother, morning, mirror.*

▶ 2. Draw the following *m* words on a sheet of paper and challenge your child to guess as many as he/she can in 3 minutes: *map, man, marble, mat, mailbox, mask, milk, mitten.*

▶ 3. Have your child complete the following sentence: *The man on the moon . . ..* Encourage him/her to use *m* words.

LANGUAGE

▶ 1. Read *Madeline* and other Madeline books by Ludwig Bemelmans.

▶ 2. Have your child bring along a writing tablet when you visit a discount store. Have him/her write *Mm* at the top. Ask your child to draw any *m* objects he/she sees as you walk through the store. After you are home, have your child identify each of the objects he/she drew.

▶ 3. Have your child recite the following poem, filling in the blanks with *m* words:

> *Mm, mm, mm,*
> *I sure love _____.*
> *Mm, mm, mm,*
> *but not as much as _____.*
> *Mm, mm, mm,*
> *M's are just the munchiest.*
> *Mm, mm, mm,*
> *M's are for ME!*

MATH (4 — Four)

▶ 1. Write the number words *zero* through *four* on five slips of paper. Fold them up and place them inside five balloons (use one slip of paper per balloon). Blow up the balloons and tie them. Let your child choose a balloon and pop it. Have him/her read the number word on each slip of paper.

▶ 2. Set out several pennies and demonstrate how to add them. Then, set up equations with the coins. Have your child add each set of pennies. (Keep the sets relatively small.)

▶ 3. Write the numerals 0 through 4 on five slips of paper. Write the number words *zero* through *four* on five other slips of paper. Pin the slips of paper onto socks. Next, hang a clothesline. Put the numbered socks in a laundry basket and hang the number word socks on the line. Have your child match the numerals to the number words and hang them side by side. Encourage your child to do this as quickly as he/she can. Then, have him/her arrange the sock pairs in numerical order.

▶ 4. Show your child a mail scale and demonstrate how it works. Give him/her various small objects to weigh. Divide a sheet of paper into two columns. Have your child draw each object weighed on the left, and record each object's weight on the right.

SCIENCE (Vegetables)

▶ 1. Have your child arrange vegetables according to color and type.

▶ 2. Prepare a big chef salad with your child. Talk about each of the vegetables as you wash and slice them.

▶ 3. Arrange vegetables according to the letter they begin with. Have your child write the beginning sound for each vegetable on slips of paper and put them in alphabetical order.

▶ 4. Play a game to test your child's memory. Start out by saying, *I'm planting a garden with green vegetables, like lettuce.* Challenge your child to repeat the sentence and add another green vegetable, such as *I'm planting a garden with green vegetables, like lettuce and cucumbers.* Continue until one of you makes a mistake or can't think of another vegetable. Try with other groups of vegetables or fruits.

▶ 5. Try growing an avocado plant. Watch how the roots form.

SOCIAL STUDIES (Calendar Skills)

▶ 1. Help your child write what he/she does each day of the week. Help him/her look for any patterns in his/her activities.

▶ 2. Have your child stack a block as he/she names each day of the week. If he/she gets to Saturday and the stack still hasn't fallen, start over with Sunday and continue until the stack comes crashing down.

▶ 3. Have your child make up a song about the days of the week and what he/she does on each day.

GROSS/FINE MOTOR SKILLS

▶ 1. Take your child for a walk. Keep it interesting by varying your style of walking. Say, for example, *I see a sign, let's skip* or *I see a house, let's run.* It won't be long until your child catches on and can join in.

▶ 2. Make a treasure map for your child that leads to a special treasure. Draw landmarks that start with *m.* Help your child follow the map.

▶ 3. Have your child draw a map of his/her favorite places to play.

Letter M, m

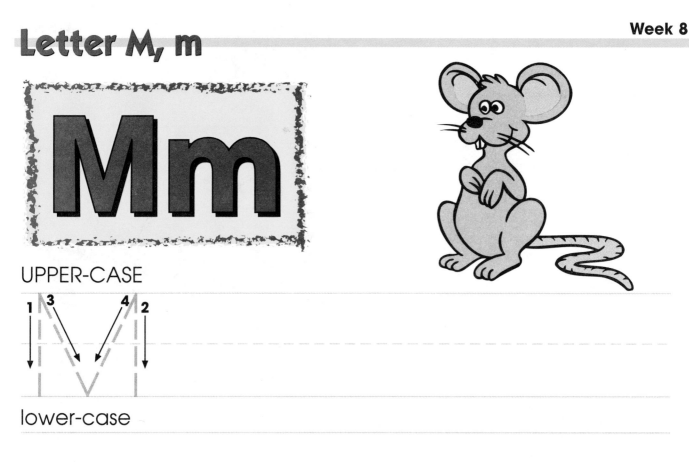

UPPER-CASE

lower-case

These pictures begin with the letter M, m. **Color** the pictures.

MILK MILK

Learn at Home, Grade K

Mouse Magic

Help Michael Mouse perform magic. **Color** only the pictures that begin with the sound of M, m.

Number 4

This is the number 4. **Color** the pictures.

How many things are in this picture? _____

Trace the 4's.

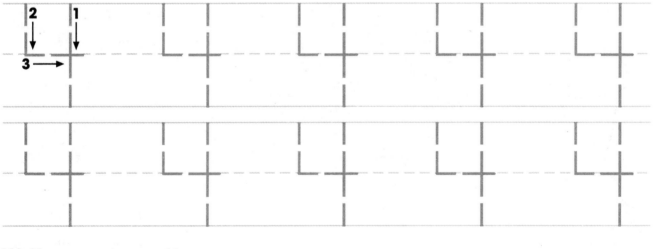

Write your own 4's.

What Belongs?

Draw an **X** on each thing which does not belong in the grocery store.

Learn at Home, Grade K

	Reading	**Language**	**Math**
Monday	**Consonant Review** Set out two objects that start with each of the review letters *b, t, c, s, d* and *m*. Have your child name the beginning sound for each object. *See* Reading, Week 9, numbers 1–4 for additional activities. Have your child complete **Consonant Review** (p. 100).	Read *How Rabbit Stole the Fire*, a book of folktales by Joanna Troughton. *See* Language, Week 9, number 1.	**5 — Five** Get out five balls. Have your child count them out loud. Help your child try to keep all five balls bouncing at the same time. Using mustard, squirt a number 5 on a napkin. Have your child do the same. Let your child continue to practice squirting 5's. Have your child complete **Number 5** (p. 103).
Tuesday	Using a jumbo box of crayons, have your child find a color that starts with each of the following letters: *b, t, c, s, d* and *m*. Then, have your child color a picture using only those colors.	Look at the **Native American Symbols** chart on page 101 and discuss with your child why each one might have been chosen. Draw a simple story using these symbols, and ask your child to interpret the symbols to tell the story. Then, help your child create his/her own story.	Have your child trace five circles on a sheet of wrapping paper and cut them out. Write the word *five* in the center of a sheet of construction paper. Have your child glue the five circles on the paper all around the word *five*. Help your child sound out the word *five*, then have him/her write a number on each of the five circles.
Wednesday	Write the following upper- and lower-case letters, each on a separate slip of paper: *b, t, c, s, d* and *m*. Pin each slip of paper to a sock. Have your child match each upper-case letter with the correct lower-case letter.	Read *Thirteen Moons on Turtle's Back: A Native American Year of Moons*, a book by Joseph Bruchac, Jonathan London and Thomas Locker. Talk about legends and myths and how they are used to explain events and natural phenomena. Encourage your child to make up his/her own legend or myth.	Set out a bunch of licorice sticks. Have your child count out groups or sets of five. Have your child complete **Cupcake Count** (p. 104).
Thursday	Ask your child to be a "letter detective." Give him/her a special hat and a magnifying lens. Say words that begin with *b, t, c, s, d* or *m*. He/she must tell you the beginning sound for each word. Repeat, this time with written words as in a story. Can your detective spot the mystery letters (d, m, s, c, b, and t)? If so, ask him/her to shout "Aha!" and point to the letter.	Read *Raven: A Trickster Tale From the Pacific Northwest* by Gerald McDermott. Enjoy the story and use the bold artwork to review color words with your child. *See* Language, Week 9, number 2.	Teach your child the finger play, "Be One, Two, Three, Four, Five." *See* Math, Week 9, number 1.
Friday	Have your child draw a picture in which each of the following letters is represented: *b, t, c, s, d* and *m*.	Ask your child what he/she thinks of when he/she thinks of black. Colors symbolized certain things to many Native Americans. Black, for instance, meant disease, sickness, death, cold and night. Spell the word *black* with a thick black marker. Sound out the word with your child. Have your child draw symbols to represent the Native American meaning of black. Have your child complete **Black** (p. 102).	Write each of the following color words on a small slip of paper: *red, yellow, blue, orange, purple, green, brown* and *black*. Have your child match each color word with the corresponding crayon in a box of crayons. Have your child complete **Make a Splash!** (p. 105).

Science	Social Studies	Gross/Fine Motor
Simple Experiments Have your child rub a balloon against his/her hair for 1 minute. Ask him/her to look in a mirror as he/she pulls the balloon away. What happens? Explain that static electricity is created by friction between two objects that are rubbed together. *See* Science, Week 9, numbers 1–3 for additional activities.	**Native Americans** Explain that Native Americans are also known as Indians because Columbus thought he had landed in the West Indies—not America. The term *Native American* means native to (or born in) America. Read *North American Indians* by Andrew Haslam and Alexandra Parsons to help your child see the way Native Americans looked, dressed and lived long ago.	Make a simple model of a Native American drum from an oatmeal container covered with construction paper. Let your child practice playing various rhythms. Then, model a rhythm for your child, and ask him/her to repeat it. Repeat, trying several patterns and rhythms. *See* Gross/Fine Motor Skills, Week 9, number 1.
Set up a drying rack in a room in your home and discuss what happens when things get wet. Explain that when something "dries," the water *evaporates* from it. Hang up wet towels, paintings and different pieces of clothing and have your child predict how long it will take the water in each one to evaporate. Then, have your child observe the evaporation and discuss the results. Ask your child: *Why did certain materials dry more quickly than others?*	Discuss how Native Americans communicated with one another. See pages 48–51 of *North American Indians* by Haslam and Parsons for pictures of some of the hand motions Native Americans used to communicate. Try communicating with your child using these same gestures. *See* Social Studies, Week 9, numbers 1–4 for additional activities.	Make fry bread, a traditional Native American quick bread, with your child. Follow a simple recipe you may have or one included in Laurie Carlson's *More Than Moccasins: A Kid's Activity Guide to Traditional North American Indian Life.*
Place a white carnation in a vase of water. Have your child add food coloring to the water. Have your child observe any changes today and note them on a chart. On the left side of the chart, label Days 1–3. Leave the right side open for your child's observations.	Explain to your child that North Americans ate a healthy diet of buffalo, fish, grain, nuts, fruit, corn, beans, popcorn and squash. They were excellent fishermen and hunters. With your child, discuss the tools Native Americans might have used to hunt and fish. Then, share a healthful Native American snack of popcorn, nuts, fruit and dried beef sticks.	Take your child fishing. If that is not possible, cut out fish shapes from construction paper. Attach a large paper clip to each fish. Simulate a pole, fishing line, and hook using a dowel rod, piece of yarn and magnet. *See* Gross/Fine Motor Skills, Week 9, numbers 2–3.
Use mealtimes and snacktimes to explore what happens when water evaporates, is boiled or frozen. For example, boil water and have your child observe what happens to the water. You may also wish to freeze water to make ice cubes or dry fruit to demonstrate what happens to fruit when the water inside evaporates. Have your child observe the carnation again today and write down his/her observations next to Day 2.	Tell your child that Native Americans enjoyed their free time. They often played games, such as "War's Little Brother," an awl game (similar to a board game) and "Post Ball." They also enjoyed music. They are known for their rhythmic drums and dances. Consult *North American Indians* for a detailed account of Native American leisure activities.	Play the Native American game of "Post Ball." The object of the game is to hit a post with a ball. Women were allowed to use their hands, but men could only use sticks. For your game, try using the post of a basketball net and a large ball, such as a soccer ball or a basketball.
Have your child observe the carnation again today and write down his/her observations next to Day 3. Once the carnation has turned the color of the food coloring, explain how the plant's special tubes, called xylem, carry the water up the roots into the stem and eventually into the flower. These tubes keep the flower beautiful by providing nourishment. The tubes carried the food coloring along with the water, causing the carnation to change color.	Explain to your child that Native American homes varied with the specific tribe and climate. Tepees, pueblos, reed houses, hogans, and lean-tos are some examples of typical dwellings. Some Native Americans were nomadic, meaning they moved from place to place. Ask your child what types of homes would be suitable for people on the move. Why does he/she think the Native Americans would want to move around?	Choose a type of Native American home to make (*see* today's Social Studies lesson). Think of ways to make your model look realistic. For example, if it was made with mud and sticks, use the same materials to make your model.

Learn at Home, Grade K

TEACHING SUGGESTIONS AND ACTIVITIES

READING (Consonant Review)

▷   1.   Spray shaving cream into the sink. Let your child write each review letter in both upper- and lower-case.

▷   2.   Play "Who am I?" with letters. Your child must try to guess a letter based only on your description of the letter's shape. Try not to use words that begin with the mystery letter.

▷   3.   Make gelatin. After it has solidified, use lightly floured alphabet cookie cutters or molds to make the review letters. Then, have your child name two words that begin with each letter.

▷   4.   List specific examples from a category whose name starts with one of the review letters. See if your child can guess the category. For the letter d, for example, list kinds of dogs. See if your child recognizes them as dogs. For the letter c, name kinds of cars. You may want to begin this activity by working through an example with your child.

LANGUAGE

▷   1.   Help your child write a short story about a Native American child. Have him/her draw illustrations to go along with the story.

▷   2.   Go to the library and look for books or videos on Native Americans. Using the books and/or video from the library as references, make a traditional Native American outfit for your child to wear. Cut a simple shape and sew it together. Allow your child to decorate it with beads, felt appliques or other materials.

MATH (5 — Five)

▷   1.   "Be One, Two, Three, Four, Five" (finger play)

Teach your child this finger play. Help your child create actions to go along with the play.

> *Be one puppy trying to catch her tail.*
> *Be two pigs that are eating from a pail.*
> *Be three mice nibbling on some cheese.*
> *Be four butterflies flying in the breeze.*
> *Be five tadpoles swimming in a pool.*
> *Be boys and girls who like to play school.*
> *Be one rabbit hopping up and down.*
> *Be two squirrels hiding nuts in the ground.*
> *Be three snow people standing in a row.*
> *Be four roosters who like to crow.*
> *Be five fishes splashing in a pool.*
> *Be boys and girls who like to play school.*

SCIENCE (Simple Experiments)

▶ 1. Consult the *Fun With Simple Science* series by Barbara Taylor and *Science for Kids* by Robert W. Wood for ideas for simple experiments to do with your child.

▶ 2. Remove the paper from several crayons and set them outside in the sun. Have your child check on them a few hours later. What happened? Ask: *What else will melt in the sun?*

▶ 3. Play, "What will happen if...?" Have your child ask him/herself, *What will happen if I _____?* and fill in the blank. Then, have your child try each thing to find out what does happen. Discuss famous inventors and how their curiosity and willingness to experiment may have led to some of their inventions.

SOCIAL STUDIES (Native Americans)

▶ 1. Teach your child how to weave a basket. If you don't know how, consult a large craft store. They may either offer classes or be able to direct you to another place to take classes.

▶ 2. Go to a museum that has a Native American exhibit. Talk with your child about what he/she observes as he/she looks at the artifacts.

▶ 3. Buy beads and show your child how to string them into necklaces, just like many Native Americans do.

▶ 4. Give your child a pair of moccasins. Ask why he/she thinks Native Americans wore these shoes. Does your child like to wear them? Why or why not?

GROSS/FINE MOTOR SKILLS

▶ 1. Cut pieces of paper into strips. Teach your child how to weave the strips together until he/she has woven a whole sheet. Discuss how Native Americans wove cloth to make mats.

▶ 2. Camp out in the woods to honor our Native American heritage. Bring along a traditional kind of snack, sing Native American songs around a campfire and, if possible, rent a canoe to paddle on a river.

▶ 3. Visit a cave. Talk about how Native Americans often lived in them. Perhaps the cave you visit may even be a Native American cave. For the location of caves, consult a state map or check the Internet.

Consonant Review

Write the beginning sound for each picture.

Native American Symbols

teepee at night

bear alive

day

teepee in the daytime

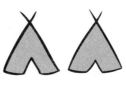

camp

stars

pony tracks

river

mountain

canoe

war

trail

days and nights

rain

deer tracks

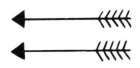

arrows

winter

fish

101

Black

Color the pictures black.

black

black

black

black

black

Write the word.

b l a c k

102

Number 5

This is the number 5. **Color** the pictures.

How many things are in this picture? _____

Trace the 5's.

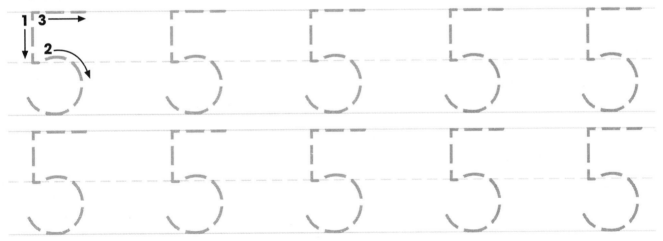

Write your own 5's.

Learn at Home, Grade K

Cupcake Count

Count aloud from 1 to 5. **Connect** the dots in order from 1 to 5.
Color the picture.

Make a Splash!

Color each can and brush. **Draw** a line to match the cans and brushes.

1 red   2 yellow   3 blue

4 brown   5 green

Learn at Home, Grade K

	Reading	Language	Math
Monday	**F, f** Fill a fish bowl or shallow container with water. Cut fish shapes out of sponges. Use a permanent marker to write an upper- or lower-case *f* on each fish. Your child will enjoy your new easy-to-care-for "pets." *See* Reading, Week 10, numbers 1–4 for additional activities. Have your child complete **Letter F, f** (p. 110).	Prepare your child for today's Science experiment with the following poem. Recite it with your child several times. See if he/she can memorize it. *Water, magic water,* *How I wonder at your style.* *You are smoky or you're icy,* *Or you're in a drippy pile.*	**Basic Concepts** Make a pattern with round cookies and square crackers. As you set up the pattern, ask your child to describe the shape of the cookies and crackers. Then, have your child complete the pattern you started. Have your child try to complete at least two or three additional patterns. *See* Math, Week 10, numbers 1–4 for additional activities.
Tuesday	Dip your pointer finger in finger paint. Paint upper- and lower-case *f*'s on a sheet of paper. Lay your finger down sideways to form the trunk of the *f*. Then, use just part of your finger to make the horizontal sticks. Model this process for your child, then let him/her try. Then, let your child put his/her foot in the paint and stamp it on the paper several times.	Read *The Foot Book* by Dr. Seuss. Have your child point to the word *foot*. Note that it starts with the letter *f*. As you read the book, read slowly and move your finger under each word as you read it. Have your child look for the word *foot* and read it with you when he/she sees it. *See* Language, Week 10, numbers 1–4 for additional activities.	Set out two pairs of socks per family member. Have your child sort them first by size, then by color.
Wednesday	Set a variety of objects on your kitchen table, making sure many of them begin with the letter *f*. Make the *f* sound for your child and have him/her repeat it after you several times. Then, have your child put all the *f* objects on one side of the table and the rest of the objects on the other side. Have your child complete **Funny Fences** (p. 111).	Help your child create an *f* tongue twister. Try to say your tongue twister five times in a row very quickly.	Set out forks for your child to count. Change the number several times and have your child count them out loud, one by one. Have your child complete **What a Winner!** (p. 112).
Thursday	*F* is for french fries! Buy Alphabet French Fries and cook them according to the directions. Have your child pick out all the *f*'s. Then, see how many other letters your child can name. See if he/she can tell you the sound each letter makes and a word beginning with that sound.	Read *Owl Moon* by Jane Yolen. Read it with the lights out in a whispery voice.	Pose a number of sequencing scenarios for your child. **Example:** Which comes first—putting away the dishes or washing the dishes? Have your child complete **What Comes First?** (p. 113).
Friday	Read *One Fish, Two Fish, Red Fish, Blue Fish* by Dr. Seuss. Have your child read the number and color words for you. Ask him/her to point to any *f*'s on the page.	*One little finger wiggles in the sun.* *Two little fingers, run, run, run!* *Three little fingers, spread wide apart.* *Four little fingers point to your heart.* *Five little fingers walk up the hill.* *Six little fingers stand straight and still.* *Seven little fingers climb up a tree.* *Eight little fingers fly like a bee.* *Nine little fingers scratch in the sand.* *All little fingers hide in my hand.*	Set out two stacks of blocks, each containing a different number of blocks. Ask which pile has more. Then, explain that the other pile has fewer. Repeat with different stacks. Then, have your child make his/her own stacks. Tell him/her which you think has more and which has fewer. Your child must determine if your answer is right or wrong.

Science	Social Studies	Gross/Fine Motor
Simple Experiments Pour a glass of water into a teakettle or saucepan. Heat it on high until steam forms. Have your child tell you what he/she observes. Next, fill an ice cube tray with water. After it freezes, show your child the ice. Talk about the three forms of water: solid (ice), liquid (water) and gas (steam). *See* Science, Week 10, numbers 1–3 for additional activities.	**Native Americans** Discuss Native American family life. Explain that a village was made up of a group of relatives called a *clan*. Explain that your child's clan would be made up of aunts, uncles, grandparents and other relatives. Children learned through play with bow, arrows and dolls. Grandparents taught the children about life. Men were usually the warriors, although some women helped in battle.	Fill your bathtub with water. Have your child get in and pretend to be a fish. Can your child put his/her head under the water? Can he/she kick his/her "fins" and blow bubbles? *See* Gross/Fine Motor Skills, Week 10, numbers 1–3.

Make crystals with your child:
1. Chop a handful of "non-starter" charcoal briquets into two or three pieces each.
2. Mix together:
  6 Tbs. laundry bluing
  6 Tbs. salt
  1 Tbs. ammonia
3. Pour the mixture over the briquets.
4. Let it sit for six days.
	Continue your discussion about Native American life. Explain to your child that Native Americans used art to please the gods, or spirits, as they called them. Many of their baskets, clay pots, jewelry and rugs were not only functional but beautifully crafted as well. Many symbols were specifically used to please different spirits. *See* Social Studies, Week 10, numbers 1–4 for additional activities.	Help your child make a clay pot. If the clay is too stiff for your child to work with, try adding water, or use play dough. Bake at 250° until it hardens. Let your child paint the completed pot with bright colors and Native American symbols. *See* Gross/Fine Motor Skills, number 10, number 4.

Have your child observe the charcoal briquets. Help your child make a two-column chart to record his/her observations. Have him/her label down the left column Days 1–6, leaving room for his/her observations in the right column. Have your child record what he/she sees today, and have him/her continue to observe for the rest of the week.	Tell your child that Native Americans typically got around by foot or canoe until Europeans introduced horses to the New World, or America. A main reason for travel was trade. Native Americans did not use money like we do today. Instead they used a barter system—they would trade something they had for something they needed or wanted. They often traded blankets, furs, tools, horses, hides, jewelry, eagle feathers and pearls.	*Cars and bikes and buses, too,* *Lots of ways I like to move.* *Boats and planes and big balloons,* *From here to there, and oh, so soon.* Repeat this chant several times with your child, then talk about the ways in which Native Americans traveled. Whose ways are faster? Ask your child which way he/she would rather travel.
Have your child continue to observe the charcoal briquets and record his/her observations.	Explain to your child that Native Americans saw their skill in hunting as extremely important. To be a skillful hunter was a great honor in the village. Native Americans used bows and arrows, rawhide shields and tomahawks to hunt. They went to war mainly to protect themselves or when others stole their horses or their land.	Explain to your child that Native Americans first showed Europeans how to grow corn. Help your child make corn bread, using a boxed mix or a recipe from a cookbook.
Have your child record today's observations on his/her chart. Have him/her continue to observe the briquets and record his/her observations throughout the weekend and into Monday.	Tell your child that Native Americans believed in a very real and active spirit world. It was as real to them as the physical world they could see. Whenever anything happened, it was because of the spirits. If a child got sick, they thought a spirit was angry with them. If they had a poor hunt, a spirit was also unhappy. Native Americans performed ritualistic dances complete with masks in order to honor and appease the spirits who were angry.	Make your own masks using paper plates, feathers, sand (dyed with food coloring) and leaves. Punch a hole in each side of a plate and use a piece of twine or yarn as strings to tie the mask on.

Learn at Home, Grade K

TEACHING SUGGESTIONS AND ACTIVITIES

READING (F, f)

▶ 1. Have your child make a family flag out of construction paper. Let him/her choose the colors for the flag and pictures to include on the flag that represent your family.

▶ 2. Draw the following *f* words on a sheet of paper and challenge your child to guess as many as he/she can in 2 minutes: french fries, finger, fox, frog, face, fish.

▶ 3. Get two grocery bags—one for you and one for your child. Set a timer for 4 minutes. See who can find the most *f* objects in that time.

▶ 4. Hide four feathers in various *f* places (fireplace, foyer, floor). Give your child clues until he/she finds the feathers. You may also help your child by saying *warm* and *cold* as he/she gets closer to or farther away from the feathers.

LANGUAGE

▶ 1. Read *Hurry Up, Franklin* by Paulette Bourgeois. There are several other books featuring Franklin that would also be perfect for *F* Week.

▶ 2. Help your child write a short poem or nursery rhyme about friends.

▶ 3. Help your child take pictures of letter *f* objects. Cut construction paper in half and staple several sheets together to form a book. Have your child write *My Letter F, f Book* on the cover. On the first page he/she can write, *F-f-f . . . these words start with f.* Then, have him/her tape the *f* pictures in whatever order he/she chooses, naming the *f* words as he/she goes.

▶ 4. Ask your child to make a commercial for the letter *f.* Help him/her plan the commercial before starting it. Record it on videotape if you have access to a camcorder.

MATH (Basic Concepts)

▶ 1. Teach your child how to estimate. Place several objects in a bowl. Ask your child which number is closest to the number of objects in the bowl: 1, 8 or 20. Repeat with other numbers to give your child practice in estimating.

▶ 2. Find a good fudge recipe. Have your child measure out each of the ingredients and do the mixing. Explain each of the measuring utensils he/she will need as you go along.

▶ 3. Talk about the ordinal numbers *first* through *fifth.* Then, have your child put the objects in size order, using the ordinal numbers.

▶ 4. Have your child tell you what he/she did this morning. Have your child say, *First I* _____.
Second, I _____ . . . .

SCIENCE (Simple Experiments)

▶ 1. Pour various amounts of water into several similar glasses. Ask your child to clink a spoon on each glass. How does each sound? Have your child put the glasses in order by pitch, from lowest to highest. Then, look at the water level in each glass. Help your child deduce: *The fuller the glass, the _____ the pitch.*

▶ 2. Have your child grow mold. Let bread mold in the refrigerator in an airtight container. Add water to help increase the mold. Help your child record observations each day. Discuss beneficial molds, such as penicillin, that are used as medicines.

▶ 3. Purchase an inexpensive microscope. If it is not possible to get a microscope, a magnifying lens will do. Your child will love observing everyday objects closely. Have your child record observations by drawing what he/she sees through the lens.

SOCIAL STUDIES (Native Americans)

▶ 1. Native Americans often hunted buffalo. See if you can find buffalo meat in a large supermarket or served at a nearby restaurant. Try a buffalo burger. Have your child compare the buffalo meat to other foods he/she has eaten. What does it taste like? Does he/she like it?

▶ 2. The Native Americans dried their own fruits and beef. You can, too, with the convenience of a food dehydrator. If you don't have one, see if you can borrow one. They are very simple to use. Your child can do most of the work, which is minimal. Be sure to follow directions for your particular machine.

▶ 3. Talk about why the Native Americans needed to dry their meat and fruit. Discuss the conveniences that we have today that Native Americans did not have.

▶ 4. Go to the library and look for a tape or CD of Native American music. Listen to it together at home. What does your child think? Does he/she like it? Why or why not? Encourage your child to dance or move to the music.

GROSS/FINE MOTOR SKILLS

▶ 1. Play "freeze tag" with your child.

▶ 2. Buy your child's favorite juice and make homemade freeze pops by pouring the juice into ice cube trays and freezing. Before the juice sets completely, add a toothpick to each cube.

▶ 3. Have your child draw a huge letter *f* on a sheet of paper. Then, have him/her turn the letter into a fantastical *f* creature.

▶ 4. Make Native American paper dolls. You may have to make the pattern for your child. Then, have him/her color and decorate the dolls, using crayons, markers, feathers and colored sand.

Letter F, f

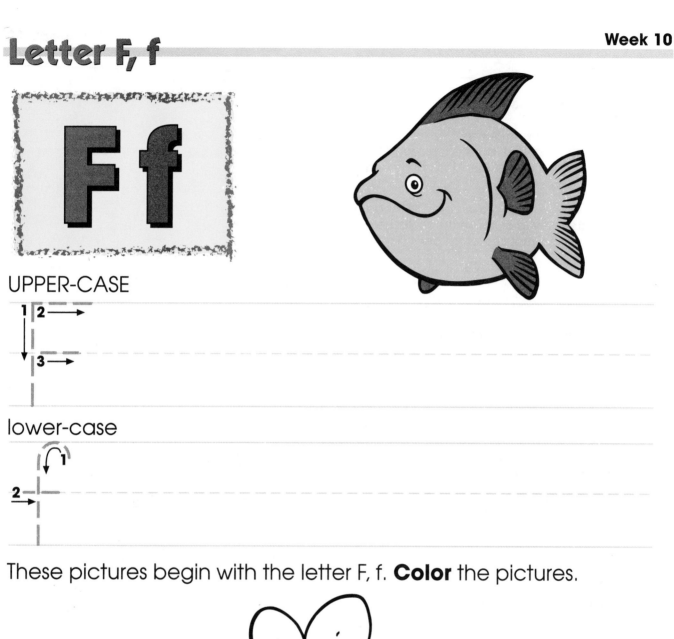

UPPER-CASE

lower-case

These pictures begin with the letter F, f. **Color** the pictures.

Learn at Home, Grade K

Funny Fences

Color and **cut out** each picture which begins with the sound of F, f. **Glue** each picture on the fence.

Learn at Home, Grade K

What a Winner!

Count the number of awards in each group. **Write** the correct number in the box.

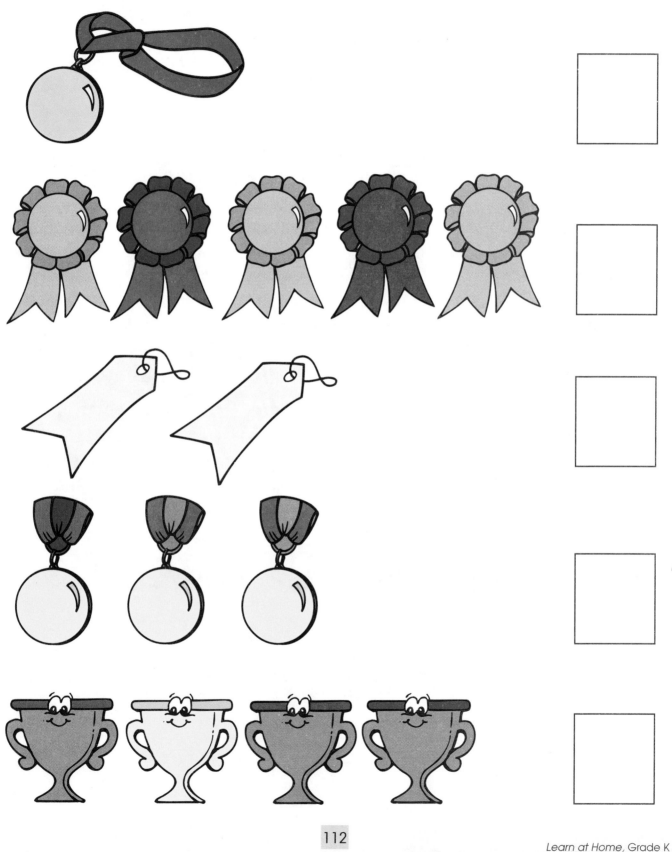

What Comes First?

Color the first picture in each row. **Circle** and **color** the picture that comes next in the story.

	Reading	Language	Math
Monday	**R, r** Arrange rocks in the shape of an upper- and lower-case *r*. Have your child trace the letters with his/her finger. Then, allow him/her to mix up the rocks and arrange them into his/her own letter *r*'s. *See* Reading, Week 11, numbers 1–4 for additional activities. Have your child complete **Letter R, r** (p. 118).	Tell your child the story of *Little Red Riding Hood* by Trina Schart Hyman. Then, act out the story with your child, playing the roles of Little Red Riding Hood and the wolf. To make it more fun, dress the part and use props. Afterwards, discuss the *r* words you used most often in the story. *See* Language, Week 11, numbers 1–4 for additional activities.	**6 — Six** Set out one die from a pair of dice, with the number 6 faceup. Have your child count the number of dots on the top of the die. Then, have him/her count the dots on each of the other sides. Play a simple game that includes a die, so your child will learn to quickly recognize the number without counting the dots each time. *See* Math, Week 11, numbers 1–4.
Tuesday	Have your child draw an upper- and lower-case letter *r* on a wide ribbon, preferably one with books printed on it. Have your child trace each *r* with glue and sprinkle it with dried rice. Your child can use this as his/her reading bookmark. Have your child complete **Remarkable Rockets** (p. 119).	Help your child tell a morality tale. Remember, the key to these stories is that good children are rewarded by pleasant surprises, while bad ones meet with unpleasant circumstances.	Thaw frozen bread dough. Have your child divide the dough into six balls and shape each one into the numeral 6. Bake the dough 6's at 350° until cooked through.
Wednesday	Discuss with your child the sound letter *r* makes. Then, have your child jump rope while chanting the "Red Rooster" rhyme. *See* Reading, Week 11, number 5.	Talk about school in the pioneer days and how it is today. Discuss some of the similarities and differences with your child. Plan a special day in which your child will experience what is was like to go to school "in the olden days."	Have your child select six different colored pencils, crayons or markers to complete **Number 6** (p. 120).
Thursday	Race against your child to see how many *r* objects each of you can find in 2 minutes. Count out the objects, then leave them on the table while you each try to beat your joint score in the next 2 minutes. Play this game several times.	Show your child a smooth object, then a rough object. Encourage him/her to feel the objects and to say the words *smooth* and *rough*. Put several rough and smooth objects in a bag. Then, have your child reach into the bag and determine by touch alone if each object is rough or smooth. Then, see if your child can correctly identify each object with his/her eyes closed.	Arrange objects in groups of one to six or point to groups of objects. Ask your child to tell you how many are in each group. Then, ask him/her to create groups with one to six objects in each. Have your child complete **Complete the Picture** (p. 121).
Friday	Celebrate *R* Day by showing your child how much he/she can read. Write words you know your child can read, such as his/her name, color words, number words; common words, such as *love, mom* and *dad;* and one-letter words, such as *I* and *a*. Then, celebrate your child's progress by doing something special, such as taking a recess from school, complete with a trip to the store to pick out a letter *r* treat.	Have your child tell a letter *r* story. Have him/her create a main character whose name begins with *r*. Help your child think of what the character could do or see that begins with *r*. Continue to help your child with each step of this activity until your child has a complete story.	Give your child a sheet of paper. Roll one die. Have your child look at it, count the dots and tally the number on the sheet of paper. Repeat several times.

Science	Social Studies	Gross/Fine Motor
Magnets Have your child record his/her final observations of the crystal experiment from last week. Read pages 1–11 of *What Makes a Magnet?* by Franklyn M. Branley. Have your child perform the experiment described. Ask your child why some things are attracted to the magnet and others aren't. *See* Science, Week 11, number 1.	**Pioneer Life** Read pages 1–11 of *A Child's Day* by Bobbie Kalman and Tammy Everts. Ask your child how a pioneer child's life was different from and similar to his/her own. Have your child keep a chart: on the right side write, *Pioneer Child*; on the left side, *Me*. Have him/her write the differences on this simple chart. *See* Social Studies, Week 11, numbers 1–4 for additional activities.	Make fried apples and onions together. Use the recipe on page 11 in *A Child's Day*. Let your child do the measuring and stirring. *See* Gross/Fine Motor Skills, Week 11, numbers 1–3 for additional activities.
Read pages 12–15 of *What Makes a Magnet?* Complete the experiment described. Discuss the results.	Read pages 12–19 of *A Child's Day*. Have your child describe more similarities and differences between the pioneer child's life and his/her own. Record them on the chart from yesterday.	Let your child try some of the pioneer games mentioned in *A Child's Day*. He/she could try rolling a hoop, using a hula hoop and stick. You might also to try making your own stilts.
Read pages 16–25 of *What Makes a Magnet?* Discuss the Earth as a giant magnet. Then, make the simple magnetic compass described.	Read pages 20–24 of *A Child's Day*. Have your child discuss the differences between his/her Sundays and a pioneer child's. Have your child write these on the chart.	Help your child make his/her own pioneer paper dolls and clothing. Make two sets of clothing: one set for everyday dress and the other for Sunday best. Make the paper dolls (one boy, one girl) out of poster board. Make the clothing out of construction or wrapping paper. Don't forget to help your child cut out tabs to help the clothes stay in place on the doll.
Read pages 25–31 of *What Makes a Magnet?* Ask your child which poles of a magnet attract and which poles repel. Have your child try the experiment on page 26 of the book.	Read pages 24–31 of *A Child's Day*. Once again, have your child discuss the similarities and differences between pioneer life and his/her own. Help him/her write the differences on the chart.	Plan a race in which you will compete against your child. Plan the event with your child, setting up an obstacle course of letter *r* events. **Example:** *Run to the road's edge. Turn around and ride a bike around the house. Jump off the bike, put on roller skates and skate down the driveway, roll across the lawn to the house,* etc. Be sure to have a blue ribbon on hand for the first-place winner and a red ribbon for the second-place winner.
Take a walk with your child and bring along the compass he/she made. Show your child how to read it. Then, as you turn down various streets, ask your child which direction you're walking. Discuss how compasses help keep people from getting lost. *See* Science, Week 11, number 2.	Visit a museum or village that depicts life in the early 1900s.	While visiting a museum or village depicting life in the 1900s, help your child try some of the hands-on activities. For example, let your child make his/her own candles.

Learn at Home, Grade K

TEACHING SUGGESTIONS AND ACTIVITIES

READING (R, r)

▶ 1. Have your child write the letter *r* on ten note cards. Have him/her find letter *r* objects, write each object's name on a card and tape the card to the object.

▶ 2. Choose a particular day of the week to be Red Day. Wear red clothes, make (and eat) red foods and play with red games or toys.

▶ 3. Have your child create his/her own red food. Make an apple creature with chunks of cheese, olives and pepperoni stuck onto it with toothpicks. Or help your child create a tomato-based pasta sauce.

▶ 4. Play a rhyme game. Say a letter *r* word and have your child say a word that rhymes with it.

▶ 5. "Red Rooster" (jump rope rhyme)

Red rooster, red rooster, turn around,
Red rooster, red rooster, touch the ground.
Red rooster, red rooster, go up the stairs,
Red rooster, red rooster, say your prayers.
Red rooster, red rooster, turn out the light,
Red rooster, red rooster, wake me when it's light.
Cock-a-doodle-do!
Cock-a-doodle-do!
Cock-a-doodle-do!

LANGUAGE

▶ 1. Borrow a riddle book from the library. Enjoy the riddles with your child. Together, create your own riddle to try and stump a friend.

▶ 2. Have your child create a book of favorite recipes, then have him/her actually make them. Let your child take pictures of the finished dishes to include in the recipe book.

▶ 3. Read Walt Disney's *Robin Hood*.

▶ 4. To practice the *r* sound, pretend you are puppies and growl at each other. If your child has trouble with *r*'s, do this daily.

MATH (6 — Six)

▶ 1. Help your child make a six-piece puzzle. A simple one can be made by using a finished page from a coloring book. Have your child brush glue onto the back of the page and attach it to a piece of poster board. Then, have your child cut it into six different puzzle pieces. Challenge him/her to put it back together again.

▶ 2. Take your child to the grocery store. Ask him/her to look for items that come in packages of six. How many can he/she find?

▶ 3. Have your child eat groups of six items. For example, at snack time, have him/her organize grapes into sets of six; or at supper, have him/her organize peas into sets of six.

▶ 4. Allow your child to call six friends or relatives this week. Help him/her prepare a list of six numbers to call. Let him/her dial the number and then check it off after completing the call.

SCIENCE (Magnets)

▷ 1. Try some of the simple magnet experiments in *Magnets* (Junior Science series) by Terry Jennings.

▷ 2. Encourage your child to create art with magnets. Spray paint iron filings (which can be found in hardware stores or science supply catalogs) several different colors, then scatter them on a sheet of paper. Let your child rub a magnet under the paper to form a design or pattern. Spray your child's creation with a clear shellac or clear acrylic spray to keep the filings in place. Be sure there are no large clumps. They will not stay in place. Frame the finished piece and display it.

SOCIAL STUDIES (Pioneer Life)

▷ 1. Show your child how to start a campfire. Let him/her help you build it. Discuss pioneers and the importance of fire in their lives. Discuss the many uses of fire.

▷ 2. Page through *Frontier Home* by Raymond Bial. Enjoy the pictures with your child. Ask him/her to describe the pioneer homes, farms, furniture and tools in the pictures. How are they different from what we have today?

▷ 3. Look at the pictures in *Nineteenth Century Clothing* by Bobbie Kalman. Have your child compare nineteenth century clothing styles to those of today. Which look more comfortable? Which pioneer styles does your child like best? The least?

▷ 4. Skim *A One-Room School* by Bobbie Kalman. Your child will enjoy learning about school life in the pioneer days.

GROSS/FINE MOTOR SKILLS

▷ 1. Have your child build a tower of red. It can be made of anything, as long as it's all red. See if your child can meet his/her goal of building the tower taller than he/she is. While building, have him/her chant:

> *Red tower, red tower,*
> *Way over my head,*
> *Red tower, red tower,*
> *"No tumbling," I said.*

▷ 2. Have races of six: hop six times, skip six steps, run back and forth six times, etc.

▷ 3. Make homemade raisin bread together. Consult your favorite cookbook.

Letter R, r

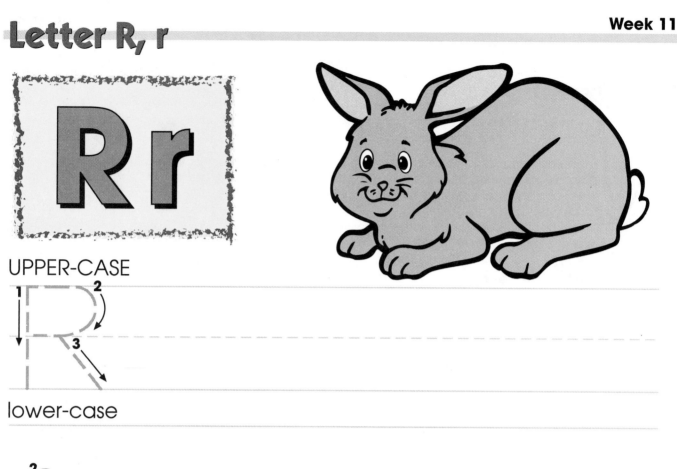

R r

UPPER-CASE

lower-case

These pictures begin with the letter R, r. **Color** the pictures.

Remarkable Rockets

Color and **cut out** each picture which begins with the sound of R, r. **Glue** each picture on a circle under the rocket.

Number 6

This is the number 6. **Color** the pictures.

How many things are in this picture? _____

Trace the 6's.

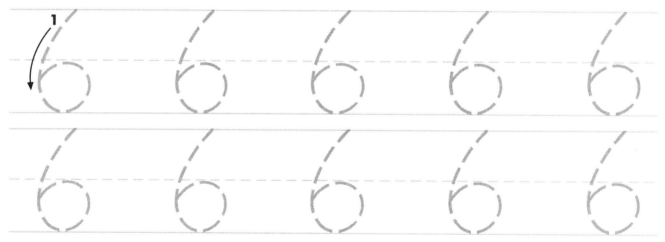

Write your own 6's.

Learn at Home, Grade K

Complete the Picture

Finish each picture.

Draw 1 balloon for the boy.

Draw 2 scoops of ice cream.

Draw 3 fish in the fish bowl.

Draw 4 legs on the horse.

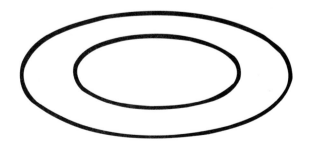

Draw 5 apples on the tree.

Draw 6 cookies on the plate.

Learn at Home, Grade K

	Reading	**Language**	**Math**
Monday	**Consonant Review** Cut note cards into eighteen smaller squares. On each square, write one of the review letters *b, t, c, s, d, m, r,* and *f,* writing upper- and lower-case letter on separate squares. Buy a roll of magnet tape and cut it into strips. Stick each letter to the magnet. Have your child match the upper- and lower-case letters on the front of your refrigerator.	Read the poem "I Am Thankful." *See* Social Studies, Week 12, number 1. Ask your child if he/she likes the poem. Are there any lines he/she would change? Which lines would they be and why? Are there any lines your child would add? Begin a discussion with your child about all the things he/she is thankful for. *See* Language, Week 12, numbers 1–4 for additional activities.	**7 — Seven** Draw a large numeral 7 on a sheet of paper. At the bottom of the page, write the word *seven*. Have your child trace the word, then turn the numeral 7 into a creature that has seven arms, legs, eyes, etc. *See* Math, numbers 1 and 2. Have your child complete **Number 7** (p. 126).
Tuesday	Set a newspaper in front of your child. Give him/her one set of directions at a time, such as *Draw a red circle around each letter r.* Then, give other directions for the letters *b, t, c, s, d, m* and *f,* both upper-case and lower-case, to see if your child recognizes them. *See* Reading, Week 12, numbers 1–3 for additional activities.	Have your child make up his/her own Native American-style dance for the corn harvest. Make it complete with authentic Native American hand motions.	Set out eight note cards with the number words *zero* through *seven* written on them. Hand your child a bag of balloons. Have your child read the number word on each note card and put that number of balloons next to it. Have your child complete **Balloons on a String** (p. 127).
Wednesday	Ask your child to think of an animal whose name begins with each of the review letters (*b, t, c, s, d, m, f, r*). Write the animal names as your child names them.	Discuss the lives of Pilgrim children. Why did wood need to be chopped? Where did children find nuts? What had to be done to the turkey before it could be roasted? Why did Pilgrim children have so much work to do? Would your child like to be a Pilgrim child? Why or why not? Ask your child to choose one or two of the Pilgrim children's jobs to do for a week. Ask if he/she would like to do that chore every day. Why or why not?	Make a fried egg with your child. Talk about each step as you do. Afterwards, ask your child to tell you the order of steps in frying an egg. Have your child complete **Ice-Cream Fun** (p. 128).
Thursday	Say a word that begins with one of the review letters. Using the magnetic review letters you made on Monday, have your child place the first letter of that word on the refrigerator. Play until all the magnets are on the refrigerator. Repeat, with a second group of words beginning with the review letters and have your child remove the magnets, one by one, as each letter is used.	Discuss what the Pilgrims brought with them on their voyage to America. Help your child make his/her own list of necessities to take on a long ocean voyage. Have your child cut out pictures of necessities from newspapers and catalogs. Discuss the things on your child's list. Ask him/her to explain why he/she chose each one.	Write the numerals 0–7 on slips of paper and put them inside plastic eggs. Give your child a bag of jelly beans and have him/her fill each egg with the number of jelly beans shown on the paper. Have your child complete **Eggs-actly!** (p. 129).
Friday	Play "I Spy a Word That Begins With Letter ___." Describe objects for your child to guess that begin with each of the review letters. Reverse roles and let your child describe the objects.	Gather different foods that were served on the first Thanksgiving Day. Blindfold your child and ask him/her to taste several foods. Can he/she guess what any of them are?	Have your child trace his/her foot seven times onto a sheet of construction paper and cut out the outlines. Have him/her write a number word, *one* through *seven*, on each foot. Then, have your child close his/her eyes while you arrange the footprints in numerical order leading to a special treat.

Learn at Home, Grade K

Science	Social Studies	Gross/Fine Motor
Magnets Take your child to a hardware store and look at the many types of magnets there are. Teach your child the correct name for each kind of magnet. Let your child purchase a few for experiments at home. *See* Science, Week 12, number 1.	**Pioneer Life/The First Thanksgiving** Read *Our Thanksgiving Book* by Jane Belk Moncure. Have your child make his/her own Thanksgiving tree with leaves on which your child has written what he/she is thankful for. *See* Social Studies, Week 12, number 1.	Have your child help you think of a good finger play using the Pilgrim finger puppets. *See* Gross/Fine Motor Skills, Week 12, number 1. Have your child make the **Pilgrim Finger Puppets** (p. 130).
Have your child fold a sheet of paper in half, lengthwise. On the right side, have him/her list different objects to try and attract with a magnet. On the left side, have him/her write *yes* if the object attracted the magnet or *no* if it did not.	Talk about the first Thanksgiving Day. Ask your child who came to the New World and why. How did they get there? Who helped them when they arrived in Plymouth, Massachusetts? What did the Native Americans teach the Pilgrims? On the first Thanksgiving, whom did the Pilgrims thank? What kinds of foods were served at the first Thanksgiving?	Teach your child a traditional Native American game. Set a basket in the center of a room. Standing back 4 feet from the basket, try throwing corncob "darts" into the basket. The person who lands the most cobs in the basket, wins the game.
Bring home a magnetized toy—the type in which a magnet is used to move loose iron filings to give a man hair, a beard, a mustache, etc. As your child enjoys playing with it, ask him/her how the toy works.	With your child, discuss what the Pilgrim children probably did on the first Thanksgiving Day. Then, read the poem, "Pilgrim Children." *See* Social Studies, Week 12, number 2.	Have your child make a zoo train of the review letter animals named in today's Reading lesson. Help him/her cut out rectangles and two round wheels per car. Have him/her draw one animal in each car. Attach the cars together by gluing two or three long pieces of yarn along the back. Have your child finish it off by gluing pieces of yarn vertically down each boxcar to look like a cage.
Read pages 4 and 5 of *Magnets* by Steve Parker with your child. Have your child gather household objects that contain magnets. How many did he/she find? Have your child count the objects.	Discuss what the voyage to the New World was like for the Pilgrims. Explain that many Pilgrims became ill and died on the voyage. Using pictures of the Mayflower, help your child make his/her own Mayflower, either on paper or using craft sticks.	Help your child make a Thanksgiving necklace. Have your child use **Thanksgiving Necklace** (p. 131).
Teach your child this rhyme: *Magnets, magnets, everywhere,* *They pull and push through our Earth's* *air.*	Read *My First Thanksgiving Book,* a book of Thanksgiving poetry by Jane Belk Moncure. After reading several of the poems, help your child write his/her own Thanksgiving poem.	Teach your child "Turkey Walk," an action poem. *See* Gross/Fine Motor Skills, Week 12, number 2.

TEACHING SUGGESTIONS AND ACTIVITIES

READING (Consonant Review)

▷ 1. Write each of the review letters on a sticky note. Give your child 3 minutes to attach each letter to an object beginning with that letter.

▷ 2. Have your child cut out leaf shapes. Ask him/her to draw a picture of an object beginning with each review letter on a leaf. Scatter the leaves on the floor. Have your child "rake" the leaves and sort them into same-sound piles.

▷ 3. Spray shaving cream in the sink. Spread it out smoothly, then have your child trace an object beginning with the sound of one of the review letters. Ask your child to write the first letter of that word.

LANGUAGE

▷ 1. Consult *Kids' Holiday Fun* by Penny Warner, a great source of Thanksgiving songs, crafts and party ideas.

▷ 2. For a more in-depth Thanksgiving story, see, *Thanksgiving: Why We Celebrate the Way We Do* by Martin and Kate Hintz.

▷ 3. To help your child gain a clearer picture of life in the pioneer days and the way they celebrated holidays, read books by Laura Ingalls Wilder to your child. Start with the first one, *Little House in the Big Woods*. Read just one chapter a night before bed. This will soon become a treasured tradition.

▷ 4. Read *The Berenstain Bears Count Their Blessings* by Stan and Jan Berenstain. Ask your child to count some of his/her blessings.

MATH (7 — Seven)

▷ 1. Challenge your child to make the highest possible stack of seven objects. Encourage your child to vary the seven objects until he/she finds the combination which makes the highest stack.

▷ 2. Read *Seven Little Rabbits* by John Becker.

SCIENCE (Magnets)

▷ 1. Try magnet experiments from *Magnets* by Steve Parker and *The Science Book of Magnets* by Neil Ardley.

GROSS/FINE MOTOR SKILLS

▶ 1. "I Am Thankful" (poem)

I am thankful for pets.
I am thankful for school.
I am thankful when I
Can swim in a pool.
I am thankful for home,
And the food that I eat.
I am thankful for all
The new friends that I meet.
I am thankful for health,
And for my family.
I'm especially thankful
That I am just ME!

▶ 2. "Pilgrim Children" (poem)

Pilgrim children did not play
On that first Thanksgiving Day.
The first chopped wood which he would take
To help his sister cook and bake.
The second took a great big sack
And brought some nuts, all he could crack.
The third one got a turkey and
She helped to roast it in a pan.
The fourth ground corn to make some bread.
The fifth made covers for the bed.
The sixth one brought a pumpkin by,
She cut it up to make a pie.
The seventh came and popped some corn.
The eighth fed horses in the barn.
The ninth watched food, or it might burn.
The tenth churned butter in a churn.
Pilgrim children did not play
On that first Thanksgiving Day.

SOCIAL STUDIES (Pioneer Life/The First Thanksgiving)

▶ 1. Plan a neighborhood play about the first Thanksgiving. Work together to make props, costumes and scenery.

▶ 2. "Turkey Walk" (action poem)

Old turkey gobbler walks so proudly.
Gobble, gobble, gobble,
Strut, strut, strut!
When he walks, he gobbles very loudly.
Gobble, gobble, gobble,
Strut, strut, strut!

Hold your head high, if you please.
Gobble, gobble, gobble,
Strut, strut, strut!
And when you walk, don't bend your knees.
Gobble, gobble, gobble,
Strut, strut, strut!

Number 7

This is the number 7. **Color** the pictures.

How many things are in this picture? _____

Trace the 7's.

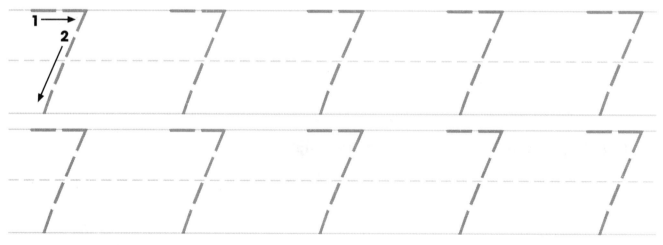

Write your own 7's.

Learn at Home, Grade K

Balloons on a String

Trace the numbers. **Draw** balloons on the strings. **Count** and **color** them.

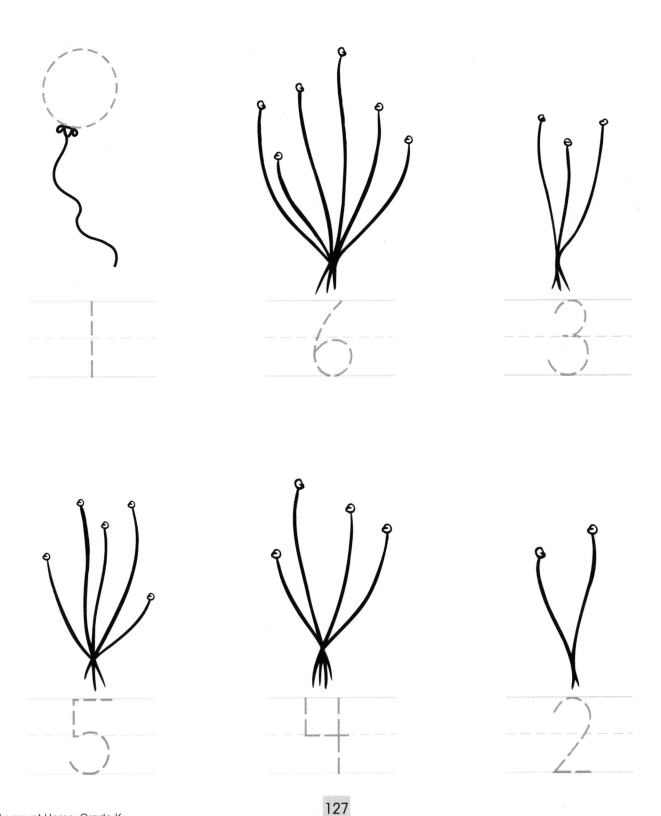

Ice-Cream Fun

Color and **cut out** the numbers. **Glue** the numbers to put the pictures in order.

Eggs-actly!

Draw the correct number of eggs for each duck.

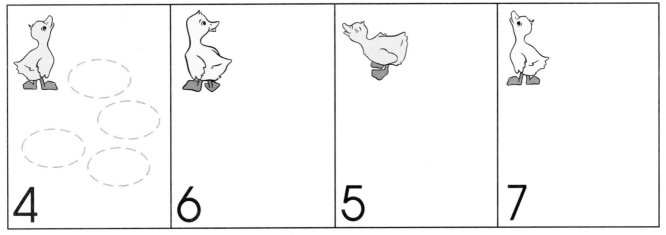

| 4 | 6 | 5 | 7 |

How many ducks? **Circle** the answer.

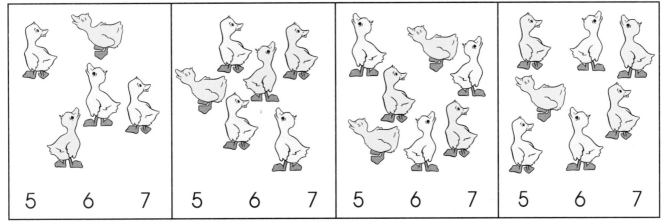

| 5   6   7 | 5   6   7 | 5   6   7 | 5   6   7 |

Match the ducks to the pond.

7

4

6

Pilgrim Finger Puppets

Copy the finger puppet pattern. **Color** and **cut out** the puppets. **Fold** and **tape** the puppets to fit your fingers.

Thanksgiving Necklace

Copy the Thanksgiving patterns. **Color**, **cut out** and **punch** a hole in each one. String them together for a colorful Thanksgiving necklace!

	Reading	Language	Math
Monday	**G, g** Shape two "gold" necklaces into an upper- and lower-case *g*. Have your child trace the necklace letters with his/her finger. Then, allow him/her to form the *g*'s him/herself. *See* Reading, Week 13, numbers 1–4 for additional activities.	Read *Curious George Visits an Amusement Park* (or any other Curious George book) by Margaret and H. A. Rey in honor of the letter *g*.	**Basic Concepts** Introduce the shape of a star by showing your child a star fruit. Cut off a half-inch slice and lay it flat. Have your child tell you how many points are on a star. Have your child dip the slice into paint and stamp it on a sheet of paper. Cut a clean slice and allow your child to eat it. *See* Math, Week 13, number 1.
Tuesday	Have your child draw a large upper- and lower-case *g* on a sheet of paper. Have him/her trace the lines of each *g* with a thick stream of glue. Then, let your child sprinkle glitter on the glue and gently shake off any excess. Have your child complete **Letter G, g** (p. 136).	Talk with your child about the number of times he/she has used each of his/her senses today. Begin a project in which your child keeps track of this information on a chart. At the end of the day, discuss which sense he/she used most often. Ask your child why he/she thinks he/she used that sense most often. Then, ask if he/she thinks he/she will use the same sense most often tomorrow. Have him/her record his/her senses to test his/her prediction.	Draw one circle, one square and one star on a sheet of construction paper for your child to cut out. Have him/her glue each shape onto the outside of a brown paper lunch bag. Then, have your child find objects of each shape and place them in the correct bag.
Wednesday	Play the "Giving Game." Take your child to a discount store. Each of you gets $3 to buy a gift for the other. Bring the gifts home to wrap before exchanging. If possible, try to find gifts that begin with the letter *g*. Have your child complete **A Great Garden of G's** (p. 137).	Teach your child the dreidel song, sung to the tune of "I Have a Little Shadow:" *I have a little dreidel.* *I made it out of clay.* *And when it's dry and ready,* *Then, dreidel I will play.* *Oh, dreidel, dreidel, dreidel,* *I made it out of clay.* *And when it's dry and ready,* *Then, dreidel I will play.*	Remind your child of three events that happened this morning. Have him/her retell the events in the order they happened, using the words *first, second* and *last*. *See* Math, Week 13, number 2. Have your child complete **What Comes First?** (p. 138).
Thursday	Cut off the top of a gallon milk jug. Ask your child to search through the house and fill the gallon jug with any *g* objects he/she finds.	Let your child taste foods that are salty, sweet, sour and bitter. Offer two or three examples of each flavor. Ask your child what he/she notices about where on the tongue those particular taste buds are. (*See* today's Science lesson.) Teach your child the poem "A Story That Never Grows Old," which tells the Christmas story. *See* Language, Week 13, number 1.	Ask your child to observe you as you get out a glass, pour milk inside and drink the milk. Ask your child what you did last. Then, describe another simple scenario and ask your child what came last. Explain to your child that *last* means at the very end. Have your child complete **What Comes Last?** (p. 139).
Friday	Play a *g* game using the following rhyme: *G word, G word,* *It's G word time.* *G word, G word,* *With [pet], what rhymes?* (**Answer:** *get.*)	Declare today Green Day. Have your child dress in green, have a green snack and, using green markers, make a Green Day banner. Make sugar cookies, frost them in green and write *g*'s on them with icing.	Give your child a golf ball. Chant, filling in the underlined portion with a direction phrase: Golf ball, Golf ball, where will you go? <u>Under the table</u>, oh no, oh no! Have your child place the golf ball wherever you say. Use directional words such as *under/over, in/out, up/down, inside/outside* and *above/below*. *See* Math, Week 13, number 3.

Science	Social Studies	Gross/Fine Motor
The Five Senses Have your child act out the following poem: *Five senses each have we,* (Hold up 5 fingers.) *To smell, to taste, to see.* (Point to nose, then mouth, then eyes.) *The other two are clear,* (Hold up 2 fingers.) *They're to touch and to hear.* (Wiggle fingers, then point to ears.) *Five senses each have we,* (Hold up 5 fingers.) *They help explore for me.* (Point to self.)	**Winter Festivals** Teach your child about Hanukkah. Explain that Hanukkah is a festival celebrated by Jews all over the world. It lasts for 8 days and 8 nights, and the days are marked by lighting candles on a candelabra called a *menorah.* Each night one candle is lit, until the eighth night when all eight candles are lit. The candles are lit with a helper candle called a *shamash,* which has a special place on the menorah.	Have your child create his/her own paper menorah with **Hanukkah Menora** (p. 141).
Read *My Five Senses* by Margaret Miller. As your child goes through the day, help him/her notice how often he/she uses each one of his/her senses. Record the information on a chart. (*See* today's Language lesson.) *See* Science, Week 13, numbers 1 and 2 for additional activities.	Read *Latkes and Applesauce: A Hanukkah Story* by Fran Manushkin. Then, make this traditional Hanukkah food with your child. *See* Social Studies, Week 13, number 1.	Help your child make a dreidel. Use a half-pint milk carton and an unsharpened pencil. Paint the dreidel or cover it with construction paper. Write a Hebrew letter ג gimmel, ה heh, ש shin or נ nun, on each side of the dreidel. Put the pencil through the center of the carton with the eraser at the bottom.
Blindfold your child and give him/her a taste test. How many times did he/she guess correctly? Which foods was he/she unable to guess? Ask your child why these ones were difficult to guess.	Play the dreidel game, a traditional Hanukkah game. It is played with a four-sided top, with a Hebrew letter on each side. You can use small candies, raisins or pennies for the "pot." Take turns spinning the dreidel. The letter facing up when the dreidel stops tells the player what to do. Use the **Dreidel Game** (p. 140) as a reference while you play. When the pot gets small, each player should add one to the pot. The person with the most at the end, wins.	Teach your child the finger play "The Dreidel." *See* Gross/Fine Motor, Week 13, number 1.
Have your child stand in front of a mirror and stick out his/her tongue. Explain that each of the little bumps on his/her tongue is a taste bud. Explain that there are four types of tastes: sweet, salty, sour and bitter. All food is made up of one or more of these tastes. The sweet and salty taste buds are located at the tip of the tongue, the sour taste buds are found along the sides and the bitter taste buds are at the back. (*See* today's Language lesson.)	Teach your child about Christmas. Explain that Christmas is a festival celebrated by Christians all over the world to mark the birth of Jesus Christ. Christians celebrate by decorating trees, singing carols, exchanging cards and gifts.	Go on a letter *g* walk. While walking with your child, shout out things you see. Your child must shout *g* if it is a *g* object or make a buzzer sound if it is not.
Have your child hold his/her nose, then eat a flavorful food. Ask him/her how it tasted and why this is so. Then, have your child eat the same food with his/her nose unplugged. Ask how the sense of smell adds to the sense of taste. Collect several fragrant objects, such as cinnamon, peppermint leaves, etc., and place each in a plastic bag. Blindfold your child. Ask him/her to guess what is in each bag using only his/her sense of smell.	Teach your child the poem "One Is for the Manger," which relates the Christmas story: *One is for the manger* *Where Baby Jesus lay.* *Two for Mary and Joseph* *On that Christmas day.* *Three is for the wise men* *Who brought three gifts of love.* *Four is for the shepherds* *And angels' songs above.*	Bake something with your child that has a distinctive aroma—perhaps some homemade bread. While it is baking, discuss the aroma and its effect on how hungry you feel.

Learn at Home, Grade K

TEACHING SUGGESTIONS AND ACTIVITIES

READING (G, g)

▶ 1. Have your child cut out magazine pictures of letter *g* objects and tape them to a gate (a baby gate, an outside fence gate or a paper one you make with your child). To finish it off, have your child cut out a large letter *g* and tape to the center of the gate.

▶ 2. Have a letter *g* scavenger hunt in which each clue will lead your child to a letter *g* object. Next to that object will be another clue for a different *g* object. At the very end, have a granola bar as your child's reward for a successful *g* hunt.

▶ 3. Challenge your child to guess as many *g* animal words as he/she can in 1 minute. Give verbal clues for each animal. **Examples:** goose, goat, gorilla, goldfish, giraffe, guinea pig.

▶ 4. Fill a glass with grapes. Before your child can eat each grape, have him/her say a *g* word.

LANGUAGE

▶ 1. "A Story That Never Grows Old" (poem)

Once a little baby lay
Sleeping in a manger.
Resting on a bed of hay,
A precious little Stranger.
Shepherds on the hillside stayed
With their sheep at night.
They heard such beautiful music played.
They saw a heavenly light.

The donkeys and the cows stood near.
Wise men came from afar.
Mary held the Baby dear,
Over them a star.
Wise men came themselves to know
Of the Baby's birth.
Wise men knelt on bended knee.
Christ had come to Earth!

MATH (Basic Concepts)

▶ 1. Play "I Spy" with shapes. Instead of describing an object by its color, say, *I spy a circle.*

▶ 2. Place several different shapes which are familiar to your child in a line. Ask your child which is first, which is second, and so on. Rearrange the order of the shapes and repeat. Alternately, give your child directions to change the order of the objects: *Put the star first and the circle second.*

▶ 3. On slips of paper, write different directions for your child to follow. Fold these up and place them in a hat. Have your child pull out a slip of paper and follow the directions as you read them aloud. Be sure to incorporate directional words, such as *up/down, over/under, in/out, inside/outside* and *above/below.*

SCIENCE (The Five Senses)

▷ 1. Visit the nearest school for the deaf. Ask if you and your child may walk around, observe the students and attend some classes. Ask your child to note the differences as well as the similarities between how he/she is taught and how deaf students are taught. Take home a sign language alphabet chart and practice learning the sign language alphabet at home.

▷ 2. For more in-depth information on senses, consult *How Our Senses Work* by Jaime Ripoll.

SOCIAL STUDIES (Winter Festivals)

▷ 1. Latke (Potato Pancake) recipe (makes 24 small pancakes)

8 large potatoes	1 large onion	2 eggs, separated
2 tablespoons of flour	1 teaspoon pepper	vegetable oil for frying

Grate the potatoes and onion and strain them to remove the liquid. Combine the potatoes and onion with the egg yolks, flour, salt and pepper. Beat and gently fold in the egg whites. Heat the oil. Fry the latkes on one side, and turn them when they are golden brown and crisp.

GROSS/FINE MOTOR SKILLS

▷ 1. "The Dreidel" (finger play)

Nun, gimmel, heh, shin.　　　　　　　(Count on four fingers.)
Put the nuts and candies in.
Take a dreidel from the shelf,
And let it spin and spin.　　　　　　(Twirl finger.)
Nun means nothing, if it shows.　　　(Make zero with thumb and finger.)
Gimmel is one, a number small.　　　(Hold up one finger.)
Heh means half of everything.　　　　(Hit open palm of hand.)
But shin means win and take it all.　　(Hold out two palms.)
Nun, gimmel, heh, shin.
Spin the dreidel on the floor.　　　　(Make spinning motion.)
Spin it like a top,
One and two and three and four.

Letter G, g

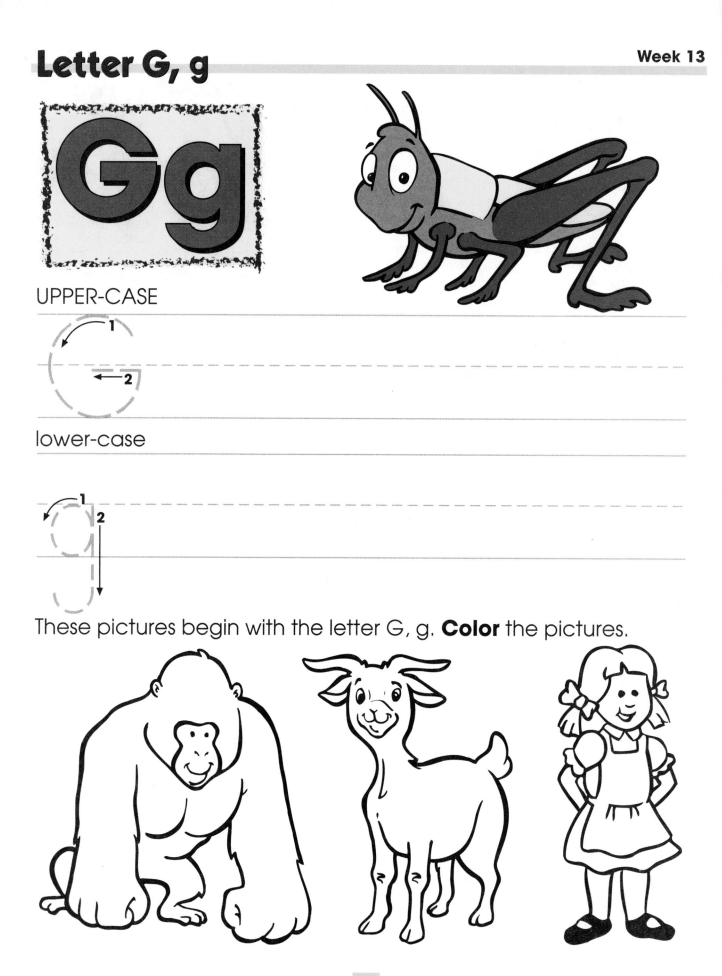

UPPER-CASE

lower-case

These pictures begin with the letter G, g. **Color** the pictures.

Learn at Home, Grade K

A Great Garden of G's

Write G, g under each picture which begins with the sound of G, g. **Color** the G, g pictures.

Learn at Home, Grade K

What Comes First?

Circle the picture in each row that shows what happened **first**.
Color the pictures.

Learn at Home, Grade K

What Comes Last?

Circle the picture in each row that shows what happened **last**.
Color the pictures.

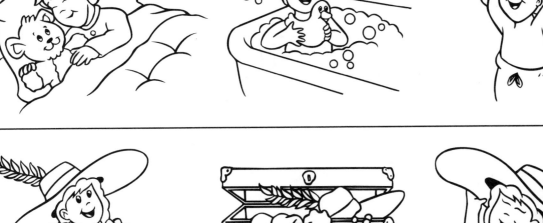

Dreidel Game

  gimmel - gets all

 shin - put in one

heh - gets half

 nun - get nothing

Decorate the dreidel.

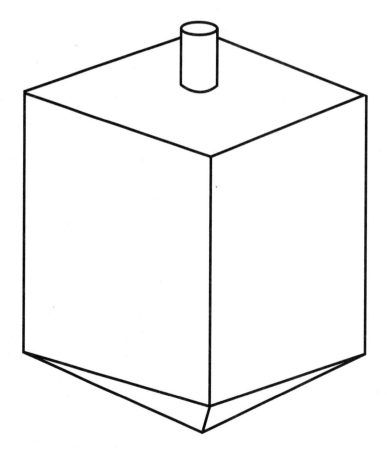

dreidel

Learn at Home, Grade K

Hanukkah Menorah

Color the menorah.
Color and **cut out** the candles.
Glue the candles on the menorah.

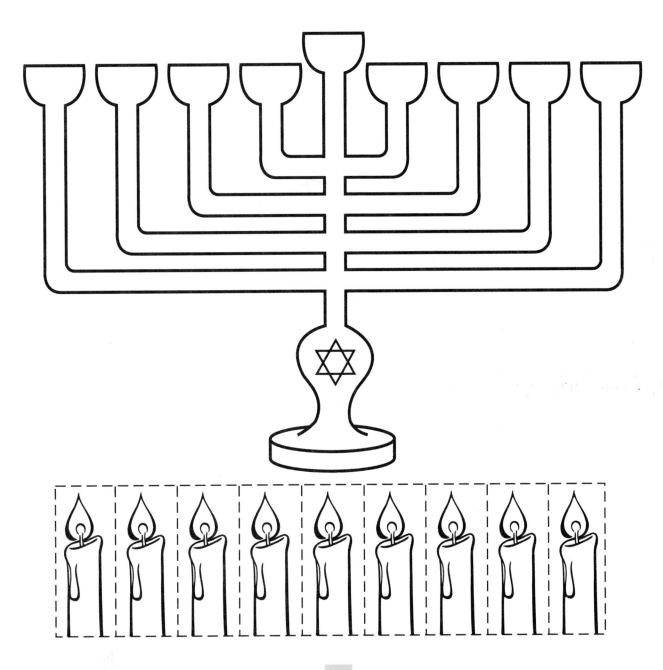

	Reading	Language	Math
Monday	**P, p** Make pancake batter. Pour it through a funnel onto a hot skillet, forming lower- and upper-case *p*'s. Flip the *p* pancakes when bubbles form around the edges. Cook them until they are golden brown. Serve the pancakes for breakfast on *P* Day and enjoy breakfast together. *See* Reading, Week 14, numbers 1–4 for additional activities.	Reread the poem, "My Five Senses." *See* Monday's Science lesson from Week 13. Also read the poem, "Licks." *See* Language, Week 14, number 1.	**8 — Eight** Spread peanut butter on two slices of bread. Using a toothpick, trace the number 8 in the peanut butter. Encourage your child to do the same with the second slices. Smooth out the peanut butter with a knife and let your child repeat several times. *See* Math, Week 14, numbers 1 and 2. Have your child complete **Number 8** (p. 148).
Tuesday	Have your child draw an upper- and lower-case letter *p* on separate paper plates. Have your child squeeze glue onto the lines of each *p* and then place popcorn over the glue. Have your child complete **Letter P, p** (p. 146).	Teach your child the poem "Gingerbread Man:" *Stir a bowl of gingerbread* *Smooth and spicy brown.* *Roll it with a rolling pin* *Up and up and down.* *With a cookie cutter,* *Make some little men.* *Put them in the oven until half past ten.*	Set out a stack of pennies. On two note cards, write **+** and **=**. Set up simple addition equations, such as 2 pennies + 1 penny = ____. (Have your child write the correct number on a note card.) Show your child how to count both sets in order to find the answer. Explain to your child that everything to the left of the **=** is the same amount as on the right. Give your child plenty of practice with basic addition.
Wednesday	Have your child shape pipe cleaners to make a letter *p* family. Encourage him/her to be creative, using fabric, paper and other materials to add eyes, hats, clothes, etc.	Read *The Bears' Picnic* by Stan and Jan Berenstain. Have your own winter picnic indoors. Have your child spread out the picnic blanket by a low window so you can enjoy the outdoors. See how many *p* words you can incorporate into your picnic, from paper plates to pickles.	Help your child make a pepperoni pizza for lunch. Have him/her spread spaghetti sauce on french bread, then count out eight pieces of pepperoni, eight mushrooms and eight of any other toppings he/she likes. Top it off with a layer of mozzarella cheese. Bake at 350° for 20 minutes. You may want to broil the pizza for the last several minutes. Have your child count as you cut the pizza into eight slices.
Thursday	Celebrate *P* Day by wearing purple and reading poetry together, including Jack Prelutsky's "Ride a Purple Pelican."	Have your child draw his/her eyes in the center of a sheet of paper. Around the eyes, have him/her draw his/her favorite things to look at or see. *See* Language, Week 14, number 2.	Set out one crayon. Below that, set out two pieces of chalk. Below that, set out three pencils. Ask your child to continue the pattern until he/she sets out eight of one object. Have your child complete **Numbers 1 to 8** (p. 149).
Friday	Set out various objects on a table. If an object starts with the letter *p*, have your child put it in a large pail. Have your child label the pail with a letter *p*. Have your child complete **Plenty of Pepperoni** (p. 147).	Have your child create an alliterative poem (a poem in which all or most of the words begin with the same letter), using the letter *p*.	Set out sets of silverware (no more than eight pieces per set). Have your child count the number in each set, write the number on a note card and place each note card next to the appropriate set. Have your child complete **What Comes First?** (p. 150) and **What Comes Last?** (p. 151).

Learn at Home, Grade K

Science	Social Studies	Gross/Fine Motor
The Five Senses Read *The Ear Book* by Al Perkins. Record several everyday sounds. Play them for your child. See how many he/she recognizes.	**Winter Festivals** Help your child create Christmas tree ornaments using cinnamon and applesauce and fill your home with the wonderful smells of the holiday season. *See* Social Studies, Week 14, number 1.	Make red and green play dough. Knead cinnamon extract or peppermint into the dough. Let your child squeeze, pull, pound and roll out the dough. Then, let him/her use a variety of cookie cutters to cut out festive holiday shapes that also smell wonderful. *See* Gross/Fine Motor Skills, Week 14, numbers 1 and 2.
Put cotton balls in your child's ears for about an hour at some point during the day. Keep a close eye on him/her during this time. After he/she takes out the cotton, ask what it felt like to not be able to hear. Which sounds did he/she miss the most? Which of his/her senses did he/she use more than usual because of his/her loss of hearing? Discuss the dangers deaf people face because of their inability to hear.	Help your child make a gingerbread house. Rinse, dry and staple shut a pint-sized milk carton. Using icing, have him/her attach several graham crackers to the milk carton to create the "walls" and the "roof" of the gingerbread house. Then, provide your child with a variety of small candies. He/she may use the icing and the candies to decorate the house. *See* Social Studies, Week 14, number 2.	Help your child make a Christmas wreath. Cut the center from a paper plate. Give your child small pieces of green tissue paper to crumple and glue onto the plate. Give him/her a few pieces of red tissue paper to place throughout the wreath as holly berries. Add a red ribbon and hang your child's wreath in a prominent place for the holiday season.
Blindfold your child. Ask him/her to do several simple tasks. After removing the blindfold, ask your child to discuss the tricks he/she used to get around without bumping into things. *See* Science, Week 14, numbers 1–3.	Explain Kwanzaa to your child. Tell him/her that Kwanzaa, which begins on December 26 and ends on January 1, is a holiday observed by some African-Americans in celebration of the African harvest, culture and the joys of family. Explain that on each of the 7 days of Kwanzaa, families gather to light a candle, discuss one of the principles of African-American culture and to exchange homemade gifts. Read *Kwanzaa* by Deborah M. Newton Chocolate.	What would *P* Week be without a piano? If you don't have one, then play songs on your child's xylophone or toy piano. Play songs that you and your child can both sing. If you don't have access to a piano or xylophone, go to the library and check out a children's tape that uses a piano and has songs your child knows.
Check out a book from the library on braille. Explain to your child how the braille alphabet was designed for people who cannot see. Show him/her how each arrangement of bumps is the equivalent of a letter of the alphabet. Using a piece of tagboard and a pin, punch out tiny holes forming your child's name. Have your child practice running his/her fingers over each letter. Can he/she recognize his/her name in braille?	Continue your discussion of Kwanzaa. Tell your child that during the Kwanzaa season, African-American children wear brightly colored clothing in the tradition of African art and life. Read *My First Kwanzaa Book* by Deborah M. Newton Chocolate. Explain the the seven principles of Kwanzaa—*unity, self-determination, collective work and responsibility, cooperative economics, purpose, creativity* and *faith*—in language your child will understand.	Visit a pet shop. Have your child take along a pencil and notebook. Have him/her see how many pets there are whose names begin with the letter *p*.
Talk about the sense of touch. Explain to your child how advanced this sense is. To demonstrate, put a variety of objects in a bag. Blindfold your child and see if he/she can determine what the objects are, based solely on touch. *See* Science, Week 14, number 4.	To help your child understand that Kwanzaa is a celebration of the harvest, prepare a box of food for a needy family. Paint a box with bright Kwanzaa colors and fill it with fresh fruits, vegetables and canned goods. Help your child write *Harambee* which is Swahili for *Let's all pull together!* Take the box of food to a local church, community center or food pantry. See Social Studies, Week 14, number 3.	Celebrate *P* Week with a pajama party. Enjoy pop, peanuts and pretzels while you watch Walt Disney's *Pocahontas*.

TEACHING SUGGESTIONS AND ACTIVITIES

READING (P, p)

▶ 1. Play charades with your child, using only *p* words, such as *peel, pig, pencil* and *pants.*

▶ 2. Have your child search the house for *p* objects he/she can place in a pocket.

▶ 3. Read *A Pocket for Corduroy* by Don Freeman.

▶ 4. Help your child make up a letter *p* tongue twister.

LANGUAGE

▶ 1. Have your child act out the following poem by licking a real lollipop:
"Licks"

> *Here is a round, sweet lollipop.*
> *I bought it today at a candy shop.*
> *One lick—mmm, it tastes so good.*
> *Two licks—oh, I knew it would.*
> *Three licks—yes, I like the taste.*
> *Four licks—I will not waste.*
> *Five licks—keep on and on.*
> *Six licks—oh! It's nearly gone!*
> *Seven licks—it's getting small.*
> *Eight licks—and still not all.*
> *Nine licks—my tongue goes fast.*
> *Ten licks—and that's the last!*

▶ 2. Have your child make a book entitled *I Love to See. . . .* Each page should begin with the sentence *I love to see. . . .* Your child should complete each sentence with a different word or phrase and draw a picture to go with each sentence.

MATH (8 — Eight)

▶ 1. Take your child to the grocery store. Have him/her count out various foods you need to buy, such as eight bananas or two tomatoes.

▶ 2. Back a picture of each family member with a magnet strip. Have your child add up family members on the refrigerator. Have your child write the numbers, plus and equal signs on note cards backed with magnet strips, so he/she can use addition equations.

SCIENCE (The Five Senses)

▶ 1. Visit a school for the blind. Have your child observe the students and some classes. What does he/she think? How is it different from the way he/she is taught? How is it the same?

▶ 2. Check out a book on sign language. Learn a few basic words with your child.

▶ 3. Have your child close his/her eyes and explore your face using only his/her hands. What are some things he/she had not noticed before? Change roles and explore your child's face.

▶ 4. Talk about different textures: smooth, rough, furry, soft, hard, bumpy, pointy, prickly, etc. Have your child find examples of each.

SOCIAL STUDIES (Winter Festivals)

▶ 1. Cinnamon-Applesauce Christmas Tree Ornaments

$3^3/_4$ ounces of ground cinnamon
$^1/_2$ cup of applesauce

Mix the cinnamon and applesauce until the mixture has the consistency of cookie dough. Roll the dough between two sheets of waxed paper. Let your child use cookie cutters to cut out the ornaments. Poke a hole in the top of each ornament. Let the ornaments dry for 36 hours. Tie a thin piece of ribbon through the hole in each ornament.

▶ 2. Icing Recipe (Gingerbread House)

1 egg white
$1^1/_2$ cups of confectioner's sugar
$^1/_2$ teaspoon of cream of tartar

Beat the egg white, gradually adding the sugar and cream of tartar. Beat the mixture until it is smooth. Keep the icing covered with a damp cloth to keep it from hardening while your child works.

▶ 3. Read *Imani's Gift at Kwanzaa* by Denise Burden-Patmon.

GROSS/FINE MOTOR SKILLS

▶ 1. Help your child make personalized gift wrap. Provide him/her with white paper bags, white butcher paper and sponges cut into Christmas shapes. Have your child dip the sponges in paint, then sponge-paint designs on the paper and bags.

▶ 2. Let your child cut up old Christmas cards and glue them onto sheets of construction paper. Your child can then dictate stories for you to write about the pictures.

Letter P, p

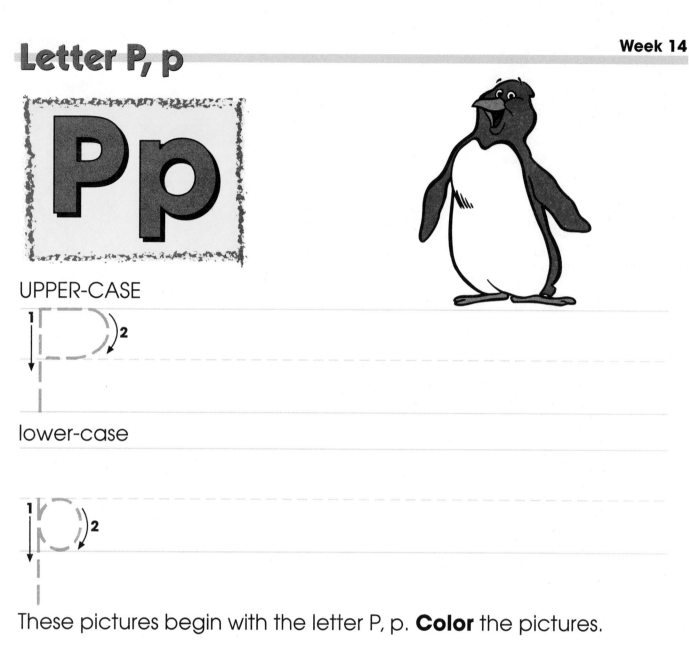

P p

UPPER-CASE

lower-case

These pictures begin with the letter P, p. **Color** the pictures.

Plenty of Pepperoni

Color and **cut out** each picture which begins with the sound of P, p. **Glue** each P, p picture on the pizza.

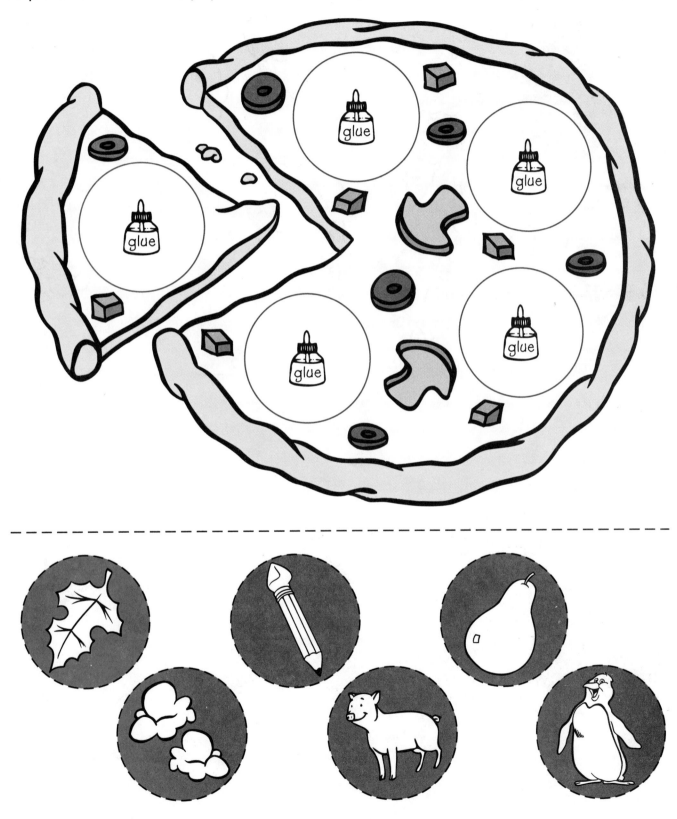

Learn at Home, Grade K

Number 8

This is the number 8. **Color** the pictures.

How many things are in this picture? _____

Trace the 8's.

Write your own 8's.

Numbers 1 to 8

Trace the number. **Color** the correct number of objects in each box.

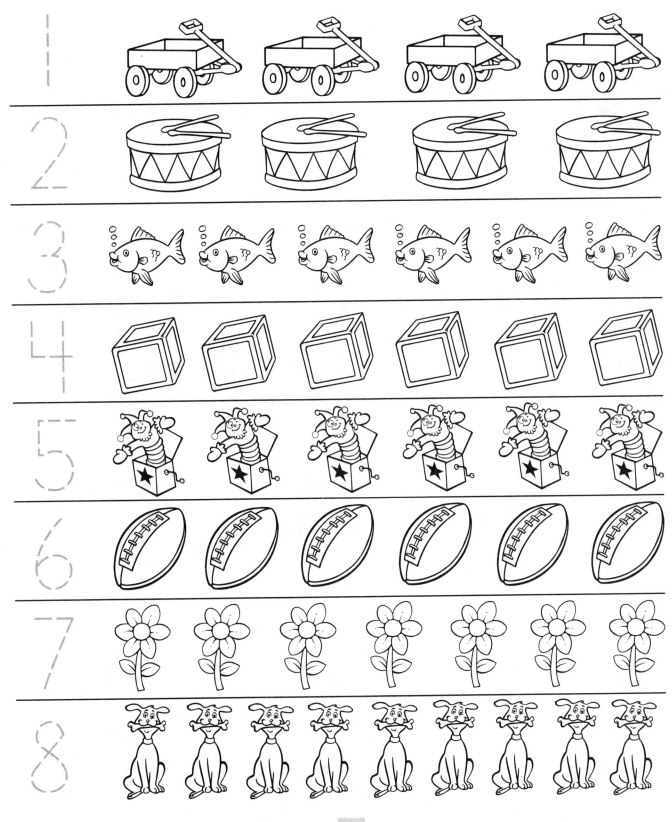

Learn at Home, Grade K

What Comes First?

Circle the picture in each row that shows what happened **first**.
Color the pictures.

Learn at Home, Grade K

What Comes Last?

Circle the picture in each row that shows what happened **last**.
Color the pictures.

	Reading	Language	Math
Monday	**Consonant Review** Have your child make a review letter booklet. Cut five sheets of construction paper in half. At the top of each page, have your child print one of the review letters — b, t, c, s, d, m, f, r, g and p — in both upper- and lower-case. Have him/her cut out and glue on pictures that begin with each of those letters. Complete b, t and c today. Then, let your child make a cover for the book.	Sing "The Wheels on the Bus" by Raffi. Discuss what it is like to ride on a bus. If your child has never been on a bus, ask him/her to imagine what it would be like. See today's Gross/Fine Motor lesson. Have your child compare a bus ride to a ride in a car. Then, teach your child the poem, "The Family Car." See Language, Week 15, number 1.	**9 — Nine** Set out nine pieces of yarn for your child to glue onto a sheet of paper in a design of his/her choice. Then, have your child use glue to draw a 9 in the center of the paper. Cut out a piece of yarn and lay it on top of the glue. Next, help your child spell out the word nine. Help your child sound it out. Have your child complete **Number 9** (p. 157).
Tuesday	Continue working on the review letter booklet. Have your child work on the letters s, d and m. See Reading, Week 15, numbers 1–4 for additional activities.	Introduce your discussion of camouflage (See today's Science lesson) with this rhyme: *Sneaky, sneaky, little frog,* *You can hide inside a log.* *I'll never see you, no I shan't,* *Because you blend in with that plant.*	Have your child roll two dice twenty times and keep track of how many 9's he/she rolls. Have him/her count the dots on the dice each time for him/herself. Have your child complete **How Many Things?** (p. 158).
Wednesday	Let your child continue working on the review letter booklet. Have him/her complete letters f, r, g and p. Keep the ten letter pages completed this week clipped together. Your child will eventually add every letter of the alphabet.	Visit a truck yard or fire station. Ask if your child may sit in one of the trucks. Let your child pretend to drive the truck. You may want to bring along your camera and take pictures. Talk about this exciting experience on the trip back home.	See Math, Week 15, numbers 1–3. Have your child complete **Eight and Nine** (p. 159).
Thursday	Play a game in which you challenge your child to guess as many words as he/she can in 2 minutes. Use verbal clues to describe each word. Your child must say the word as well as the first letter of that word before moving on to the next word. Keep playing until the 2 minutes are up. **Words:** stand, book, tree, candle, dog, money, fruit, rabbit, girl, perfume, belly, table, candy, soup, dragon, milk, frog, ring, gift, pen.	Visit the airport. Watch the airplanes take off and land. Teach your child an action poem about flying, called "The Airplane." See Language, Week 15, number 2. Let your child create movements to go along with the poem.	Set out marbles and the + and = note cards made on Tuesday of Week 14. Set up basic addition equations. Be sure the sums equal nine or less.
Friday	Find objects to represent each of the eight basic colors. Prepare note cards ahead of time with each of the basic colors written out. Have your child match them. Have your child complete **Green, Purple, Orange and Black** (p. 156).	Read The Airplane Alphabet Book by Jerry Pallotta.	Have your child make nine homemade muffins or biscuits using your favorite recipe. Help your child read the directions, and have him/her do all the measuring and mixing.

Learn at Home, Grade K

Science	Social Studies	Gross/Fine Motor
Forest Animals Take a short brisk walk in the woods. Look for animals to photograph. What kinds of animals did you and your child find? *See* Science, Week 15, numbers 1–3 for additional activities.	**Transportation** Go on a "transportation sight-seeing tour" with your child to see how many types of transportation you can find. Explain to your child that *transportation* is any way of getting from one place to another. Have your child draw his/her findings from your tour. How many types of transportation did he/she find? *See* Social Studies, Week 15, numbers 1–5 for additional activities.	If your child has never been on a bus, take him/her on a short trip. Remember to ask questions that encourage him/her to observe his/her surroundings. *See* today's Language lesson. *See* Gross/Fine Motor Skills, Week 15, numbers 1–5 for additional activities.
Discuss why your forest trip may not have been a success. Although many animals live in the forest, you may not always see them. Explain the concept of camouflage (*see* today's Language lesson). Read *Nature Hide & Seek: Woods & Forests* by John Norris Wood. Your child will enjoy this lift-a-flap book.	Discuss car safety. Talk about wearing seat belts, using car seats for babies, keeping voices low, etc. Have your child come up with his/her own list of car safety rules.	Have your child make a hopscotch grid using tape. Have him/her cut out and tape down a picture inside each square that begins with a review letter. For side-by-side squares, have your child draw pictures that begin with the same letter. As your child jumps on each square, he/she must call out the beginning letter of the picture.
Continue your discussion of camouflage. Read *Animals and Their Hiding Places* by Jane R. McCauley.	Talk about trucks. What are they used for? What can they haul? What kind does your child like best? What kind of workers use trucks every day at their jobs?	Cut out various shapes. Have your child make a fleet of trucks by gluing rectangles, squares and circles together.
Read *Animals That Live in Trees* by Jane R. McCauley. Go upstairs, if you have a second story and look at the birds in neighboring trees. What do they look like? Have your child describe them.	Read the first 20 pages of *First Flight* by George Shea. It tells the story of the Wright Brothers.	Have your child make several paper airplanes and test them to see which flies the farthest.
Read *Creatures of the Woods* by Toni Eugene. After reading, go back through the book and have your child name as many of the animals as he/she can remember. What else can he/she tell you about each of the animals?	Read pages 21–48 of *First Flight*. Talk about the many trials it took before the Wright Brothers came up with a plane that worked well.	Recite and act out "I'm a Plane" with your child: *I'm a plane with wings so bright,* *Waiting here to take a flight.* *Now I sail up straight and high,* *Now I sail around the sky.* *Now I land upon the ground,* *With a very quiet sound.* Afterwards, have your child draw a plane and trace its path as described in the poem.

Learn at Home, Grade K

TEACHING SUGGESTIONS AND ACTIVITIES

READING (Consonant Review)

▶ 1. Have your child draw a picture in which each of the review letters is represented.

▶ 2. Set out several objects whose names begin with the review letters, including a box, tie, cookie, sock, doll, map, fork, rug, gum and a purse. Have your child place the objects with the same first letter together.

▶ 3. Write each of the review letters on a slip of paper. Have your child tape each slip to an object beginning with that letter.

▶ 4. Play the "Sign Game." While traveling in the car, look for a sign with an *a* on it. Then, have your child find a sign with a *b* on it, and so on. The person who gets to *z* first, wins.

LANGUAGE

▶ 1. "The Family Car" (an action poem)

Sometimes I ride in the family car.
The engine jerks, so we cannot go far.
Pop, pop, pop, pop, pop, pop, pop!
Pop, pop, pop! Juggle, jiggle, JAT!
What is the matter?
Why, the tire is flat! Sssssssssssss!

▶ 2. "The Airplane" (an action poem)

The airplane has big, wide wings.
Its propeller spins around and sings.
Vvvvvvv!
The airplane goes up in the sky.
Then, down it goes, just see it fly!
Vvvvvvv!
Up, up and up—down, down and down,
Over every housetop in our town!
Vvvvvvv!

MATH (9 — Nine)

▶ 1. Make a pattern with spoons and forks. Have your child continue the pattern up to the ninth piece of silverware.

▶ 2. Have your child find a recipe that requires nine of something. Have fun looking through cookbooks. Then, work together to make the recipe.

▶ 3. Write down the numerals and the number words from zero to nine. Have your child match each numeral to the correct number word.

SCIENCE (Forest Animals)

▶ 1. Check a state map for wildlife preserves or bird sanctuaries in your area. Visit one of these and look for forest animals.

▶ 2. Visit a cave. Look for bats and other animals.

▶ 3. Check out some library books about your child's favorite forest animal.

SOCIAL STUDIES (Transportation)

▶ 1. Display many kinds of toy vehicles. Discuss each, allowing your child to contribute his/her thoughts and ideas. Let your child play with the toys.

▶ 2. Obtain several large boxes from the grocery store. Let your child paint the boxes to represent different vehicles, such as a car, boat, airplane, etc.

▶ 3. Use a hanger to make a transportation mobile. Have your child draw or cut out pictures of various forms of transportation. Using yarn, attach them to the hanger at varying lengths.

▶ 4. Help your child make his/her own *Transportation Alphabet Book*. Use your child's own drawings or pictures cut from magazines and newspapers.

▶ 5. Read *The Glorious Flight* by Alice and Martin Provensen about Louis Bleriot's historic flight across the English Channel.

GROSS/FINE MOTOR SKILLS

▶ 1. Have your child make a paper plate mask of his/her favorite forest animal.

▶ 2. Using gelatin boxes, cereal boxes, plastic "tires and axles" from frozen push-up treats, and other scrap items, help your child make his/her own transportation collection.

▶ 3. Have your child jump rope. On every other jump, challenge him/her to name a different type of transportation.

▶ 4. Visit a museum where antique cars or other modes of transportation are on display. Discuss the differences between those vehicles and the ones people drive today.

▶ 5. Play transportation charades. Have your child act out a type of transportation for you to guess. Switch roles and act out modes of transportation for your child to guess.

Learn at Home, Grade K

Green, Purple, Orange and Black

Use green, purple, orange and black crayons to **color** the picture.

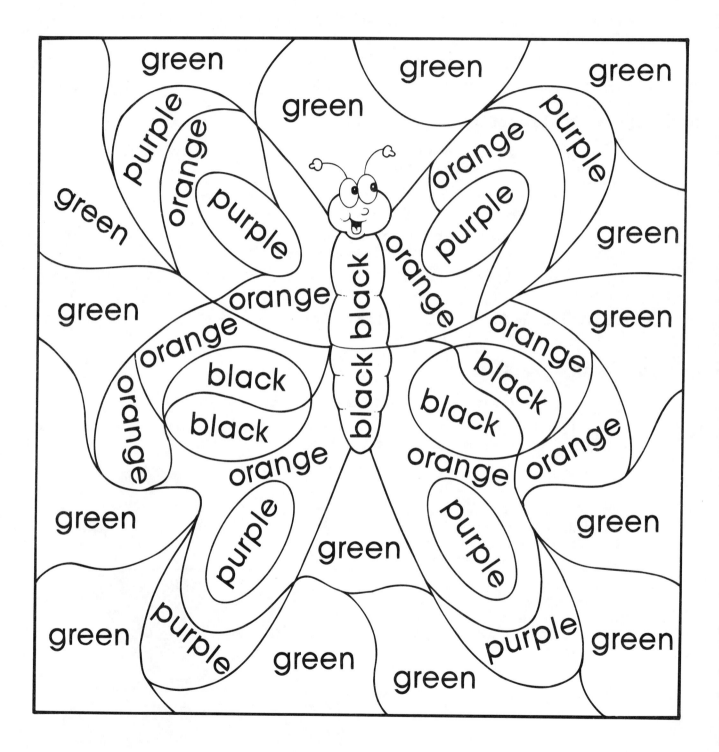

156

Number 9

This is the number 9. **Color** the pictures.

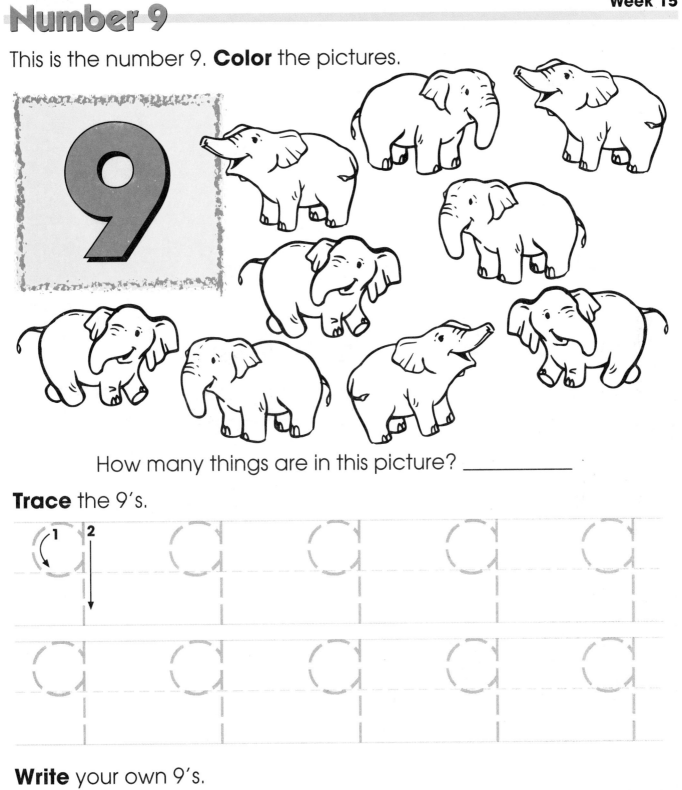

How many things are in this picture? _____

Trace the 9's.

Write your own 9's.

Learn at Home, Grade K

How Many Things?

Count the things in each box. **Cut out** the numbers. **Glue** the
correct number in each box. **Color** the pictures.

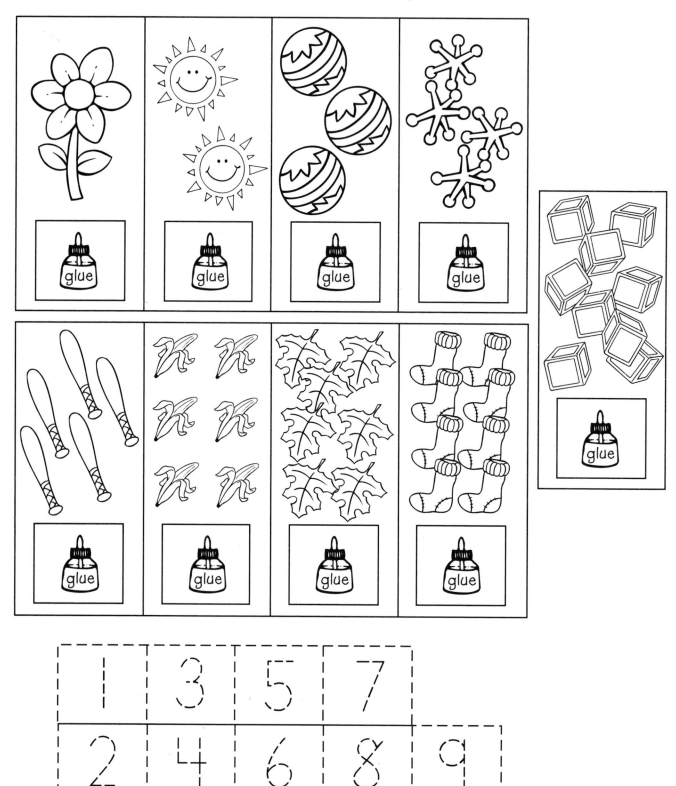

Eight and Nine

Use counters. Put 7 on the tree. Put in 1 more.
How many? _____

Put in 1 more counter. How many now?_____

Draw an apple for each counter on the tree.
How many apples?_____
Count again. **Write** a number on each apple as you count.

Learn at Home, Grade K

	Reading	**Language**	**Math**
Monday	**W, w** Use a paintbrush to brush water on a window in the shape of an upper- and lower-case *w*. Then, let your child do the same, repeating the procedure several times. *See* Reading, Week 16, numbers 1–3 for additional activities. Have your child complete **Letter W, w** (p. 164).	Read *Where the Wild Things Are* by Maurice Sendak. Ask your child to listen and watch for words beginning with *w*. Have him/her point to each *w* word as you read the story.	**Basic Concepts** Set out clothes, shoes, socks, etc. Have your child lay out the clothing on the bed in the order he/she would put them on. As he/she lays out each article of clothing, emphasize the ordinal words *first*, *second*, *third*, *fourth*, *fifth*, etc. *See* Math, Week 16, numbers 1–4 for additional activities.
Tuesday	Have your child shape bread dough into upper- and lower-case *w*'s. Mix one egg white with two tablespoons of water and brush the mixture over the dough. Bake the letters at 350° until they are golden brown. Let them cool and eat them with your child.	Celebrate *W* Week by wearing white, eating waffles and playing relay races with wheels and wagons.	Show your child how to read a scale. Have your child weigh him/herself. Then, have him/her use a postal scale to weigh smaller items. Help your child make a chart to record each object's weight in ounces. Be sure to explain to your child the difference between ounces and pounds. Then, have him/her make comparisons by saying which weighs more and which weighs less.
Wednesday	Teach your child the *w* sound. It is one of the most difficult consonant sounds for many children to master. Set *w* objects, such as water, a washcloth, window cleaner, whistle, watch, wallet or a wheel on a table. Have your child say the name of each object and then say *w*. Have your child complete **Wonderful Watches** (p. 165).	Practice the *w* sound with your child by repeating the following rhyme: *Wa, wa, wa, wa,* *What says wa?* *W, W,* *Window, wash, we.*	Set out objects that go together, such as a hat and mittens, peanut butter and jelly, a fork and a spoon. Then, set out single objects, such as a plate, sock, toothbrush or comb and have your child find a match for each one. Have your child complete **What Goes Together?** (p. 166).
Thursday	Act out the following *w* words and challenge your child to guess as many as he/she can in 3 minutes: worm, wheel, whisper, wiggle, window, wagon, wash, work, woman, wind. Be sure to emphasize that they all begin with *w*.	Help your child create a *w* tongue twister. See how many times in a row your child can repeat the twister.	Write a variety of directions for your child using directional words, such as *under, on, between* and *over*. Write each direction on a separate slip of paper and place the directions in a hat. Then, have your child choose a slip of paper and do what it says. Be sure to include *w* words in the directions whenever possible. Have your child complete **Where Does It Go?** (p. 167).
Friday	Go on a *w* walk. Have your child load up a wagon with *w* objects in your home.	Teach your child the poem "Rocket Ships." *See* Language, Week 16, number 1. Recite the poem with your child. Then, ask him/her to imagine where the rocket is headed and what kinds of creatures and planets it will encounter.	Have your child bring you foods. Then, have him/her bring you things to help clean. Continue asking him/her to bring you things that fit into broad categories. Have your child complete **Let It Shine!** (p. 168).

Science	Social Studies	Gross/Fine Motor
Forest Animals Talk about your home. Ask your child why it fits your family so well. Tell your child that today he/she will learn about animal homes and why they fit them so well. Read *Animals That Build Their Homes* by Robert M. McClung. Read the book a second time, asking your child to name each animal and its home. *See* Science, Week 16, numbers 1–4 for additional activities.	**Transportation** Talk about boats today. Look through books that have pictures of all types of boats. Explain the purpose of different parts of a boat, including the rudder, oars, etc.	Help your child make a boat using a foam meat tray, meat skewer and construction paper. Give your child the option of designing his/her own boat. Have him/her test potential boat bases in the sink to see if they will float. Have boat races in the tub. *See* Gross/Fine Motor Skills, Week 16, numbers 1–3 for additional activities.
Read *Animal Homes* by Tammy Everts and Bobbie Kalman. Have your child complete **Home You Go!** (p. 169).	Visit your county's maintenance facility. Arrange to have someone show your child around and explain the purpose of each of their big trucks. Maybe your child can even sit in one of them. *See* Social Studies, Week 16, number 1.	Help your child make wax design pictures for *W* Week. This activity must be carefully supervised. Light a colored candle. Allow your child to hold the candle, tipping it at an angle away from him/her. Let the wax drip onto a sheet of paper. Have your child repeat with various colors to form a wax design.
Read the poem "Animal Homes" aloud. *See* Science, Week 16, number 5. Reread the poem several times, until your child is familiar with the words. Then, read it again, this time pausing at each underlined section to let your child finish the line. Can he/she remember the different animal homes?	Read *Polar Express* by Chris Van Allsburg. Talk to your child about trains. Ask what types of cars make up a train (flat car, coal car, caboose, engine, etc.). *See* Social Studies, Week 16, number 2.	Have your child act out the following poem: *Chugga-chugga goes the train,* *Barreling down the tracks.* *Chugga-chugga goes the train,* *We all know where it's at.* *Chugga-chugga goes the train,* *Our favorite part is coming.* *Chugga-chugga goes the train,* *Toot-toot!* *Our train is singing.*
Skim *Endangered Forest Animals* by Dave Taylor. Discuss with your child the meaning of the terms *extinct* and *endangered*. Ask your child why he/she thinks some animals are becoming extinct. Talk about how their habitats and homes are being destroyed. Look through the book, pointing out interesting facts to your child.	Look through *Visual Timeline of Transportation* edited by Stephen Setford. Look at the pictures and discuss those that most interest your child. Ask him/her to count some of the pictures and to describe and classify others. *See* Social Studies, Week 16, number 3.	Have your child make a personal time line of transportation. What did he/she first do as a baby to get around? Continue all the way up through today. (**Basic stages:** crawling, walking, scooter toys, tricycle, big wheel, two-wheeler, scooter, etc.) Have your child complete **Let's Go Around the Block!** (p. 171).
Visit a nearby zoo. Have your child look for animals that are endangered. Which ones does he/she see? Talk to a worker at the zoo about what you can do to help save endangered animals.	Skim *Wings, Wheels & Sails* by Tom Stacy. This is a great question-and-answer book about transportation. Read through the table of contents. When your child wants to know the answer to a particular question, turn to the appropriate page and read about it. Have your child use **Transportation Patterns** (p. 170) to create a transportation lotto or memory game.	Play "Teacher Says" using as many *w* words as possible. **Examples:** *Teacher says wink while washing your hands. Teacher says whisper, 'I love you.' Teacher says wiggle as you say a w word.*

TEACHING SUGGESTIONS AND ACTIVITIES

READING (W, w)

▶ 1. Draw a large *w* at the top of a chalkboard or dry-erase board. Have your child guess *w* words as you draw them on the board. See how quickly he/she can guess all eight words: *watermelon, wheat, wave, wolf, worm, watch, wheel, wet.*

▶ 2. Learn about the Wild, Wild West. Check out western books from the library. Dress up like cowboys and enjoy learning about them.

▶ 3. Have your child find as many ways as possible to wear *w*. Give your child a wig, a waterproof coat or a watch to wear. Brainstorm together other *w* articles of clothing he/she could wear.

LANGUAGE

▶ 1. "Rocket Ships" (poem)

Our rocket ship is standing by,
And very, very soon,
We'll have a countdown, then we'll blast
Ourselves off to the moon.
Begin to count: ten, nine, eight,
Be on time, don't be late.
Seven, six, five and four,
There aren't many seconds more.
Three, two, one! Zero! Zip!
The rocket is off on its first moon trip.

MATH (Basic Concepts)

▶ 1. Ask your child to estimate the weight of each family member. Ask: *Who weighs less, Daddy or you?* Continue until your child has a list of family members, from lightest to heaviest. Weigh everyone to see if your child was correct.

▶ 2. Write counting directions on slips of paper. **Example:** *Give your mom 9 kisses* or *Put away 8 toys.* Each day this week, have your child choose one of the slips and perform the action written on it.

▶ 3. Create addition story problems using real objects. **Example:** *You have three apples and I give you two more. How many apples do you have now?*

▶ 4. Have your child put away the silverware after it has been washed. This is great sorting practice. Ask him/her to count the number of forks, knives and spoons.

SCIENCE (Forest Animals)

▶ 1. Read *Snow Babies* by Eric Rosser.

▶ 2. Let your child use face paint to make his/her face look like a favorite forest animal.

▶ 3. Have your child make his/her own animal information cards using large note cards and resources from the library. On each card, have him/her dictate the name, a physical description, the eating habits and the habitat of the animal.

▶ 4. See how many forest animals your child can name. How many begin with *w*?

▶ 5. "Animal Homes" (poem)

> *Birds live <u>in nests</u>,*
> *Squirrels live <u>in trees</u>,*
> *Beavers live <u>in lodges</u>,*
> *And a house is for me.*
> *Prairie dogs live <u>in tunnels</u>,*
> *Owls live <u>in trees</u>,*
> *Bats live <u>in caves</u>,*
> *And a house is for me.*

SOCIAL STUDIES (Transportation)

▶ 1. Read *Snow Day* by Betsy Maestro. Discuss the different types of trucks in the story.

▶ 2. Have your child help you read *Pano, the Train* by Sharon Holaves. The picture words will help your child to read along with you.

▶ 3. Read aloud *You Are There: Transportation From Cars to Planes* by Gare Thompson.

GROSS/FINE MOTOR SKILLS

▶ 1. Have your child sort his/her toy vehicles, first by color, then by type. Ask your child: *Is there any other way you can sort these vehicles?*

▶ 2. Take an imaginary bus ride with your child. Arrange kitchen chairs in a column to look like seats on a bus. Talk about where you would go, what you would pack, etc.

▶ 3. Take your child on a short train or boat ride.

Letter W, w

UPPER-CASE

lower-case

These pictures begin with the letter W, w. **Color** the pictures.

Wonderful Watches

Color each of the watches. **Color** and **cut out** each picture that begins with W,w. Then, **glue** them on the watches.

Learn at Home, Grade K

What Goes Together?

Draw a line to match the things that go together.

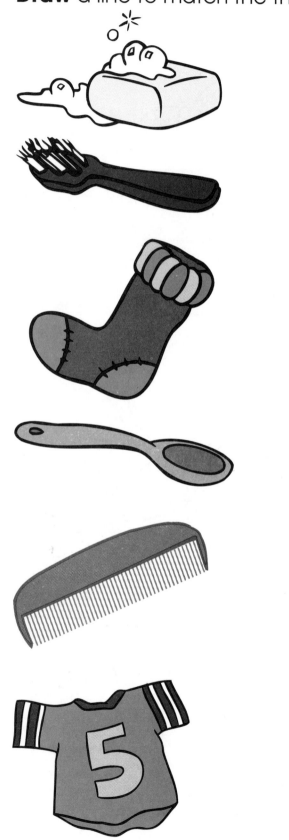

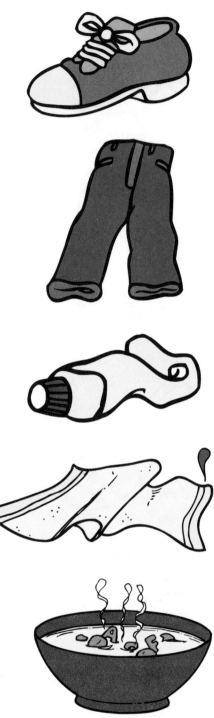

Where Does It Go?

Color and **cut out** the pictures at the bottom of the page. **Glue** them in the correct place.

under

on

between

in

Let It Shine!

Circle 10 things that give light.

Learn at Home, Grade K

Home You Go!

Help the animals get home! **Draw** a line from each animal to its home.

Transportation Patterns

Train

Car

Bus

Airplane

Ship

Balloon

Truck

Bicycle

Helicopter

Learn at Home, Grade K

Let's Go Around the Block!

Draw straight lines. Stop at each dot.

Learn at Home, Grade K

	Reading	Language	Math
Monday	**J, j** Shape a jump rope into a letter *j* on top of a table. Dip your finger in jelly and give your lower-case *j* a dot of jelly on top. Then, change the jump rope into an upper-case *J*. Help your child do the same. *See* Reading, Week 17, numbers 1–3 for additional activities.	Teach your child the "Head, Shoulders, Knees and Toes" action rhyme. *See* Language, Week 17, number 1. Recite the rhyme with your child several times.	**10 — Ten** Have your child count out ten pieces of cereal and glue them onto a sheet of paper. In the center of the page, have your child write the numeral 10 and the word *ten*. Have your child complete **Number 10** (p. 179).
Tuesday	Have your child spread jelly onto a slice of bread in the shape of an upper-case *J*. On the other slice of bread, have him/her spread a lower-case *j*. Put both sides together to make a sandwich. Have your child complete **Letter J, j** (p. 176).	Read *Alexander and the Terrible, Horrible, No Good, Very Bad Day* by Judith Viorst. Have your child tell you about a time he/she had a really bad day.	Provide your child with counters to complete the activity sheet **Ten** (p. 180).
Wednesday	Introduce the sound of letter *j* with this chant: *I know a j word, a j word, a j word.* *I know a j word.* *Do you want to play?* Give one-word hints for *j* words, such as *jump, jar, jam, jacket, jokes, juice* and *jack-in-the-box.* For example, for the word *jump,* give your child the hint *hop.* Have your child complete **Jumping Jacks** (p. 177).	Read *The Berenstain Bears and Too Much Junk Food* by Stan and Jan Berenstain. With your child, brainstorm to see how many kinds of junk food he/she can name. Discuss how junk food got its name.	Let your child count to ten with this action rhyme: *1, 2, 3, 4, 5, 6, 7, 8.* *See me swinging on the gate.* *1, 2, 3, 4, 5, 6, 7, 8, 9.* *My clothes are flopping on the line.* *1, 2, 3, 4, 5, 6, 7, 8, 9, 10.* *Let us count all over again.* Have your child complete **Counting From 1 to 10** (p. 181).
Thursday	Have your child think of *j* words and draw them on a chalkboard while you try to guess them as quickly as possible.	Explore feelings and expression with the following rhyme: *When my heart is happy,* *My face gives a smile.* *When my heart is sad,* *Tears fall down in a pile.* *When my heart is angry,* *My face is very tight.* *But when my heart is excited,* *My eyes are big with delight.*	Give your child a fun introduction to subtraction with the finger play "Ten Huge Dinosaurs." *See* Math, Week 17, number 1.
Friday	Cut out a large letter *j* from poster board. Then, have your child look through old magazines and calendars for *j* pictures to glue inside the giant *j*. Have your child complete **Letters W, w and J, j** (p. 178).	Celebrate *J* Day by going to the library and checking out joke books.	Set out ten crackers and the cards with a + and = on them. Set up basic addition equations with sums of ten or less.

Learn at Home, Grade K

Science	Social Studies	Gross/Fine Motor
My Body Have your child point to and name all the body parts he/she knows. Talk about how his/her body has changed since he/she was a baby. Look at photos from when your child was a baby, and ask if he/she has grown any new body parts. Explain that human babies are born with all their body parts, and they just continue to grow.	**My Feelings** Read *My Many Colored Days* by Dr. Seuss. With your child, discuss days when he/she feels "blue," "orange" or "red." *See* Social Studies, Week 17, numbers 1–3 for additional activities.	Teach your child the following rhyme. Have him/her repeat it with you several times. Then, have him/her try saying the rhyme while jumping up and down. *Jump, jump,* *Jump for joy,* *Jump for letter J-J.* *Jump, jump,* *Jump for joy,* *For J's we say "Hooray!!"*
Talk to your child about ways to care for his/her body. What are some of the ways he/she keeps him/herself clean? Ask how often your child does each of these. Why is it important to stay clean? Talk about thorough cleaning. Check behind your child's ears and in his/her mouth. How good of a job is he/she doing? *See* Science, Week 17, numbers 1 and 2.	Talk with your child about the many different feelings he/she has. Have him/her name as many as he/she can. Then, discuss how we might be able to tell what another person is feeling just by watching his/her body. Demonstrate a few looks and gestures. Explain that bad days are normal and everyone has them.	Have your child draw a picture of him/herself when he/she is having a bad day. What does his/her face and body look like? *See* Gross/Fine Motor Skills, Week 17, number 1.
Talk about good nutrition. Explain to your child that it is just as important to keep the inside of the body healthy as it is the outside. Discuss the food pyramid and set out several foods from each food category. Have your child search the kitchen and pantry for more foods in each category. Talk about the importance of eating well for staying healthy and feeling good. Have your child complete **Good To Eat!** (p. 182).	Read *I Was So Mad!* by Norma Simon. Discuss times when you felt angry. Then, have your child share times when he/she was mad.	Celebrate *J* Week by wearing jams (long, colorful shorts) or jeans and dancing to jazz music together.
Ask your child what else is important besides keeping his/her body clean and eating healthful foods. Guide your child to the answer that exercise is also important. Discuss why it is important. Then, talk about fun ways to exercise. Have your child name the kinds of exercise he/she likes best. Have your child complete **Staying Fit** (p. 183).	Have your child show you a sad face. Ask: *What makes you sad?* Ask if your child feels like crying when he/she is sad. Reassure him/her that tears are a necessary and healthy part of life and that it is okay to cry when he/she is sad or upset. Also reassure your child that you are there for him/her when he/she is sad, because you love him/her.	Have your child jump rope while saying: *Cousin Anna, dressed in 'jamas* *Went upstairs to find her flannels.* *Made a mistake,* *Kissed poor Jake.* *How many doctors did it take?* *1, 2, 3, 4, 5, 6, 7, 8,....* Have your child keep counting until he/she misses a jump or can't count any higher.
Read *Your Skin and Mine* by Paul Showers. Discuss points which may be new to your child. *See* Science, Week 17, number 3.	Talk with your child about feeling afraid. Ask your child what scares him/her. Explain that everyone has fears. Read *Franklin in the Dark* by Paulette Bourgeois.	Read and perform the action rhyme "Hands on Shoulders." *See* Gross/Fine Motor Skills, Week 17, number 2.

Learn at Home, Grade K

TEACHING SUGGESTIONS AND ACTIVITIES

READING (J, j)

▶ 1. Ask your child to design a January calendar picture. Write *January is . . .* at the top of the page. Have your child complete the sentence with a *j* word, then draw a January scene.

▶ 2. List special jobs on slips of paper and place them inside a jar. Call this the "job jar." Have your child pick one slip each day—this will be his/her job for the day.

▶ 3. Set out a variety of objects on the table. Have your child pick out all the letter *j* objects and form a *j* with them.

LANGUAGE

▶ 1. Have your child point to each part of his/her body as he/she says this action rhyme:

"Head, Shoulders, Knees and Toes"

Head and shoulders, knees and toes, knees and toes.
Head and shoulders, knees and toes, knees and toes.
Eyes and ears and mouth and nose.
Eyes and ears and mouth and nose.
And that's the way this rhyme goes!

MATH (10 — Ten)

▶ 1. "Ten Huge Dinosaurs" (finger play)

Ten huge dinosaurs were standing in a line.
One tripped on a cobblestone and then there were _____.
Nine huge dinosaurs were trying hard to skate.
One cracked right through the ice, and then there were _____.
Eight huge dinosaurs were counting past eleven.
One counted up too far, and then there were _____.
Seven huge dinosaurs learned some magic tricks.
One did a disappearing act, and then there were _____.
Six huge dinosaurs were learning how to drive.
One forgot to put in gas, and then there were _____.
Five huge dinosaurs joined the drum corps.
One forgot the drumsticks, and then there were _____.
Four huge dinosaurs were wading in the sea.
One waded out too far, and then there were _____.
Three huge dinosaurs looked for Mister Soo.
One gave up the search, and then there were _____.
Two huge dinosaurs went to the Amazon.
One sailed in up to his head, and there was _____.
One lonesome dinosaur knew his friends had gone.
He found a big museum, and then there were _____.

SCIENCE (My Body)

▶ 1. Take your child to a doctor for a physical exam. Help your child become familiar and comfortable with his/her doctor and the doctor's office.

▶ 2. Take your child to a nearby mall to walk in the winter. Walking is great exercise and the mall provides a warm place to do it.

▶ 3. Have your child lie down on a sheet of butcher paper. Trace around his/her body. Then, have him/her complete his/her body outline by drawing the clothes he/she is wearing today.

SOCIAL STUDIES (My Feelings)

▶ 1. Read *Don't Feed the Monster on Tuesday* by Adolph Moser.

▶ 2. Discuss with your child a plan of action for when he/she is angry. Discuss things that make him/her angry. Ask your child what he/she can do to appropriately express his/her angry feelings. Brainstorm together for ideas.

▶ 3. Role-play specific situations with your child. How will he/she respond? Role play the same situation several times for reinforcement.

GROSS/FINE MOTOR SKILLS

▶ 1. Sing songs about feelings with your child. There are many tapes and CD's on this subject in the library.

▶ 2. "Hands on Shoulders" (action rhyme)

> *Hands on shoulders, hands on knees,*
> *Hands behind you, if you please!*
> *Touch your hips and touch your nose,*
> *Bend way down and touch your toes.*
> *Hands up high, now, in the air,*
> *At your sides, and touch your hair.*
> *Hands up high as you did before,*
> *Clap your hands: one, two, three, four!*

Learn at Home, Grade K

Letter J, j

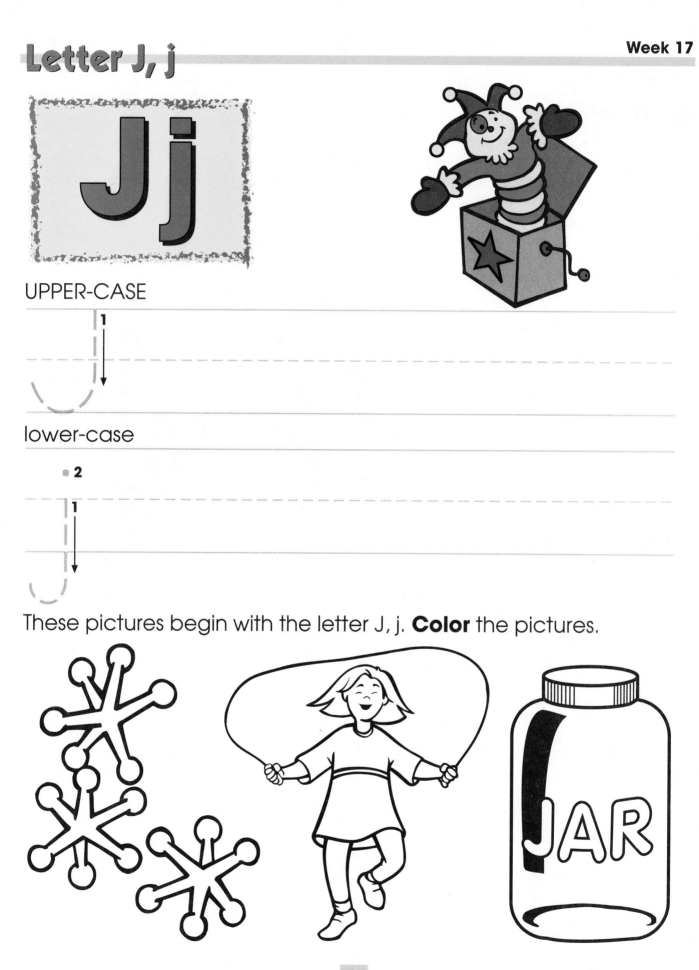

J j

UPPER-CASE

1

lower-case

2

1

These pictures begin with the letter J, j. **Color** the pictures.

JAR

176

Jumping Jacks!

Color each picture which begins with the sound of J, j. **Cut out** and **glue** the J, j pictures on the circles.

Learn at Home, Grade K

Letters W, w and J, j

Circle the beginning sound for each picture. Color the pictures.

w   j

w   j

w   j

w   j

w   j

w   j

w   j

w   j

w   j

Learn at Home, Grade K

Number 10

This is the number 10. **Color** the pictures.

How many things are in this picture? _____

Trace the 10's.

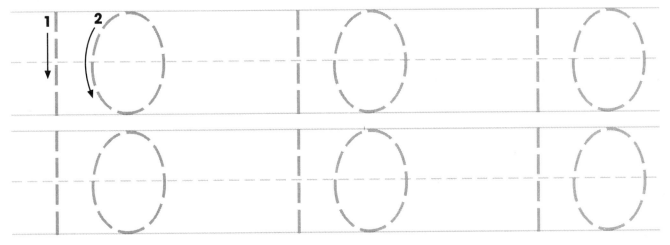

Write your own 10's.

_____

_____

Learn at Home, Grade K

Ten

Use counters. Put 9 counters in the space picture. Put in 1 more.

Count. **Write** how many: _____

Draw a ☆ for each counter.

How many ☆'s? _____

Count again. **Write** a number for each ☆ as you **count**.

☆ ☆ ☆ ☆ ☆ ☆ ☆ ☆ ☆ ☆

Write 1-10 again.

_____ _____ _____ _____ _____

_____ _____ _____ _____ _____

Learn at Home, Grade K

Counting From 1 to 10

Count how many are in the picture. **Write** the number. **Color** the picture.

Learn at Home, Grade K

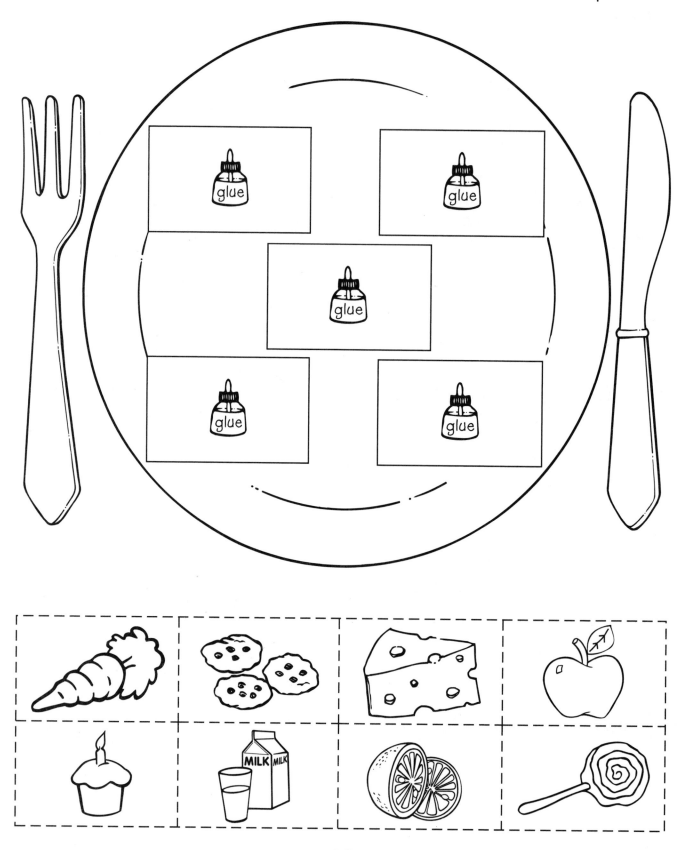

Good To Eat!

Color and **cut out** the healthful foods. **Glue** them on the plate.

Staying Fit

Circle each child who is staying healthy with exercise. **Color** the children.

	Reading	**Language**	**Math**
Monday	**Consonant Review** Have your child cut a sheet of construction paper in half. Have him/her write *W, w* at the top of one half and *J, j* at the top of the other. Have your child look through magazines and cut out pictures of objects beginning with the letters *w* and *j*. Have him/her glue each picture onto the correct page and add the pages to the review letter booklet.	Play "I'm Thinking of a Letter." Describe a review letter and see if your child can guess it. Then, have him/her describe a review letter for you to guess.	**11 — Eleven** Set out eleven napkins for your child to count. Then, have him/her number each of the napkins. Show him/her the word *eleven*. Help your child sound it out and write it on the eleventh napkin. *See* Math, Week 18, numbers 1–3 for additional activities. Have your child complete **Number 11** (p. 188).
Tuesday	Play "Review Letter Charades" with your child. Act out several words beginning with review letters, and challenge your child to guess each word and say the first letter in it. Possible words might include *bat, top, cold, sock, dizzy, monster, frog, raincoat, gum, pop, winner* and *jack-in-the-box. See* Reading, Week 18, numbers 1–4 for additional activities.	Read *Dr. Seuss's A B C.* As you read, help your child review the sounds of the letters. He/she can also read along with you, saying most, if not all, the letters.	Have your child complete **Zoorific!** (p. 189).
Wednesday	Have your child draw a picture in which each of the review letters is represented.	Read *There's an Alligator Under My Bed* by Mercer Mayer. This book addresses the issue of fear and ways in which to confront it.	Set out ten forks and eleven spoons. Have your child pair them up. Ask: *Is there one spoon for each fork?* Have your child complete **One for Each** (p. 190).
Thursday	Write each of the letters of the alphabet on a card. Have your child put the letters in alphabetical order. Encourage him/her to sing the alphabet song to help him/her remember the correct order.	Read and discuss the book *Annie Bananie* by Leah Komaiko. This book addresses the issues of loneliness and anxiety.	Ask your child to name his/her eleven favorite things to do, in order from most favorite to least favorite. Help your child make a list of these activities, but instead of listing them by number, have your child list them by the number word. **Example:** *One. Play musical chairs.* *Two. Play checkers.*
Friday	Use the alphabet cards constructed yesterday as flash cards. Use only the letters your child has learned so far. As you "flash" each letter, have your child say the sound it makes.	Teach your child the action rhyme "Who Feels Happy Today?" *See* Language, Week 18, number 1.	Make homemade alphabet soup using your favorite vegetable soup recipe and alphabet letters found in the pasta section of your supermarket. Be sure to have your child measure ingredients in order to capitalize upon the mathematics inherent in this activity.

Learn at Home, Grade K

Science	Social Studies	Gross/Fine Motor
My Body Read *The Magic School Bus* by Joanna Cole. This book gives a good overview of the inside of the human body. *See* Science, Week 18, number 1.	**My Feelings** Discuss times your child has been very happy. Then, talk about the feeling of excitement. What makes your child excited? Have him/her show you a happy face and an excited face. Discuss times you have felt happy or excited.	Have your child slice refrigerated sugar cookie dough into eleven thick sections. Have him/her press each one flat onto a cookie sheet. Then, have your child add eleven chocolate chips or other small chocolate candies to each cookie. Bake the cookies at 300° until they are cooked in the center.
Discuss the skeleton. Consult pages 6–11 of *Make It Work: Body!* by Liz Wyse. Point out the basic bones listed in the book. Help your child find them in his/her own body. *See* Science, Week 18, number 2.	Read *Dandelion* by Don Freeman. Discuss the importance of being yourself. Explain that when we aren't ourselves, we aren't as happy. We need to be true to ourselves.	Have your child act out the following poem: *Free to be me, free to be me,* *Free to be crazy, kooky me.* *Free to be quiet, thinking me.* *Free to be jokey, giggly me.* *Free to be me, free to be me,* *Free to be who I was made to be!* *See* Gross/Fine Motor Skills, Week 18, number 1.
Discuss the heart and circulatory system. Consult pages 52–55 of *The Body* by Steve Parker. Show your child where his/her heart is. Have him/her jog in place for several minutes, then check his/her heartbeat. Also show your child where to check his/her pulse (the side of the neck or the wrist). Explain that the heart pumps blood throughout the body. Show your child his/her veins, the "tunnels" that transport blood.	Read pages 1–25 of *Handling Feelings* by Joy Berry. Discuss in greater depth each of the feelings mentioned.	Do a variety of exercises with your child, such as jumping jacks, sit-ups, leg lifts and push-ups. Then, help your child find his/her pulse and count the number of beats per minute. *See* Gross/Fine Motor Skills, Week 18, number 2.
Talk about the respiratory system. Consult pages 24 and 25 of *Make It Work: Body!* by Liz Wyse. Have your child take a deep breath. Explain that what he/she is feeling is air filling the lungs. Have your child fill a balloon with air to demonstrate how the lungs hold air. Discuss interesting facts from the book.	Read and discuss the remaining pages of *Handling Feelings*. *See* Social Studies, Week 18, number 1.	Give your child activity directions that incorporate both the review letters and the Social Studies unit on feelings. **Example:** *If you're jolly, jump for joy. If you're sad, slump down low.*
Talk about the brain. See pages 32–35 of *Make It Work: Body!* by Liz Wyse. Explain that the brain controls the entire body. It is also in charge of storing memories. Have your child tell you about his/her earliest memory. *See* Science, Week 18, number 3.	Discuss the importance of being sensitive to other people's feelings. Read *Horton Hears a Who!* by Dr. Seuss. *See* Social Studies, Week 18, numbers 2 and 3. Have your child complete **What Should I Do?** (p. 191).	Test your child's memory by bringing out a tray of ten objects. Let him/her study the objects for 5 minutes, then remove the tray. See how many of the objects your child can remember.

Learn at Home, Grade K

TEACHING SUGGESTIONS AND ACTIVITIES

READING (Consonant Review)

▶ 1. Help your child take pictures of objects that begin with each of the review letters. Put a magnet on the back of each picture. Then, have your child match the object pictures with the alphabet note cards on the refrigerator.

▶ 2. Read a short story. Ask your child to listen closely, giving him/her directions such as *Clap if you hear the sound of c* or *Jump if you hear the sound of j.*

▶ 3. Give your child a large basket or bin. See if your child can find an object for each review letter to put into the basket.

▶ 4. Have your child practice matching lower-case letters to upper-case letters.

LANGUAGE

▶ 1. "Who Feels Happy Today?" (poem)

Who feels happy today?
If you do, snap your fingers this way.
Who feels happy today?
If you do, clap your hands this way.
Who feels happy today?
If you do, wink your eye this way.
Who feels happy today?
If you do, jump up and shout, "Hooray!"

MATH (11 — Eleven)

▶ 1. Set out eleven objects and the + and = cards. Have your child give you addition equations. Have your child be the "teacher" and praise you if you give the correct answers.

▶ 2. Make a pattern with five objects. Then, ask your child to continue the pattern up to the eleventh piece.

▶ 3. Show your child how to use a ruler. Have your child measure eleven objects.

Learn at Home, Grade K

SCIENCE (My Body)

▶ 1. Read from *The Human Body* by Gilda Berger.

▶ 2. Schedule a trip to a hospital. Ask permission for your child to see a model skeleton. Have him/her point out and name all the bones that he/she can remember.

▶ 3. Talk about safety. Ask your child how he/she can protect his/her body.

SOCIAL STUDIES (My Feelings)

▶ 1. Help your child practice verbalizing his/her feelings. When your child is angry, for example, encourage him/her to express his/her feelings by asking questions.

▶ 2. Teach your child to respect others' feelings by giving him/her different scenarios. What would he/she do or say in a given situation?

▶ 3. Make "happy" and "sad" hand puppets out of small paper plates and craft sticks. Draw a happy face on one plate and a sad face on the other. Glue a craft stick to the back of each plate. Have your child hold these up as a quick way to show how he/she is feeling.

GROSS/FINE MOTOR SKILLS

▶ 1. "Me" (action poem)

> *Here are my fingers, and here is my nose.*
> *Here are my ears, and here are my toes.*
> *Here are my eyes that are open and wide.*
> *Here is my mouth with my white teeth inside.*
> *Here is my pink tongue that helps me to speak.*
> *Here are my shoulders and here is each cheek.*
> *Here are my hands that help me to play.*
> *Here are my feet that go walking every day.*

▶ 2. "Active Me" (action poem)

> *I wiggle my thumbs and clap my hands,*
> *And then I stamp my feet.*
> *I turn to the left, I turn to the right,*
> *And make my fingers meet.*
> *I raise them high and let them down,*
> *I give another clap.*
> *I wave my hands and fold my hands,*
> *And put them in my lap.*

Number 11

This is the number 11. **Color** the pictures.

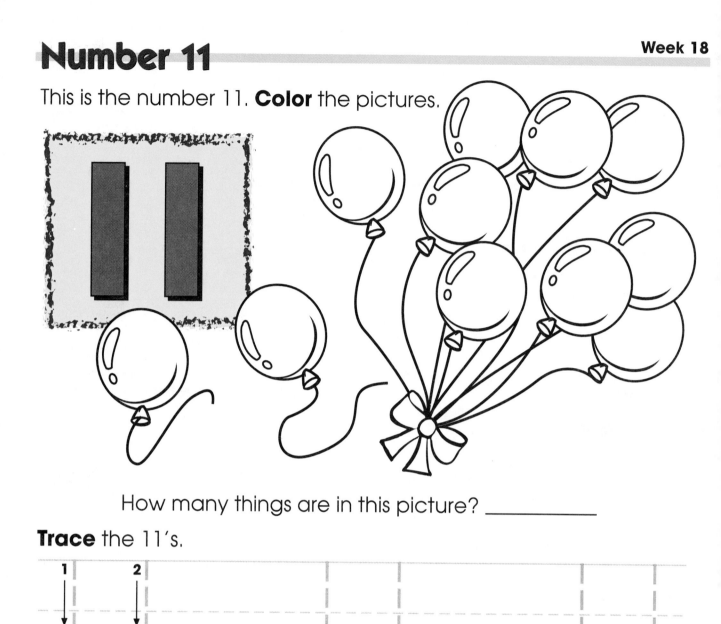

How many things are in this picture? _____

Trace the 11's.

Write your own 11's.

Learn at Home, Grade K

Zoorific!

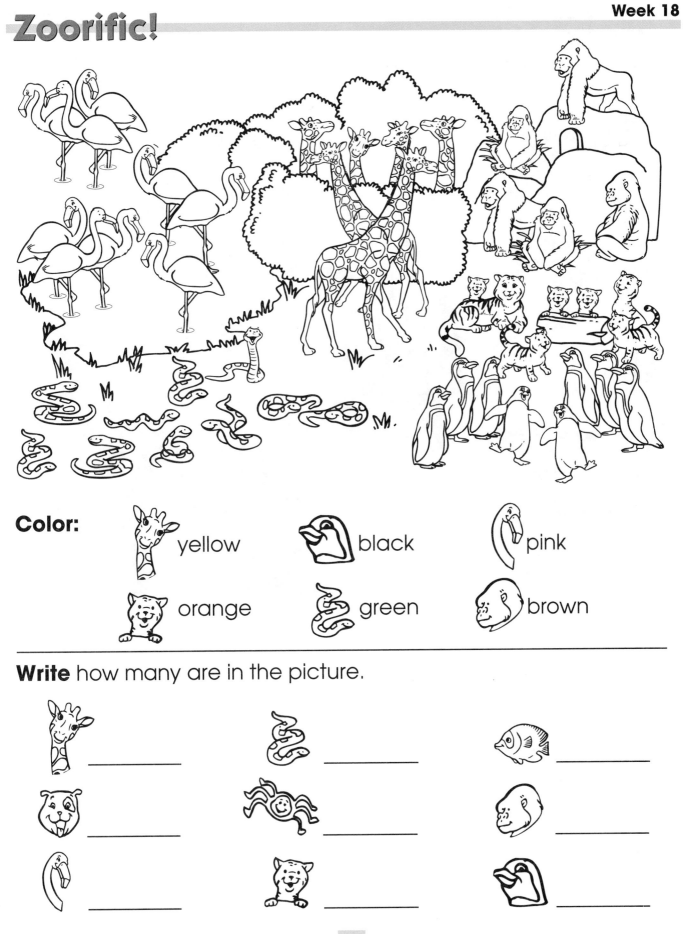

Color:

yellow   black   pink

orange   green   brown

Write how many are in the picture.

_____   _____   _____

_____   _____   _____

_____   _____   _____

One for Each

Draw one bone for each dog.

What Should I Do?

Color the picture that shows what each child should do.

Learn at Home, Grade K

	Reading	Language	Math
Monday	**H, h** Have your child sing the alphabet song. Then, have him/her sing it again, emphasizing the letter *h*. Shape several handkerchiefs into upper- and lower-case *h*'s. Have your child trace over the letters with his/her fingers, then shape the *h*'s by him/herself. *See* Reading, Week 19, number 1. Have your child complete **Letter H, h** (p. 196).	Read *Count-A-Saurus* by Nancy Blumenthal. As you read each page, have your child count the dinosaurs out loud. *See* Language, Week 19, numbers 1–3 for additional activities.	**Basic Concepts** Read *All About Where* by Tana Hoban. On each page, discuss the following location concepts: *above, on, behind, under, out, against, across, between, in, through, beside, among, below, over* and *around*. *See* Math, Week 19, numbers 1–4 for additional activities.
Tuesday	Have your child spread glue on a sheet of paper in the shape of a house. Inside the house, have him/her write an upper- and lower-case *h* with a crayon.	Read *Old Hat, New Hat* by Stan and Jan Berenstain. Be sure to point out that the word hat starts with an *h*. Have your child make the *h* sound along with you. Discuss the silly hats in the story. Look back through the book and ask your child questions about which hat is tallest or shortest, or which has more things on it and which has fewer.	Have your child count as high as he/she can. Then, show him/her how to count by tens. Set out 100 objects in sets of ten. Have him/her count each set. Then, have him/her count them all. Count with him/her to 100 by tens, pointing to each set and moving it aside as it is counted. Do this several times. Learning to count by tens will help your child anticipate the number that comes after 19, 29, 39, etc.
Wednesday	Have your child write the alphabet in capital letters on a sheet of paper. Encourage him/her to sing the alphabet song to help remember the order. As you hold up different objects, have him/her clap his/her hands if the object begins with the letter *h*. **Examples:** head, hair, hand, hook, house, hat, heart, hanger, horse. *See* Reading, Week 19, numbers 2.	Write each upper-case letter of the alphabet on a separate card. Have your child place the letters in the correct order.	Practice counting by tens with this finger play. *10, 20, 30, 40* *Count by tens, it's sure less wordy.* *50, 60, 70, 80* *Quicker than ones, my little matey.* *90, 100—we did it,* *We did it!* *We counted by tens in less than a minute.* Have your child complete **Gingery Treat!** (p. 198).
Thursday	Give your child a hat. Have him/her fill the hat with as many letter *h* objects or letter *h*'s as it can hold. Afterwards, discuss the full hat and the empty hat.	Read *Dinosaur Encore* by Patricia Mullins. Afterwards, flip back through the pages and have your child point out the tallest, fastest, smallest, etc.	Set out groups of pencils, crayons, slips of paper of different sizes and pieces of yarn of different lengths. Ask your child to pick out the longest and the shortest in each group. Have him/her count the objects in each group, then put the groups in order from least to greatest. Let your child create patterns with the objects. Then, have him/her complete patterns you begin. **Example:** *pencil, yarn, yarn....*
Friday	Play charades with your child using letter *h* words, such as *hen, horse, hammer, hit, hole, hippopotamus*. Have your child complete **Home We Go!** (p. 197).	Celebrate *H* Week by watching the movie *Homeward Bound*. Before watching it, tell your child to look and listen for objects that begin with the letter *h*. Keep a running list of letter *h* objects as you watch the movie or see how many you both can remember after the movie.	Have your child count by tens for review. Then, have him/her count various groups of objects by ones and by tens. Discuss how numbers come in order, just like activities. Have your child tell you the order in which he/she does things in the morning. Have your child complete **Ducky Destination** (p. 199).

Learn at Home, Grade K

Science	Social Studies	Gross/Fine Motor
Dinosaurs Read *The Magic School Bus in the Time of the Dinosaurs* by Joanna Cole. Discuss the following terms: *paleontologist, predator, prey, fossil, extinct*. *See* Science, Week 19, numbers 1–5 for additional activities.	**Martin Luther King, Jr.** Introduce the topic of prejudice. *See* Social Studies, Week 19, number 1. Read chapters 1 and 2 of *Martin Luther King, Jr. Day* by Dianne M. MacMillan. Discuss how Martin Luther King, Jr. felt growing up as a child. *See* Social Studies, Week 19, numbers 2–4 for additional activities.	Have your child measure and mix the ingredients for your favorite sugar cookie recipe. Then, using dinosaur cookie cutters, have your child make his/her own collection of dinosaurs. Bake them as the recipe directs. Have your child count out the cookie dinosaurs and sort them by type. Let them cool, then frost them. *See* Gross/Fine Motor Skills, numbers 1 and 2 for additional activities.
Talk about the two main types of dinosaurs: meat eaters (carnivores) and plant eaters (herbivores). *See* page 35 of *The Magic School Bus in the Time of the Dinosaurs* for information on this topic. See also *Dinosaur*, pages 22–27, by David Norman, Ph.D. and Angela Milner, Ph.D. Your child may enjoy looking at the other pictures in the book as well.	Read chapter 3 of *Martin Luther King, Jr. Day*. Discuss how Martin must have felt when he was told he had to give up his seat on the bus because of the color of his skin. Ask your child if he/she thinks that was fair. Why or why not?	Have your child design a hat. Allow him/her to decorate an old baseball hat or knit cap, or have him/her use newspaper to construct the base of a hat and work from there. Encourage your child to add interesting things to the hat.
Help your child make his/her own dinosaur book. Have your child begin by creating a cover for the dinosaur book. Provide construction paper, scissors, glue and markers. Once the cover is complete, have your child begin working on the first two pages of the book. *See* Science, Week 19, number 5. Choose one dinosaur per day to focus on, beginning with tyrannosaurus rex.	Read chapter 4 of *Martin Luther King, Jr. Day*. Discuss Rosa Parks' brave refusal to sit in the back of the bus. Ask your child how she might have felt. What gave her the courage to take a stand?	Trace the outline of a dinosaur onto a piece of poster board and cut it out for your child. Have your child cut small 1" squares from different wrapping papers. Have him/her glue these squares onto the dinosaur, overlapping the squares in random fashion to get a patchwork quilt effect. When all the white spaces have been covered, have your child trim around the edge of the dinosaur.
Have your child focus on allosaurus today. Have him/her draw a picture on one page and complete the fact sheet on the other.	Read chapter 5 of *Martin Luther King, Jr. Day*. Explain the word *nonviolent* to your child. Ask him/her to describe some of the ways Martin Luther King, Jr. urged people to take a stand against prejudice.	Celebrate *H* Week by playing hockey with your child. Get two brooms and a plastic disk and you'll be set to go. Mark the goals with tape, making a small square at each end of the room.
Help your child learn more about triceratops today. Have your child draw a picture on one page and complete the fact sheet on the other.	Read chapter 6 of *Martin Luther King, Jr. Day*. Discuss Martin Luther King, Jr.'s dream. Ask your child why that dream is so important.	Play "_____ (your child's name) Says" in which your child gives you directions that involve the letter *h*. **Example:** *Sally says move your head back and forth. Sally says hurry to the refrigerator. Sally says get five hangers.*

TEACHING SUGGESTIONS AND ACTIVITIES

READING (H, h)

▶ 1. Have your child make a letter *h* mobile using a hanger. Attach a small piece of yarn to the bottom of the hanger. Tie the free end of the yarn to a paper plate with a hole punched in the top. Next, have your child punch several holes along the bottom edge of the plate. Help him/her tie yarn through each of these holes. Hang letter *h* objects (or pictures of these objects) from the yarn.

▶ 2. To help your child better match upper- and lower-case letters, make the following game. Glue old greeting cards front to back. On the back of each card, write (in fat marker) an upper-case and lower-case letter. Cut these apart in a puzzle fashion, with a curvy line between the two letters. Repeat until each letter is made. Spread out the pieces, letter side up, and have your child match the letters. Your child can check his/her own work by turning over the card to match the picture on the other side.

LANGUAGE

▶ 1. Read *The Last Dinosaurs* by Dougal Dixon.

▶ 2. Read *Dinosaurs* by Gail Gibbons.

▶ 3. Go to the library and have your child find books about storybook or real-life characters who got well along with others. Discuss actions of the characters.

MATH (Basic Concepts)

▶ 1. Introduce the term *half* to your child. Cut a sandwich in half. Show your child how two halves make a whole. Explain that the halves are also equal in size. Then, cut several slices of bread into halves, each cut a different way (across, up and down, diagonally). Have your child put the correct halves together, then make his/her own halves.

▶ 2. Read *Four & Twenty Dinosaurs* by Bernard Most. Have your child count the dinosaurs on each page. Then, have him/her count the dinosaurs in the entire book.

▶ 3. Have your child stack building blocks in sets of ten. Have him/her count by tens, stacking each set of ten on top of the other sets, while counting.

▶ 4. Put slips of paper with directional instructions written on them in a hat. Have your child pull one out and do what it says. Have a special treat for him/her if he/she gets them all correct. **Examples:** *Place a penny between two spoons* or *Put a doll on top of the table*. Directional words to use: top, bottom, above, below, near, far, between, beside, high, low, over, under.

SCIENCE (Dinosaurs)

▶ 1. Go on a fossil hunt. Visit a local stone quarry and see what kinds of fossils you and your child can uncover.

▶ 2. Scientists now believe that birds are direct descendants of dinosaurs. Visit a pet store and observe the birds with your child. See if he/she notices any similarities between today's birds and flying dinosaurs such as pteranodons. Then, have him/her explain the differences.

▶ 3. Have your child name other animals that remind him/her of dinosaurs. He/she may mention reptiles, such as lizards or alligators. Explain that they are related to the family of dinosaurs but not as closely as birds.

▶ 4. Help your child make a dinosaur book. Devote two pages of the book to each kind of dinosaur—one page for a picture and the other for a fact sheet. Keep the fact sheet simple, using only key words and phrases to describe the dinosaur's physical features and diet, as well as the meaning of its name and any other unusual facts. Help your child find and use resources from the library or the Internet.

▶ 5. Have your child create his/her own dinosaur. What would he/she name it? What would it eat? Have your child draw this dinosaur and tell you all about it.

SOCIAL STUDIES (Martin Luther King, Jr./Getting Along With Others)

▶ 1. Introduce the subject of prejudice. Tell your child that you are better than he/she is because you have green eyes (if your child's are a different color) or brown hair (if your child's is a different color). Eat a special treat in front of your child to emphasize your "specialness." Tell your child that he/she will be your servant because of your special coloring. Give him/her several easy jobs to do. Then, ask how this makes him/her feel.

▶ 2. Have your child research people who helped fight slavery and racism. Potential subjects might include Rosa Parks, Harriet Tubman, Harriet Beecher Stowe, Frederick Douglass and W.E.B. Du Bois.

▶ 3. Discuss ways to get along with other people. Give your child different scenarios and have him/her tell what he/she would do.

▶ 4. Talk about prejudices your child may have. Does he/she dislike people who are physically handicapped, unattractive or overweight? Discuss your child's feelings about these people. Does he/she dislike them simply because they are different?

GROSS/FINE MOTOR SKILLS

▶ 1. Have your child use frozen bread dough to form the letter *h*, hats and other *h* objects. Bake the dough as directed and enjoy.

▶ 2. Let your child use play dough to shape different dinosaurs. Bake them at 250° until they are hardened. Then, let your child paint his/her dinosaurs.

Learn at Home, Grade K

Letter H, h

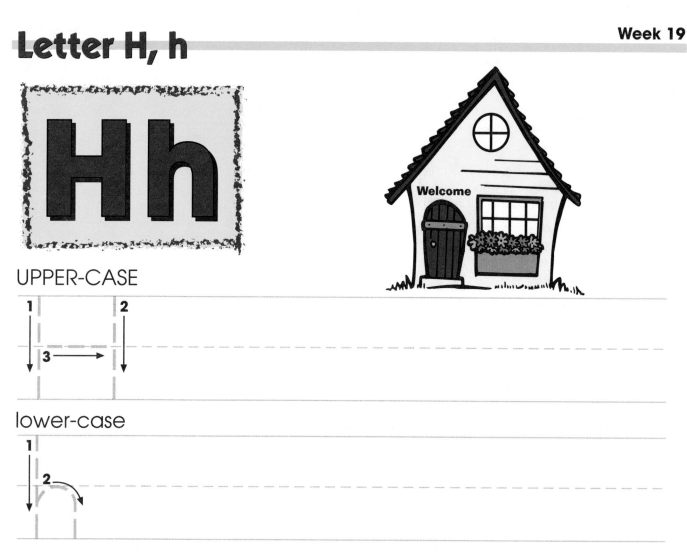

UPPER-CASE

lower-case

These pictures begin with the letter H, h. **Color** the pictures.

Home We Go!

Help Homer and his dog get home! **Color** the pictures which begin with the sound of H, h. Then, follow the path to Homer's house.

Gingery Treat!

Color the spaces: 10 — white

⠿ ⠿ — yellow

ten — brown

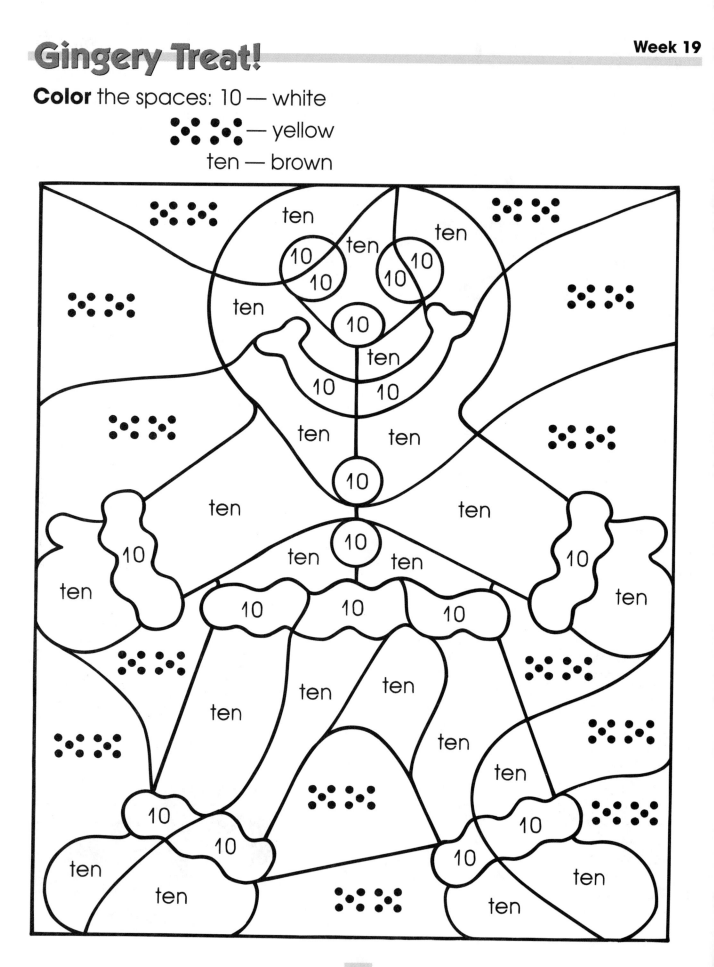

Ducky Destination

Help Ducky have a great vacation. Number the pictures 1, 2, 3 and 4 to show the correct order.

Learn at Home, Grade K

Reading	Language	Math
Monday **N, n** Cut a sheet of newspaper in the shape of upper- and lower-case *n*'s. Have your child trace over each letter with his/her fingers. *See* Reading, Week 20, numbers 1–4 for additional activities. Have your child complete **Letter N, n** (p. 204).	Have your child make a card for Martin Luther King, Jr.'s widow, Coretta Scott King. Help your child write the message he/she would like to send. Address the envelope to: Coretta Scott King King Center 449 Auburn Ave. N.E. Atlanta, GA 30312 *See* Language, Week 20, numbers 1 and 2.	**12 — Twelve** Have your child measure out and mix his/her favorite cookie recipe. Have him/her make one large cookie with twelve chocolate chips and twelve other small candies on it. Bake it at 300° until it is cooked in the center. *See* Math, Week 20, numbers 1–4 for additional activities. Have your child complete **Number 12** (p. 207).
Tuesday Have your child squeeze glue onto a sheet of newspaper in the shape of upper- and lower-case letter *n*'s. Have him/her place nickels on the glue.	Give your child a page from the newspaper. Have him/her draw a circle around each upper-case *n* and a square around each lower-case *n* he/she finds.	Write the numeral 12 and the number word *twelve* on a sheet of paper. Help your child sound out the letters in the word *twelve*. Then, have him/her rip the paper into twelve pieces. Have your child complete **Buffy's Cookies** (p. 208).
Wednesday Make the letter *n* sound for your child and have him/her repeat it with you. Then, give descriptions for the following *n* words for your child to guess: *nurse, nut, nap, nail, neighbor, nose, nod, nine, note, number, new, necklace.* Have your child complete **Nice Nests** (p. 205).	Skim *I Wonder Why Triceratops Had Horns and Other Questions About Dinosaurs* by Rod Theodorou. Read through the questions and answers with your child.	Using finger paint, have your child write the numbers one through twelve on a sheet of newsprint. Have your child complete **Numbers 1 to 12** (p. 209).
Thursday Set out various objects on the floor, many of which begin with the letter *n*. Have your child scoop up as many *n* objects as he/she can in 10 minutes. Have your child complete **Letters H, h and N, n** (p. 206).	Read *Dinosaur Dances* by Jane Yolen. Enjoy the dinosaur poetry together. Ask your child which poem he/she liked best and why.	Review counting by ones and counting by tens. Have your child complete **Dino-mite!** (p. 210).
Friday Have your child "follow his/her nose" to the letter *n*. See how many letter *n* foods and other objects he/she can find in your house.	Read *Pterodactyl Tunnel* published by TimeLife for Children.	Point to a clock. Show your child that there are twelve numbers on it. As you point to each number, have him/her tell you what it is. Then, take the clock off the wall. As you say a number, have your child move the big hand to that number.

Learn at Home, Grade K

Science	**Social Studies**	**Gross/Fine Motor**
Dinosaurs Help your child learn about brachiosaurus. Have your child draw a picture on one page of his/her dinosaur book and complete the fact sheet on the other. *See* Science, Week 20, numbers 1–4 for additional activities.	**Martin Luther King, Jr.** Read chapters 7 and 8 of *Martin Luther King, Jr. Day* by Diane M. MacMillan. Ask your child what special prize Dr. King received. Ask your child if he/she thinks Dr. King deserved such an award. Talk about the work that Martin Luther King, Jr. did to earn the prize.	Have your child think of a person with whom he/she last had a disagreement. Ask your child how he/she could "make peace" with that person. Brainstorm many ideas and have your child choose his/her favorite. Then, help him/her follow through with it. *See* Gross/Fine Motor Skills, Week 20, numbers 1–4.
Help your child research ankylosaurus. Have your child draw a picture on one page and complete the fact sheet on the other.	Read chapter 9 of *Martin Luther King, Jr. Day*. Explain to your child the term *national holiday*. Ask your child how Martin Luther King, Jr. Day came to be a national holiday.	For letter *N* Week, have your child visit the nurse at your doctor's office. See if the nurse will show your child some basic duties of nursing, such as taking blood pressure, weighing patients, listening to heartbeats, measuring height and conducting ear and eye examinations. See if he/she will allow your child to help with some of these tasks.
The final dinosaur for your child's dinosaur book is pteranodon. Have your child draw a picture on one page and complete a fact sheet on the other. He/she can then staple all the sheets inside the cover to complete the book. Enjoy reading together and looking at your child's book.	Read chapter 10 of *Martin Luther King, Jr. Day*. Discuss the peaceful ways Dr. King wanted to make our country fair for all. Explain that Dr. King is buried in Atlanta, Georgia, and show your child where this is on a map. Also point out the different states and countries mentioned in the book that honor Dr. King by using his name.	Have your child jump rope while saying: *Peace, peace, peace,* *Keep the peace* *And get along!* *Fighting, fighting* *Just shows we both* *Are wrong.*
Read *Let's Go Dinosaur Tracking!* by Miriam Schlein. Discuss how paleontologists can learn information about dinosaurs just by looking at their footprints.	Read chapter 11 of *Martin Luther King, Jr. Day*. Talk with your child about what he/she can do to help spread peace. Help your child think of concrete ways to help and then carry these out. **Examples:** donate food and clothing to homeless shelters, donate money to a worthy cause (such as the King Center).	Celebrate the letter *n* by staying in nightclothes all morning, playing letter *n* games and reading books by letter *n* authors or with letter *n* characters.
Visit a museum that has a dinosaur exhibit. Enjoy looking at dinosaur bones together. Discuss how paleontologists know how to put the bones together. Allow your child to ask the museum curator questions about dinosaurs. Have your child complete **Dinosaur Match** (p. 211).	Read chapter 12 of *Martin Luther King, Jr. Day*. Ask your child to tell you about Martin Luther King, Jr.'s dream. Ask how he/she can help make that dream come true. *See* Social Studies, Week 20, numbers 1 and 2.	Have your child draw a picture of his/her favorite dinosaur from your museum trip.

TEACHING SUGGESTIONS AND ACTIVITIES

READING (N, n)

▶ 1. Cut out a large letter *n* from poster board. Have your child fill it in with magazine pictures of letter *n* objects.

▶ 2. Write each lower-case letter of the alphabet on a separate sheet of construction paper. Mix up the letters, then have your child put them in order on the floor. Ask your child to step on each letter of the alphabet as he/she sings the alphabet song.

▶ 3. Learn about musical notes for *N* Week. Set out glasses with different amounts of water in them. Have your child gently clink each one with the end of a spoon. Talk about the sound each glass makes. Ask your child which glasses sound higher and which sound lower. Have him/her arrange the glasses in order of pitch from low to high. Allow your child to create his/her own songs.

▶ 4. Have your child create a letter *n* centerpiece for the table. Have him/her arrange a group of letter *n* foods neatly and creatively.

LANGUAGE

▶ 1. Help your child write a poem about peace.

▶ 2. Videotape your child interviewing different people about how they try to keep peace.

MATH (12 — Twelve)

▶ 1. Take your child to a grocery store. Have him/her make a list of things that come in packages of twelve.

▶ 2. Explain that a dozen is equal to twelve. Have your child make treats by the dozen to give to friends.

▶ 3. Using thawed bread dough, have your child make twelve homemade pretzels. Have him/her brush the pretzels with an egg and water mixture, then sprinkle them with coarse salt. Bake the pretzels at 350° until they are golden brown.

▶ 4. Have your child stack several sets of twelve objects. Ask your child which stack is the tallest and which is the shortest.

SCIENCE (Dinosaurs)

▶ 1. Have your child create his/her own "prehistoric peek box." Cut a hole in the end of a shoe box. Then, have your child arrange plastic plants, sand and plastic dinosaurs in a prehistoric scene.

▶ 2. Using pudding as finger paint, have your child paint a dinosaur scene on a sheet of newsprint.

▶ 3. Spread out a strip of banner paper or tape together several sheets of 8¹/₂" x 11" paper. Have your child make a dinosaur time line.

▶ 4. Read *Tyrannosaurus Was a Beast*, a collection of dinosaur poems by Jack Prelutsky.

SOCIAL STUDIES (Martin Luther King, Jr./Getting Along With Others)

▶ 1. Invite a friend over who is of an ethnic background different than yours. Have your child ask him/her questions to get to know him/her better and to learn about his/her heritage.

▶ 2. Look through your family tree. Talk about the different ethnic backgrounds in your own family.

GROSS/FINE MOTOR SKILLS

▶ 1. Have your child crack open several large nuts, such as walnuts, and take out the "meat" of the nut. Then, help your child make a fleet of sailing "nut boats" using toothpicks, construction paper, pipe cleaners and tape.

▶ 2. See how many objects your child can make out of newspaper for letter *N* Week. For help, check out a book on origami, the Japanese art of paper folding.

▶ 3. Let your child invent letter *n* races, such as pushing a nickel with his/her nose to the finish line. Enjoy competing in the races with your child.

▶ 4. Ask your child to hold a net while you toss objects to him/her. If the object starts with the letter *n*, he/she should try to catch it; if it starts with a different letter, he/she can let it fall.

Letter N, n

Nn

UPPER-CASE

lower-case

These pictures begin with the letter N, n. **Color** the pictures.

204

Nice Nests

Color and **cut out** each picture which begins with the sound of
N, n. **Glue** each N, n picture on a nest.

Learn at Home, Grade K

Letters H, h and N, n

Color each picture the correct color.

H — red   N — yellow   H — orange   N — blue

H — green   N — purple   H — yellow   N — green

 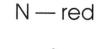  

H — blue   N — red   H — purple   N — orange

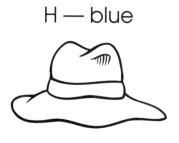  

Number 12

This is the number 12. **Color** the pictures.

How many things are in this picture? _____

Trace the 12's.

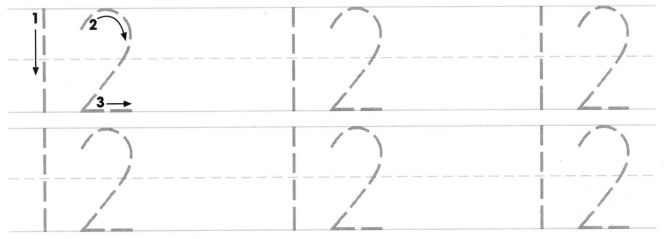

Write your own 12's.

Learn at Home, Grade K

Buffy's Cookies

Buffy Bear loves to munch on cookies. **Color** 12 cookies for Buffy to munch.

Numbers 1 to 12

Trace the numbers with different colors. **Draw** a line from the number to the correct group of objects.

Dino-mite!

Color the picture of the dinosaurs.

Count each thing. **Write** the number in the box.

Learn at Home, Grade K

Dinosaur Match

Draw a line to match each dinosaur with its skeleton.

Learn at Home, Grade K

	Reading	Language	Math
Monday	**Consonant Review** Have your child make pages for letters *h* and *n* for his/her letter review book. Have him/her cut a sheet of construction paper in half. At the top of one half, have your child write an upper- and lower-case *h* and an *n* on the other half. Help your child cut out magazine pictures that begin with each of these letters and glue them onto each sheet. *See* Reading, Week 21, numbers 1–4 for additional activities.	Take your child to the library. Help him/her check out a variety of alphabet books. Enjoy reading them together. *See* Language, Week 21, numbers 1–4 for additional activities.	**13 — Thirteen** Using finger paint, write a large 13 on a sheet of paper. Then, write the word *thirteen* and help your child sound it out. Have him/her dip a thumb into the finger paint and make thirteen thumbprints around the number 13. *See* Math, Week 21, numbers 1–3 for additional activities.
Tuesday	Have your child write the lower-case alphabet on paper with writing lines. Check to see that he/she forms each letter correctly and that each letter is positioned correctly on the line. Have him/her rewrite any difficult letters. If your child has trouble remembering what letter comes next, have him/her sing the alphabet song.	Discuss real and make-believe events. Read *The Magic School Bus: Lost in the Solar System* by Joanna Cole. Ask your child if Ms. Frizzle could really make her bus fly into outer space. Why or why not? Have your child tell you the true parts of the story as well as the make-believe parts. Have your child complete **Reality and Fantasy** (p. 216).	Draw a large wheel on a piece of poster board. Have your child write the number 13 in the center of the wheel. Then, have him/her glue thirteen small objects, such as dried beans or cereal, on each of the spokes. Have your child complete **Number 13** (p. 218).
Wednesday	Write each letter of the alphabet on a card (upper- and lower-case letters on separate cards). Shuffle the cards and use them as flash cards. As you hold up a card, have your child shout out the letter. Continue until he/she has gone through the entire deck. Pull out any letters that were difficult for him/her and review those letters.	If your child has trouble remembering the color words, review them now. Ask him/her questions about colors: *Can you think of other things that are green? Red? Orange? Yellow?* Have your child complete **Color Review** (p. 217).	Have your child write the numbers 1 through 13 on a sheet of paper. Have your child complete **Dandy Donuts** (p. 219).
Thursday	Lay out the review letter cards on the floor. Tell your child he/she has 14 minutes—1 minute per letter—to find an object that begins with each of those letters and to place it on the correct letter card.	Read and discuss *Papa, Please Get the Moon for Me* by Eric Carle.	Set up basic addition equations with sums through 10 using objects and the + and = cards. Reinforce the concept of zero.
Friday	Play "I'm Thinking of a Letter That Begins With...." Your child must guess the letter, then hold up the appropriate card. Reward your child if he/she guesses all fourteen sounds correctly.	Listen to the CD, *Follow the Drinking Gourd*, read by Morgan Freeman. Talk about how the slaves used the North Star (part of the Big Dipper constellation, called "the drinking gourd" here) to find their way north to freedom.	Review counting by ones and by tens with the goal of helping your child count to one hundred. Begin by helping your child review the number words *one* through *ten*. Have your child complete **Number Words** (p. 220).

Learn at Home, Grade K

Science	Social Studies	Gross/Fine Motor
Solar System Set out a globe. Explain to your child that the globe is a model of the Earth. Teach your child basic facts about the Earth: Earth is the planet we live on, it revolves around the sun, it is the only planet with people on it and it moves so fast we cannot even tell it is moving.	**Manners/Character Building** Read *The Berenstain Bears Say Please and Thank You* by Stan and Jan Berenstain. Discuss the proper times to say these words and encourage your child to use these words when it is appropriate. *See* Social Studies, Week 21, numbers 1–2.	Help your child make a papier-maché Earth. First, have him/her blow up a balloon and tie it. Next, make a wet paste of flour and water. Have your child tear newspaper into strips and dip one strip of newspaper at a time in the paste. Have him/her wipe off the dripping paste and wrap the strip around the balloon, smoothing the strip on the surface of the balloon. Continue until the balloon is fully covered and let it dry. Continue the project tomorrow.
Read *The Magic School Bus: Lost in the Solar System* by Joanna Cole. Discuss the following space-related terms: *solar system, Earth, planet, spaceship* and *gravity*. *See* Reading, Week 21, numbers 1–4 for additional activities.	Read *No Bad Bears* by Michele Durkson Clise. Focus on the chapter about table manners. At supper tonight, be sure your child places his/her napkin in his/her lap, passes food politely, chews with his/her mouth closed, uses his/her silverware properly and waits until everyone is finished before asking to be excused. Reinforce table manners at every meal until they become second nature.	Add another layer of papier-maché to your Earth balloon and let it dry. *See* Gross/Fine Motor Skills, Week 21, numbers 1–4 for additional activities.
Read and discuss *Our Friend, the Sun* by Janet Palazzo.	Read *Perfect Pigs* by Marc Brown. Focus on telephone manners. Evaluate how your child answers the phone. Could he/she improve his/her telephone manners? Also discuss the importance of not interrupting someone while they are on the phone.	Teach your child the following poem about the Sun: *Sun, dear Sun,* *You're just perfect,* *Don't you know?* *Your distance* *From Earth is just right—* *Not too hot* *And not too cold!*
Talk to your child about the Moon. Talk about when it appears, how it changes in appearance and how it revolves. Have your child draw a picture of what the Moon looks like tonight. Wait 1 week and have him/her draw another picture of the Moon. How has it changed?	Read *Manners Can Be Fun* by Munro Leaf. Discuss the importance of using good manners at home with family.	Once your child's papier-maché Earth is fully dried, have your child paint it blue. Let the blue paint dry, then have your child add green for the land. Have your child use a globe to help him/her paint the land masses.
Read *The Sky Is Full of Stars* by Franklyn M. Branley. Try some of the experiments mentioned. Go stargazing with your child tonight. Point out the Big Dipper and other easily recognizable constellations. Have your child complete **Space Patterns** (p. 221).	Read *Mind Your Manners!* by Peggy Parish. Discuss using good manners around friends.	Make an "alphabet train." Have your child line up alphabet sponges in order from A to Z. Have him/her dip them in finger paint and press them onto a long sheet of paper in the correct order. After they dry, have him/her connect each letter with a short line. Lastly, have your child draw an engine at the beginning of the train and a caboose at the end.

Learn at Home, Grade K

TEACHING SUGGESTIONS AND ACTIVITIES

READING (Consonant Review)

▶ 1. Set out objects that begin with each of the review letters. Have your child sort the objects into piles according to beginning sounds.

▶ 2. Have your child draw a picture in which each of the review letters is represented. As he/she draws each part of the picture, have your child write the letter that is represented.

▶ 3. Act out words that begin with each of the review letters. Have your child guess the word, then name the beginning letter.

▶ 4. Buy alphabet french fries and cook them as directed. Ask your child to pick up a particular letter. Repeat with other letters. Be sure your child recognizes them all.

LANGUAGE

▶ 1. Read *Dinosaur Do's and Don'ts* by Jean Burt Polhamus.

▶ 2. Read *Manners* by Aliki.

▶ 3. Read *Good Manners* by Joy Berry.

▶ 4. Have your child name five basic good manners, naming each one as he/she counts them on his/her fingers.

MATH (13 — Thirteen)

▶ 1. Have your child paint thirteen boxes blue. Have your child write a number from 1 to 13 on each box. Shuffle the boxes. Challenge your child to stack them in order as quickly as he/she can.

▶ 2. Write the number 13 on a sheet of paper and have your child create a picture around the number. Encourage him/her to show how many thirteen is by drawing a creature with 13 legs, 13 eyes, etc.

▶ 3. Set out a long flat container of sand. Give your child a variety of directions using the number 13. **Examples:** *Trace a 13 in the sand. Poke your finger in the sand 13 times. Build 13 little hills in the sand, then knock down 2. How many are left?*

SCIENCE (Solar System)

▶ 1. Have your child make a list of all the things he/she knows about the Sun.

▶ 2. Using chalk, have your child draw a constellation on a large blue ball.

▶ 3. Have your child draw a night sky scene using a sheet of black construction paper and colored chalk.

▶ 4. Show your child the results of gravity. Hold objects in the air, then let them go. Ask your child what happens each time. Ask your child how many times the same thing will happen. Explain that gravity always works on Earth. Ask your child what he/she thinks happens in outer space.

SOCIAL STUDIES (Manners/Character Building)

▶ 1. Carefully observe your child's manners. Which ones need improving? Be consistent in teaching good manners and your child will soon use them automatically.

▶ 2. Ask your child why manners are important. Begin a "manners jar." Every time you notice your child using good manners, put a dime in the jar. When your child uses bad manners, take one away. When your child accumulates twenty dimes, go on a special outing or let him/her buy a small prize.

GROSS/FINE MOTOR SKILLS

▶ 1. Have your child draw a star on a sheet of black construction paper. Have him/her fill it in with glue and sprinkle it with glitter or tiny beads. When the glue dries, have your child use fabric paint to write his/her name in the center of the star.

▶ 2. Have your child turn a grapefruit into a "Sun." Have him/her push in toothpicks around the edges and add triangular pieces of cheese to each toothpick.

▶ 3. Have relay races in which your child must "orbit" you while moving ahead. This can be done while standing or while on his/her knees.

▶ 4. Have your child bend pipe cleaners into star shapes.

Reality and Fantasy

Circle the 10 things in the picture which are not real.

Color Review

Color each picture the correct color.

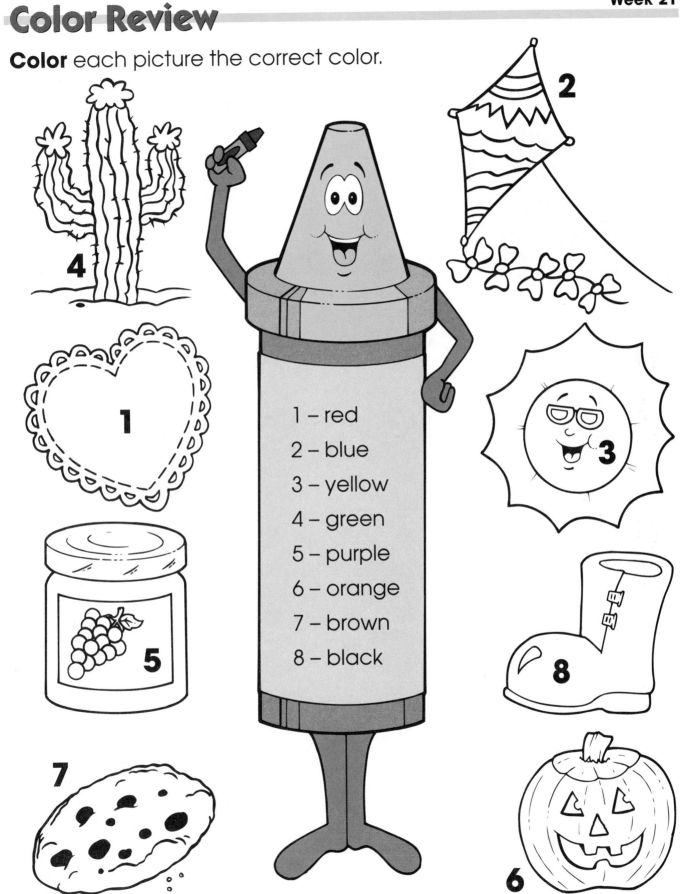

1 – red
2 – blue
3 – yellow
4 – green
5 – purple
6 – orange
7 – brown
8 – black

Learn at Home, Grade K

Number 13

This is the number 13. **Color** the pictures.

How many things are in this picture? _____

Trace the 13's.

Write your own 13's.

Learn at Home, Grade K

Dandy Donuts

Draw 13 donuts in the box.

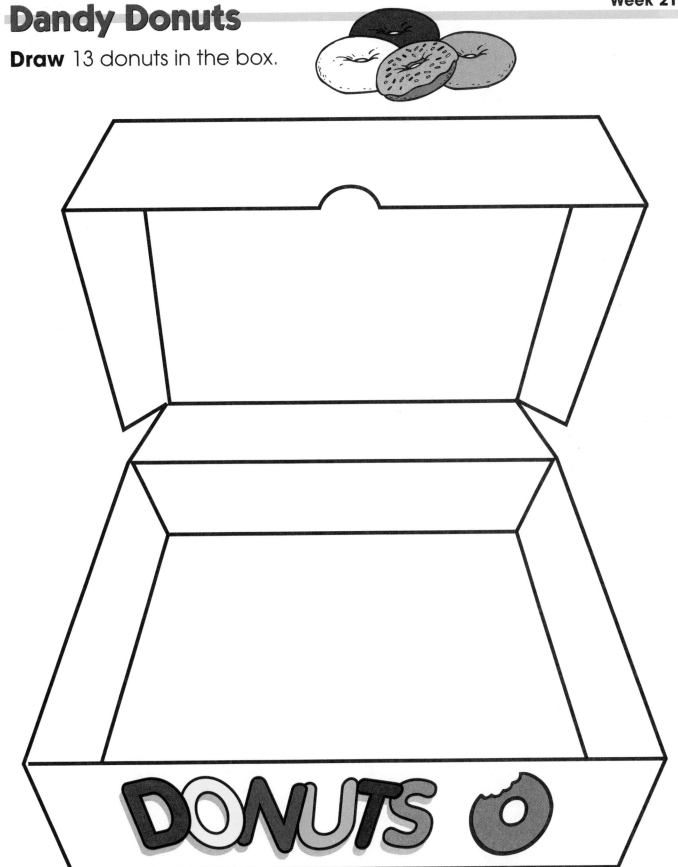

Learn at Home, Grade K

Number Words

Write how many. Then, **match** the number with the word.

one

two

three

four

five

six

seven

eight

nine

ten

Space Patterns

Draw the pictures to continue the pattern in each row.

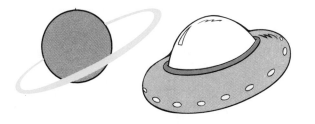

Learn at Home, Grade K

	Reading	Language	Math
Monday	**K, k** Put on lipstick and kiss a sheet of paper several times until you form upper- and lowercase letter k's. Have your child trace the letters with a finger. If your child wants to, let him/her "kiss" out a letter k, or he/she may want to draw a letter k using the lipstick. Have your child complete **Letter K, k** (p. 226).	Teach your child the poem "Three Astronauts." *See* Language, Week 22, number 1.	Introduce triangles by cutting a slice of pizza or pie or by cutting a triangle out of bread. Have your child count the number of points and sides a triangle has. Ask your child how many sides a circle and square have. Then, have your child make a triangle sandwich out of bread. *See* Math, Week 22, numbers 1–4 for additional activities. Have your child complete **Magic Triangles** (p. 228).
Tuesday	Have your child use kite string to make upper- and lower-case letter k's. Glue the string k's onto a kite shape cut from construction paper. While your child works, cut various shapes from construction paper for him/her to glue onto the kite. Have him/her name each shape as he/she glues it onto the kite. *See* Reading, Week 22, numbers 1 and 2	Videotape or audiotape your child describing what it would be like to be an astronaut. You may want to prepare a list of questions ahead of time and interview your child to keep the conversation flowing.	Have your child conduct a "triangle search" in your house and make a list of the objects found.
Wednesday	Tell your child the sound a letter k makes. Have him/her repeat it with you. Then, draw the following letter k words while he/she tries to guess them: *king, kangaroo, key, kick, kid, kitchen, kitten* and *kiss.*	Read *Alexander and the Terrible, Horrible, No Good, Very Bad Day* by Judith Viorst a second time. Ask your child if any of those things have ever happened to him/her.	Make a geoboard for your child by hammering nails in straight lines and rows onto a square piece of wood. Have your child stretch rubber bands around some of the nails to form a triangle. Ask your child what shape it is. Then, make a square with another rubber band. See if you can make a star. Then, encourage your child to make shapes for you to guess.
Thursday	Cut out a kite shape from a piece of felt. Have your child glue on pictures of k objects or draw k pictures with fabric paint pens.	Teach your child the song "It's a World of Laughter, It's a World of Tears." *See* Language, Week 22, numbers 2 and 3.	Introduce rectangles to your child. Show your child a book and have him/her count the points. Explain the difference between a square and a rectangle. Ask your child to look for rectangles around the house and outside. Have your child complete **Rectangle Robot** (p. 229).
Friday	Tell your child that today he/she is "the King of K." Make him/her a crown from construction paper and staple it so it fits his/her head. Tell your child that, as the King of K's, it is his/her job to make a list of every k object in his/her kingdom. Have your child complete **King's Castle** (p. 227).	Read *Shapes* by Henry Pluckrose. Discuss each of the questions in the book with your child.	Review the following shapes with your child by making them on the geoboard: *circle, square, star* and *rectangle*. Then, give your child practice forming each of the shapes him/herself. Have your child complete **Rectangle Roundup** (p. 230).

Science	Social Studies	Gross/Fine Motor
The Solar System Read *Space: Stars, Planets and Spacecraft* (pgs. 18–23, 26 and 27) by Sue Becklake. Discuss the experience of traveling in space. Talk about weightless- ness, dehydrated food and the responsi- bilities astronauts have. Ask your child if he/she would like to go to the Moon. Why or why not? What would be the best and most difficult parts of space travel?	**Manners/Character Building** Read *The Berenstain Bears Get the Gimmies* by Stan and Jan Berenstain. Discuss the importance of accepting "no" peacefully and respecting your parents. *See* Social Studies, Week 22, numbers 1.	Teach your child this action rhyme: *Our rocket ship is standing by* *And very, very soon* *We'll have a countdown, and we'll blast* *Ourselves up to the Moon.* *Begin to count: ten, nine, eight,* *Seven, six, five, four,* *There aren't many seconds more.* *Three, two, one, zero, zip!* *The rocket is off on a Moon trip!*
Read pages 28–31 of *Space: Stars, Planets and Spacecraft* to give your child a brief overview of each of the planets. Then, discuss why Earth is so special. *See* Science, Week 22, numbers 1–3 for additional activities.	Talk with your child about people in authority. Explain that these are people who are in charge of others. Have your child help you make a list of authority figures in his/her own life. Discuss why each of these people is important. Discuss the importance of obeying them and abiding by their rules. Talk about what happens when people break these rules. Ask your child how he/she can do his/her best to obey people in authority.	Give your child practice developing fine motor skills. Have your child complete **Outer Space Race** (p. 231).
Help your child begin a two-day planet mobile project. *See* Science, Week 22, number 4. Continue working on the mobile tomorrow.	Read *The Berenstain Bears Get the Grouchies* by Stan and Jan Berenstain. Discuss what makes your child grouchy. What does he/she do when he/she is grouchy? What do you do when you're grouchy? Talk about ways to cheer up each other when one or both of you are grouchy.	Look through *Shapes* by Ivan Bulloch. Have your child select a craft or project to do. *See* Gross/Fine Motor Skills, Week 22, numbers 1–4 for additional activities.
Have your child finish the planet mobile.	Help your child brainstorm ways to show kindness to family members. Create a list of your ideas and post it on the refrigerator as a reminder.	Play "flying saucer." Provide your child with a variety of plastic lids of all sizes. Discuss their common shape (circle). Then, let your child use the lids as "flying saucers," sending them into "outer space."
Field Trip: Visit a planetarium with your child. Help your child prepare questions ahead of time to ask the guides.	Read *The Berenstain Bears and the Truth* by Stan and Jan Berenstain. Discuss why telling the truth is so important.	Have your child create a shape mobile using boxes, cans and other recyclables. Discuss the different shapes he/she used.

TEACHING SUGGESTIONS AND ACTIVITIES

READING (K, k)

▶ 1. Draw a picture of a kangaroo or cut out one from a coloring book. Make a construction paper pouch and glue it onto the kangaroo just around the side and bottom edges. Have your child write upper- and lower-case letter k's on the pouch. Have your child fill the kangaroo's pouch with letter *k* pictures from magazines.

▶ 2. Challenge your child to find as many letter *k* objects as he/she can in the kitchen.

LANGUAGE

▶ 1. "Three Astronauts" (poem)

> *One astronaut climbs up the stair*
> *To the capsule hatch which we see there.*
> *Two astronauts sit side by side.*
> *Three astronauts prepare for the ride.*
> *The first one says, "We have checked controls."*
> *The second one says, "We will reach our goals."*
> *The third one says, "Turn the oxygen on."*
> *All three say, "We will soon be gone."*
> *The first one says, "We have checked things well.*
> *Our system is working. We can tell."*
> *The second one says, "I hear the motor sound.*
> *Our ship is lifting off the ground."*
> *The third one says, "We are high in the sky.*
> *We are already ten miles high."*
> *Three astronauts sit quietly in place,*
> *All at their work in outer space.*

▶ 2. "It's a World of Laughter, A World of Tears" (song) Sing to the tune of "It's a Small World".

> *It's a world of laughter, a world of tears.*
> *We need to give and share while we're here.*
> *Instead of pushes and shoves*
> *We need to show each other more love.*
> *Live together kindly.*
> *Live together helpfully.*
> *Live together truthfully.*
> *In the world and at home.*

▶ 3. Read *Christina Katerina and Fats and the Great Neighborhood War* written by Patricia Lee Gauch. Discuss how working to get along with others shows character.

MATH

▶ 1. Set out a collection of objects of various shapes. Have your child group them by shape.

▶ 2. Play "I Spy the Shape of a _____." When your child guesses correctly, switch roles.

▶ 3. Cut sponges into shapes. Allow your child to dip them in finger paint and use as stamps to create designs or pictures.

▶ 4. Make cutout cookies in different shapes (square, circle, star). Let your child enjoy decorating them.

SCIENCE (Solar System)

▶ 1. Let your child use binoculars or a telescope to observe stars in the sky.

▶ 2 Try activities from *Astronomy* by Robin Kerrod.

▶ 3. Read *I Wonder Why Stars Twinkle?* by Carole Stott. Read the answers to questions that interest your child.

▶ 4. Help your child make a planet mobile. Straighten two hangers and twist them together at the ends to make one long wire. Help your child tie ten pieces of yarn onto the wire. Use construction paper, foam balls or fruit to make the planets and the Sun in correct proportion to each other. Attach the planets to the yarn in the correct positions. Then, have your child add details, such as pipe cleaner rings for Saturn or a Great Red Spot on Jupiter.

SOCIAL STUDIES (Manners/Character Building)

▶ 1. Be on the lookout for teachable moments. When your child is being truthful or accepts your authority graciously, be sure to praise him/her. When he/she makes poor choices, point these out and talk together about what he/she could have done differently.

GROSS/FINE MOTOR SKILLS

▶ 1. Make cardboard patterns for a circle, square, triangle and rectangle. Have your child trace the patterns on sheets of construction paper to make a total of 27 shapes. Have your child make an alphabet shape caterpillar. Set aside one circle. Have your child write one letter of the alphabet on each of the remaining shapes, then glue them together in the correct order. Have your child draw a face on the first circle and attach antennae.

▶ 2. See how long you and your child can keep a balloon in the air by kicking it. Try several times. What is the greatest length of time you kept the balloon in the air?

▶ 3. Have your child get together with a friend to work on a project, such as putting a difficult puzzle together or building a sugar cube pyramid. Discuss rules for working together.

▶ 4. Put a variety of objects of different shapes into a bag. Have your child close his/her eyes and pull one out. Ask him/her to name the shape without looking at it. Repeat with the other shapes.

Learn at Home, Grade K

Letter K, k

UPPER-CASE

1 2 3

lower-case

1 2 3

These pictures begin with the letter K, k. **Color** the pictures.

Learn at Home, Grade K

King's Castle

Help the king color the correct picture for his castle. **Color** each picture which begins with the sound of K, k.

Learn at Home, Grade K

Magic Triangles

This is a triangle △. **Color** each triangle the correct color.

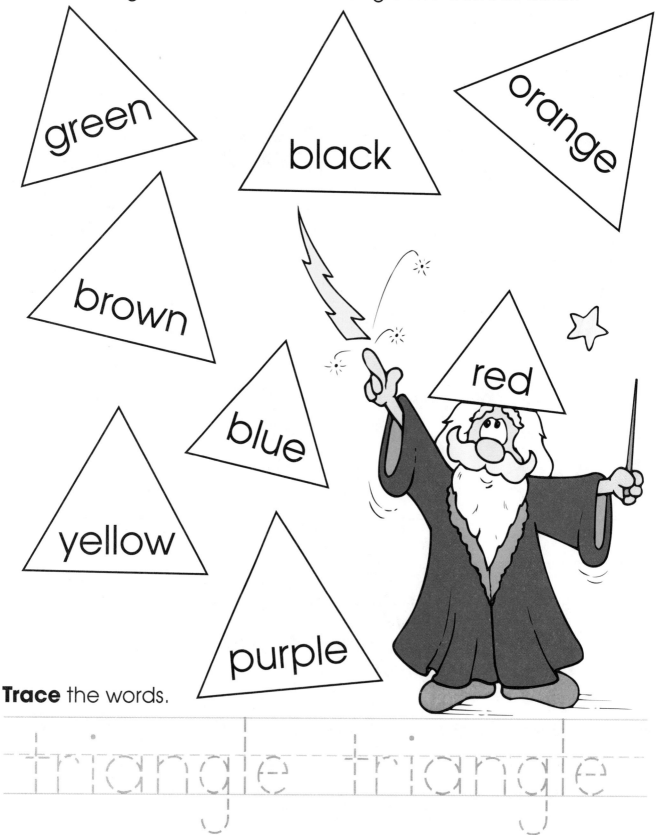

green

black

orange

brown

red

blue

yellow

purple

Trace the words.

triangle triangle

Rectangle Robot

This is a rectangle ⬚. **Color** each rectangle the correct color.

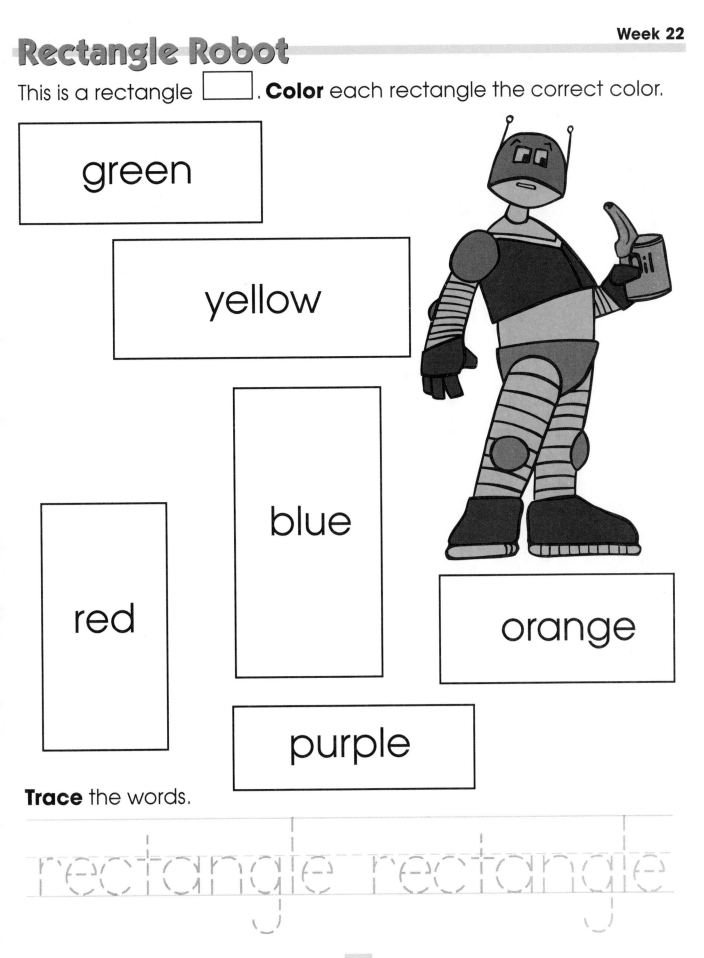

green

yellow

blue

red

orange

purple

Trace the words.

rectangle rectangle

Learn at Home, Grade K

Rectangle Roundup

Color and **cut out** each rectangle. **Glue** the rectangles in the correct places in the picture.

Outer Space Race

Help each rocket find its planet. **Draw** a line between each rocket and planet. Stay on the course so the rockets don't crash!

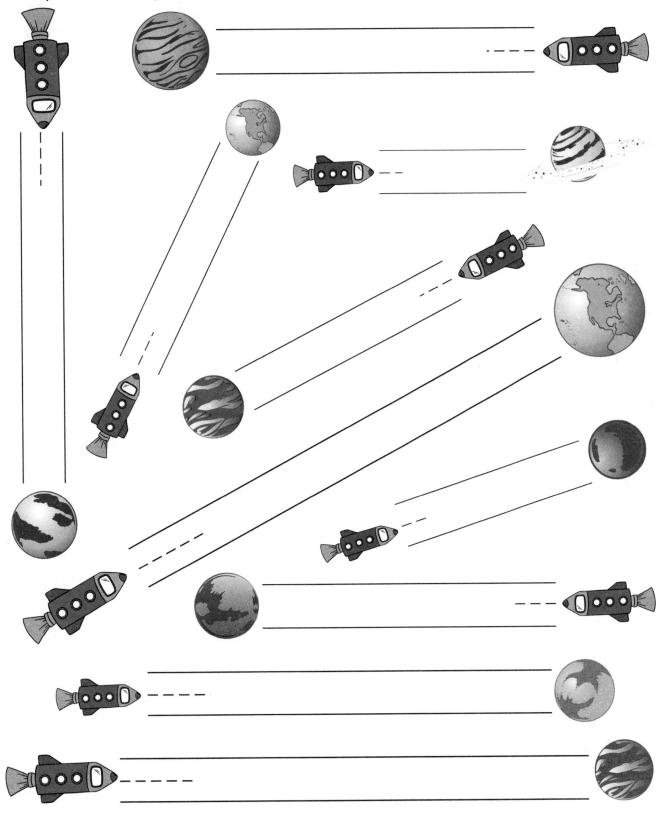

	Reading	**Language**	**Math**
Monday	**V, v** Choose a vegetable, such as a carrot or celery stick to dip into finger paint, and paint upper- and lower-case letter *v*'s on a valentine. Then, have your child do some "vegetable painting" as well. Have your child complete **Letter V, v** (p. 236).	Read *The Lifesize Animal Counting Book* edited by Djinn von Noorden. Have your child count the animals on each page. After reading through the book, randomly flip through the pages, covering up the numbers to see if your child can read the number words. Have him/her count the 100 creepy crawlers on the last page. Then, have him/her count by tens to one hundred.	**14 — Fourteen** Have your child count out fourteen straws, then use them to form the number 14. Write out the word *fourteen* and help him/her sound it out. Show him/her the two words in *fourteen*. Help your child see how the "teen words" are often just the number plus *teen*. Have your child complete **Number 14** (p. 238).
Tuesday	Have your child write upper- and lower-case *v*'s on a sheet of construction paper. Cut several carrots and celery sticks crosswise. Have your child glue these onto his/her *v* lines. *See* Reading, Week 23, numbers 1–3 for additional activities.	Have your child use white and yellow play dough to make egg shapes. As he/she shapes his/her eggs, have him/her tell you a pretend story about them. Where did the mother live? What was her name? Were there children that helped gather her eggs? What were they like?	Set out a variety of objects for your child to count. After he/she counts them, have him/her write that number on a card. *See* Math, Week 23, numbers 1–3 for additional activities. Have your child complete **How Many?** (p. 239).
Wednesday	Help your child create a *v* "word vine." Draw a tall vining plant on a large piece of butcher paper or newsprint. Have your child color it green with markers or paint. Then, have him/her draw or cut out and glue pictures of *v* objects on the vine's leaves.	Teach your child the "Hatching Chickens" finger play. *See* Language, Week 23, number 1.	Have your child write the numbers 1–14 on lined paper. Help him/her correct any mistakes in the formation of the numbers.
Thursday	Have your child complete **Very Vivid V's** (p. 237).	Read *My Hen Is Dancing* by Karen Wallace. As the book describes the hen's actions, have your child imitate them. *See* Language, Week 23, number 2.	Have your child count out fourteen pennies. Explain to him/her that each penny is worth one cent. Give him/her different amounts of pennies to count. Then, use the **+** and **=** note cards to create simple addition equations for your child to solve with pennies.
Friday	Using fabric paint, have your child write the upper-case alphabet on a plain t-shirt.	Watch the movie *The Ugly Duckling*, based on the story by Hans Christian Andersen. Ask your child to note the farm environment and the way the duckling was treated. Talk about the correct way to treat everyone.	Go to a penny candy store. Have your child count out the pennies he/she needs to buy the candies. Have your child complete **It Makes "Cents!"** (p. 240).

Learn at Home, Grade K

Science	Social Studies	Gross/Fine Motor
Baby Animals Read *Babies, Babies, Babies* by Tessa Dahl. After reading, go back through the story and have your child retell the story. *See* Science, Week 23, numbers 1–3 for additional activities.	**George Washington/Abraham Lincoln** Introduce your child to the term *president*. Explain that the president is the leader of our country, the United States of America. Discuss the responsibilities of running our country, making laws and keeping peace with other countries. Tell your child who the president is. Ask your child what he/she would do if he/she were the president.	Teach your child the finger play, "Five Yellow Ducklings." *See* Gross/Fine Motor Skills, Week 23, number 1.
Read pages 8 and 9 of *Egg* by Robert Burton. Discuss the different types of eggs. Show your child a chicken's egg. Allow him/her to handle it. Then, teach him/her how to crack it open. Let your child observe the inside of the egg. Then, cook it and have him/her taste it.	Talk about Presidents' Day. Explain that it honors George Washington and Abraham Lincoln, two American presidents born in February. Washington was the first president, nicknamed "the father of our country." Show your child his picture on a nickel. Explain that Lincoln was president during the Civil War. Show your child his picture on a penny. Read chapter 1 of *George Washington, First President of the United States* by Carol Greene.	Have your child color and cut out the presidents on **George Washington and Abraham Lincoln** (p. 241). Then, help your child make an American flag out of an 11" x 17" sheet of white construction paper. Cut out red strips for the stripes and a blue square for the corner. Use star stickers for the 50 stars. Have your child glue the presidents' heads onto his/her American flag.
Read pages 10 and 11 of *Egg*. Have your child describe each of the hens in the pictures. Discuss their nests and the hatching process.	Read chapter 2 of *George Washington, First President of the United States*. Discuss Washington's strategy for fighting. Ask your child if he/she thinks that was a good idea. Why or why not? *See* Social Studies, Week 23, numbers 1–3 for additional activities.	Have your child make a vase out of play dough. Then, help your child make "egg shell flowers." Break open two eggs to get four egg shell halves. Dye these with Easter egg dyes or food coloring. Have him/her poke a little hole in the center of each shell half. He/she may insert a green pipe cleaner for the stem and mold the stems into the vase. *See* Gross/Fine Motor Skills, Week 21, numbers 1–4 for additional activities.
Flip through *Eggs*. Give your child an overview of the different animals that hatch from eggs. Follow your child's lead. If he/she is interested in a particular animal, stop and read about it.	Read chapter 3 of *George Washington, First President of the United States*. Discuss the difficult times George Washington faced along with his army.	Teach your child the "Chicken Dance" and do the dance together.
Visit a farmer that raises hens. See if your child can gather the eggs in the morning and pet the hens. Have your child take note of what the hens eat, where they live, how they smell, etc.	Read chapters 4 and 5 of *George Washington, First President of the United States*. Discuss Washington's accomplishments.	Play balloon volleyball with your child. Lay a strip of masking tape across the middle of the floor for a boundary. Enjoy!

◀━━━━━ **TEACHING SUGGESTIONS AND ACTIVITIES** ━━━━━▶

READING (V, v)

▶ 1. Set out plastic eggs. Write an alphabet letter on a slip of paper and put it in one egg. Put an object that begins with that letter in a second egg. Do this for each of the letters your child has learned so far. Then, play a matching game. The person with the most matches, wins.

▶ 2. Have your child create a letter *v* vehicle. He/she could use an already existing vehicle, like a van, adding more *v* objects to it. If it is too difficult to find *v* objects, have your child tell a *v* story about the vehicle instead. **Example:** *This van is on its way to a vacation in Virginia.*

▶ 3. Get out vanilla sandwich cookies. Have your child use a small frosting tip to write a lowercase letter on each cookie, until he/she has completed the alphabet. Have him/her arrange the alphabet cookies in order.

LANGUAGE

▶ 1. "Hatching Chickens" (finger play)

Five eggs and five eggs	**(Hold up one hand and then the other.)**
Are underneath a hen.	
Five eggs and five eggs,	
And that makes ten.	**(Hold up all fingers.)**
The hen keeps the eggs warm for three long weeks.	**(Hold up three fingers.)**
Snap! go the shells with the tiny little beaks.	**(Snap fingers.)**
Crack, crack the shells go.	**(Clap four times.)**
The chickens, every one,	
Fluff out their feathers	
In the warm spring sun.	**(Make circle with arms.)**

▶ 2. Have your child act out *The Little Red Hen*. One of you can be the little red hen and the other can switch characters.

MATH (14 — Fourteen)

▶ 1. Stack blocks in several groups with a different number of blocks in each group. Have your child use chalk and write on the top block the number of blocks in that group.

▶ 2. Have your child count out fourteen valentine candy hearts. Have him/her use these in a *Number 14* picture.

▶ 3. Set up addition equations using candy hearts. If your child gets hungry, you may need to do subtraction as well!

SCIENCE (Baby Animals)

▶ 1. Request a mail-order chicken catalog. Enjoy looking through it with your child. To find a mail-order catalog, contact your local county extension office.

▶ 2. Show your child what chicken looks like when you buy it at the store. Talk about how it is prepared to get to this point. Make a favorite chicken dish together with your child.

▶ 3. Discuss the difference between a hen, a rooster and a baby chick.

SOCIAL STUDIES (George Washington/Abraham Lincoln)

▶ 1. Show your child American coins. Tell him/her the name of each coin and the president on the front of it.

▶ 2. With your child, make a cherry pie in honor of George Washington's birthday. While working, tell your child the story in which George Washington could not tell a lie about chopping down the cherry tree.

▶ 3. Make homemade play dough. Have your child press a coin into the dough, forming an imprint of the coin. Have him/her cut it out and make pretend money.

GROSS/FINE MOTOR SKILLS

▶ 1. "Five Yellow Ducklings" (finger play)

Five yellow ducklings,	
Dash, dash, dash!	**(Clap three times.)**
Jumped in the duck pond,	**(Make jumping motion.)**
Splash, splash, splash!	**(Clap three times.)**
Heads went down	**(Move hand down.)**
And tails went swish.	**(Move palms upward quickly.)**
They all said, "Hello!"	
To a big, black fish.	**(Make swimming motion.)**
Mother duck called them,	
"Quack, quack, quack,"	**(Clap three times.)**
And all five ducklings	
Swam right back.	**(Make swimming motion.)**

▶ 2. Help your child make a fancy valentine using a heart-shaped doily, red construction paper and dried or silk flowers. Encourage your child to give the valentine to a special family member or friend.

Letter V, v

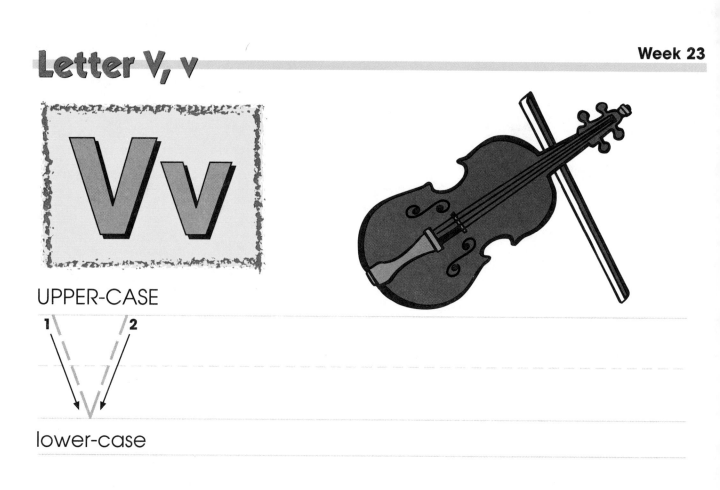

UPPER-CASE

lower-case

These pictures begin with the letter V, v. **Color** the pictures.

236

Very Vivid V's

Draw a line from V, v to each picture which begins with the sound of V, v. Then, **color** the V, v pictures.

February 14

V, v

Learn at Home, Grade K

Number 14

This is the number 14. **Color** the pictures.

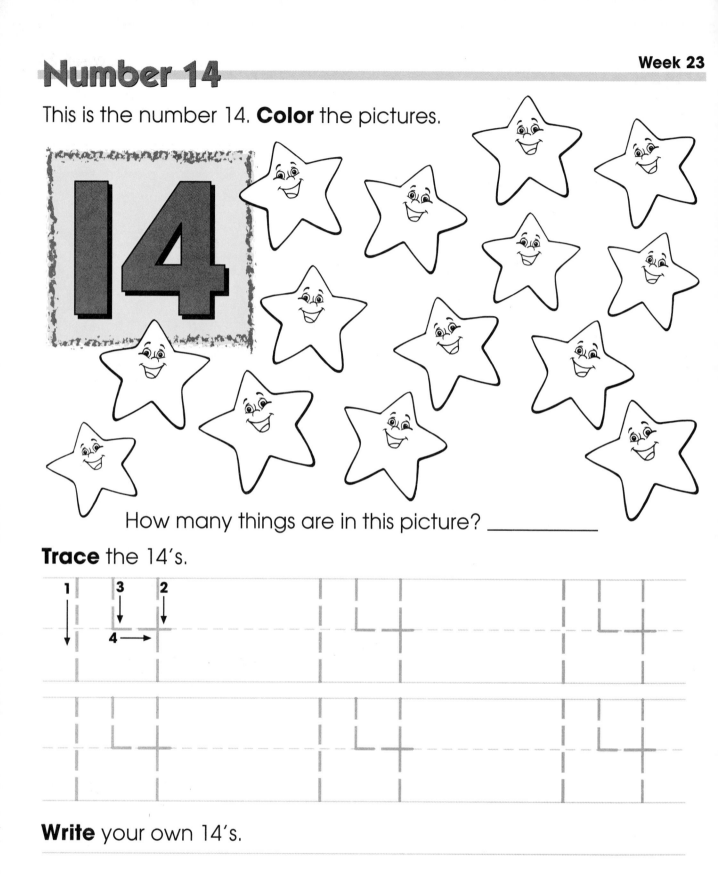

How many things are in this picture? _____

Trace the 14's.

Write your own 14's.

Learn at Home, Grade K

How Many?

Circle the correct number of things in each box.

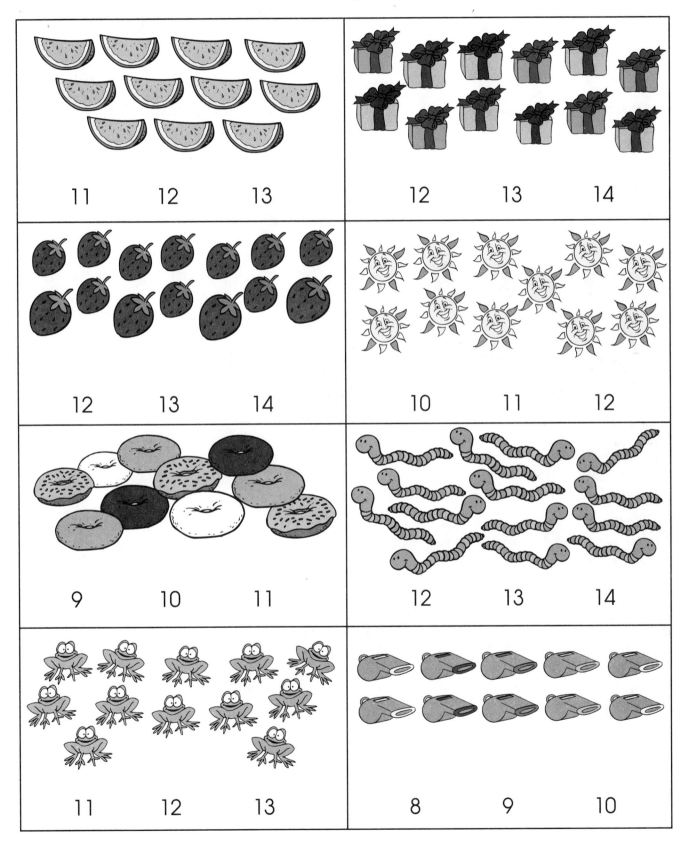

11   12   13

12   13   14

12   13   14

10   11   12

9   10   11

12   13   14

11   12   13

8   9   10

239

Learn at Home, Grade K

It Makes "Cents"

Count the pennies. How many cents?

Example:

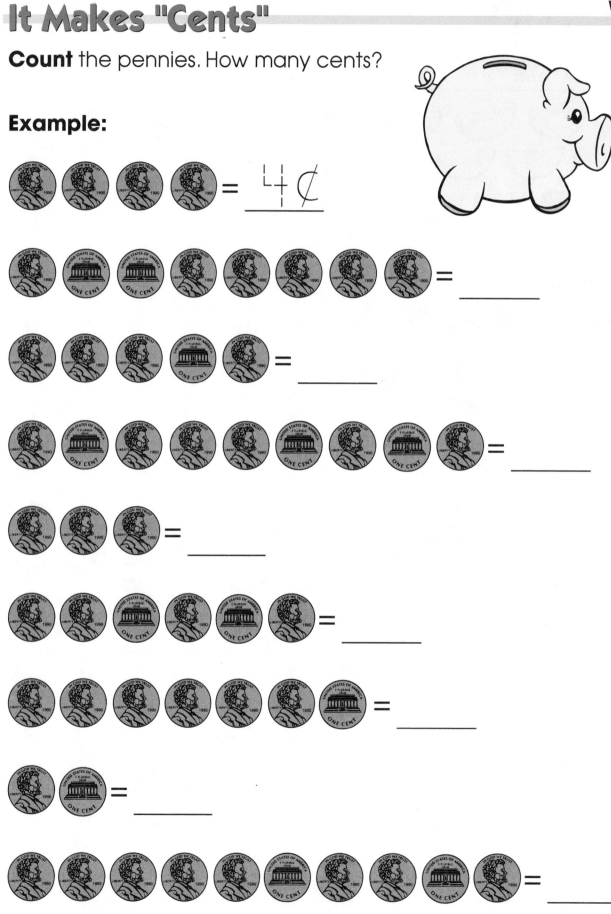

$= \underline{4 ¢}$

ABRAHAM LINCOLN

GEORGE WASHINGTON

Learn at Home, Grade K

	Reading	Language	Math
Monday	**Consonant Review** Have your child cut a sheet of construction paper in half. At the top of one sheet, have him/her write upper- and lower-case *k*'s, on the other upper- and lower-case *v*'s. Have your child glue magazine pictures of objects beginning with *k* and *v* onto the sheets. Add these pages to your child's alphabet review booklet. *See* Reading, Week 24, numbers 1–4 for additional activities.	Read *The Cat in the Hat Comes Back* by Dr. Seuss. When you come to the parts in which cats are named after letters of the alphabet, point to the letters and have your child say them. Note which letters your child does not recognize. If some of them are ones that have been covered, take time to review those letters.	**15 — Fifteen** Set out fifteen pieces of pepperoni in the shape of the number 15. Have your child do the same. Introduce the number 15, then write out the word for your child. Have your child complete **Number 15** (p. 247).
Tuesday	Read a beginner book to your child. Read it slowly. As your child hears a word and recognizes the first letter, have him/her shout it out.	Chant the following poem while marching around the house with your child. Repeat until your child has it memorized. *Read, read, read, Read, read, read, Books are great! Books are neat! Read, read, You will succeed!*	Read *Animal Numbers* by Bert Kitchen, and have your child count the objects on each page. *See* Math, Week 24, numbers 1–3 for additional activities.
Wednesday	Play a game in which you say the following short poem, then point to several objects in your house that begin with a particular letter. Your child must guess the letter. Then, switch roles. Play this game several times. *I'm thinking of a letter, A letter, a letter. I'm thinking of a letter, One that you can guess.*	Teach your child the finger play "Five Little Bunnies." *See* Language, Week 24, number 1.	Set up a penny store for your child. Set out several objects for sale, each with a price tag of between one and fifteen cents next to it. Tell your child that he/she may count out thirty pennies to buy whatever he/she wants from your store.
Thursday	Make two bingo cards and invite a second player to join the game. Instead of numbers, write lower-case letters of the alphabet in the squares. On small slips of paper, write the upper-case alphabet letters. Put these in a small plastic bag. Choose a slip of paper and hold it up. Your child must figure out which letter it is and place a penny on the matching lower-case letter on the bingo card. Also try using pictures to represent each letter.	Read *A Picture Book of Harriet Tubman* by David A. Adler. Discuss how cruelly Tubman was treated as a slave. *See* Language, Week 24, number 2.	Give your child twenty pennies and a "shopping list." List several objects and their prices, ranging from one to fifteen cents. Ask your child to count out the correct number of pennies to purchase each object. Have your child complete **Toy Time** (p. 248).
Friday	See how many of the alphabet letters you and your child can form with your bodies. Have your child complete **Consonant Review** (p. 246).	Watch the movie *The Velveteen Rabbit.* Then, read the book by Margery Williams. Have your child use the pictures to retell the story.	Make up simple addition story problems for your child. **Example:** *You have 5 pennies. I give you 3. How many do you have now?*

242

Learn at Home, Grade K

Science	**Social Studies**	**Gross/Fine Motor**
Baby Animals Read *A Time for Babies* by Ron Hirschi. After reading, have your child go back through the book, page by page, naming the baby animals. *See* Science, Week 24, number 1.	**George Washington/Abraham Lincoln** Read chapter 1 of *Abraham Lincoln, President of a Divided Country* by Carol Greene. As you read about Lincoln's move from Kentucky to Indiana, point out these places on a map. Explain that in Lincoln's day, people couldn't travel quickly by car or plane. Travel by horse and wagon took much longer. *See* Social Studies, Week 24, numbers 1–5 for additional activities.	Have your child make his/her own Lincoln cabin using **Lincoln's Log Cabin** (p. 249). *See* Gross/Fine Motor Skills, Week 24, number 1.
Help your child prepare a list of questions to ask a pet store owner about rabbits. Visit the store. Let your child spend time observing the rabbits. Then, have him/her ask the pet store owner the questions he/she prepared.	Read chapter 2 of *Abraham Lincoln, President of a Divided Country*. Find a map and trace Lincoln's move to Illinois, then to Washington, D.C. Ask if your child knows how Lincoln would have traveled. Also ask how Lincoln knew how to do so many things.	Have your child use pudding as finger paint to paint a picture of the rabbits he/she saw at the pet store. *See* Gross/Fine Motor Skills, Week 24, number 2.
Have your child set out every toy rabbit he/she owns. Have him/her compare them, then sort them by categories. They could be sorted by color, size, type of toy, etc. Then, suggest to your child that he/she re-sort them according to different criteria.	Read chapter 3 of *Abraham Lincoln, President of a Divided Country*. Point out to your child that Lincoln was often defeated in life, but he never quit. Discuss how it feels to fail or to not get something right the first time. Ask your child if this has ever happened to him/her. How did he/she feel? Explain that it is important to work at something even if it is difficult.	Help your child build a small house with sugar cubes and glue by holding the sugar cubes together for a few seconds as the glue sets. Encourage your child as you work, and explain the importance of completing a job once you've started. Make a roof with a sheet of black construction paper, creased down the middle. Put the roof on top of the four walls.
Go to the library and help your child do research on rabbits. Help him/her find information in books, magazines, videos, CD's or on the Internet.	Read chapter 4 of *Abraham Lincoln, President of a Divided Country*. Talk with your child about how Lincoln knew it was worth the price of war to free the slaves. Discuss some of the cruelties of slavery.	Play "Baby Animal Charades." Have your child think of an animal and act like the animal while you try to guess what animal it is. Then, switch roles. Play several times. If one of you cannot guess the animal, allow the other person to give a clue, such as the first letter of the animal's name.
Look through the rabbit information you have collected. Which forms of information interest your child the most? Have your child record the information he/she has learned on a rabbit outline shape. *See* Science, Week 24, numbers 2 and 3.	Read chapter 5 of *Abraham Lincoln, President of a Divided Country*. Discuss how people must have felt when they heard Lincoln had died. Ask your child how it makes him/her feel. Talk about the great things Lincoln accomplished in his lifetime.	Have your child make his/her own velveteen rabbit out of cotton balls glued onto construction paper. Ask your child to give the rabbit a name. Ask why he/she chose that name. Discuss what his/her rabbit is like and what it likes to do.

TEACHING SUGGESTIONS AND ACTIVITIES

READING (Consonant Review)

▶ 1. Give your child a basket. Have him/her place objects in it, each representing one of the review letters.

▶ 2. Set out a large shallow container of sand. Give your child various directions for the review letters of the alphabet. **Example:** Trace a lower-case letter *k* in the sand. Under the *k*, trace an upper-case *V*.

▶ 3. Write the color words and have your child read them to you. For each color word, ask your child to name one object that is that color.

▶ 4. Write out the number words *one* to *ten*. Have your child read these aloud, then write the corresponding numeral below each word.

LANGUAGE

▶ 1. "Five Little Bunnies" (finger play)

   Five little bunnies are such dears!
   The first little bunny has pink ears. **(Hold up a finger at each side of head.)**
   The second little bunny has soft toes. **(Point to feet.)**
   The third little bunny sniffs with her nose. **(Sniff twice.)**
   The fourth little bunny is very smart. **(Point to forehead.)**
   The fifth little bunny has a loving heart. **(Place hand over heart.)**

▶ 2. On videotape or audiotape, record your child telling what he/she would do if he/she were president of the United States.

MATH (15 — Fifteen)

▶ 1. Make number flash cards from 1 to 15. Show them to your child one at a time to see how fast he/she can identify the number.

▶ 2. Look through a cookbook with your child and find a recipe that calls for fifteen ingredients. Make it together, and let your child help you count, measure and mix.

▶ 3. Set out two groups of objects for your child to look at. Put more objects in one group than in the other. Ask your child to tell you, without counting, which pile contains more objects. Repeat this activity several times.

SCIENCE (Baby Animals)

▶ 1. Go to the library and check out a book about adult and baby animals. Help your child learn the names for several animals.

▶ 2. Trace an outline pattern of a rabbit on a sheet of construction paper and have your child cut it out. Have your child write rabbit facts in the shape.

▶ 3. Have your child compare rabbits and chicks and tell you the similarities and differences among them.

SOCIAL STUDIES (George Washington/Abraham Lincoln)

▶ 1. Using building logs, have your child build a model of Abraham Lincoln's home.

▶ 2. Take a trip to Washington, D.C. and show your child the Lincoln Memorial and Ford's Theatre.

▶ 3. Read *Abraham Lincoln: A Man for All the People* by Myra Cohn Livingston.

▶ 4. Read *A Picture Book of Abraham Lincoln* by David A. Adler.

▶ 5. Read *Honest Abe* by Edith Kunhardt.

GROSS/FINE MOTOR SKILLS

▶ 1. Have your child make a stovepipe hat like the one Abraham Lincoln wore. Roll a long sheet of black construction paper into a tube and tape it closed. Cut out a big black circle for the brim. Cut a hole in the center for the crown of your child's head. Tape the brim onto the bottom of the tube. Put a black circle on the top of the tube and tape it down.

▶ 2. Teach your child the following Spanish poem about rabbits:

Conejo, conejo, salta, salta,
Conejo, conejo, detente, detente.
Disculpame, hoy.
No puede jugar.
Estoy buscando las hojas de las zanahorias.

(In English:)
Rabbit, rabbit, hop, hop,
Rabbit, rabbit, stop, stop.
Excuse me today.
I cannot play.
I am off to look for a carrot top.

Consonant Review

Write the beginning sound for each picture on the lines. Then, **color** the picture.

Number 15

This is the number 15. **Color** the pictures.

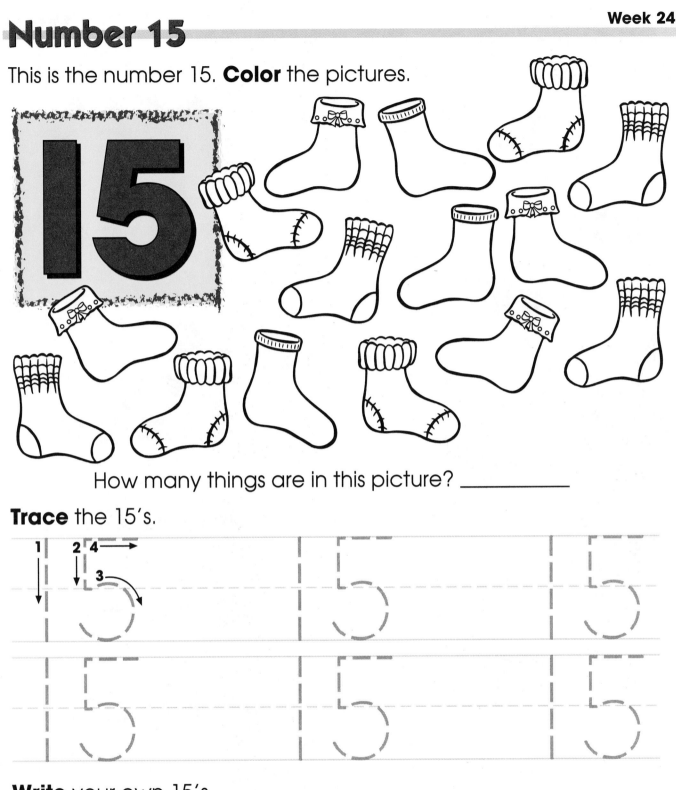

How many things are in this picture? _____

Trace the 15's.

Write your own 15's.

Learn at Home, Grade K

Toy Time

Match.

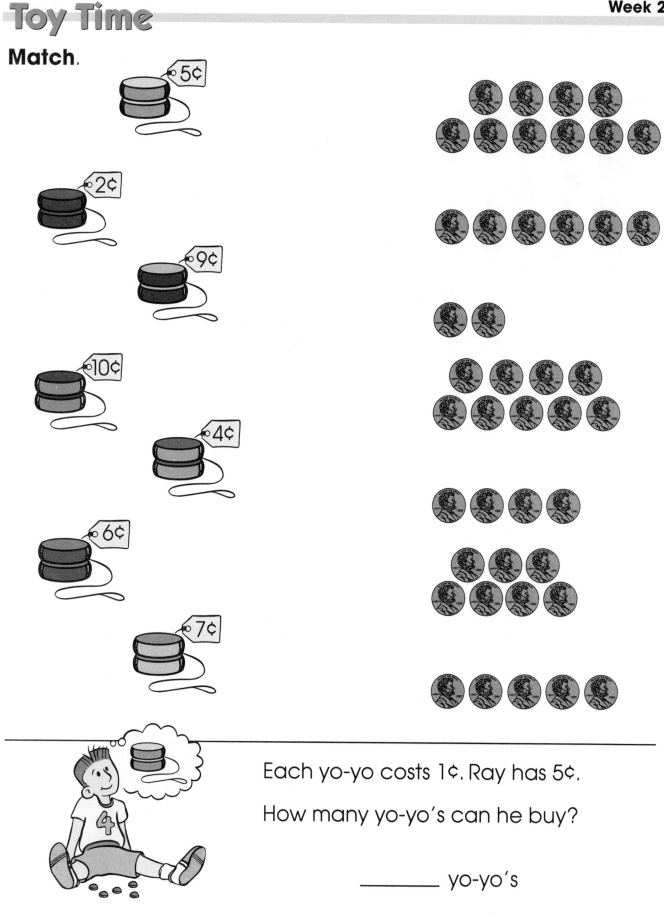

Each yo-yo costs 1¢. Ray has 5¢.

How many yo-yo's can he buy?

_____ yo-yo's

Learn at Home, Grade K

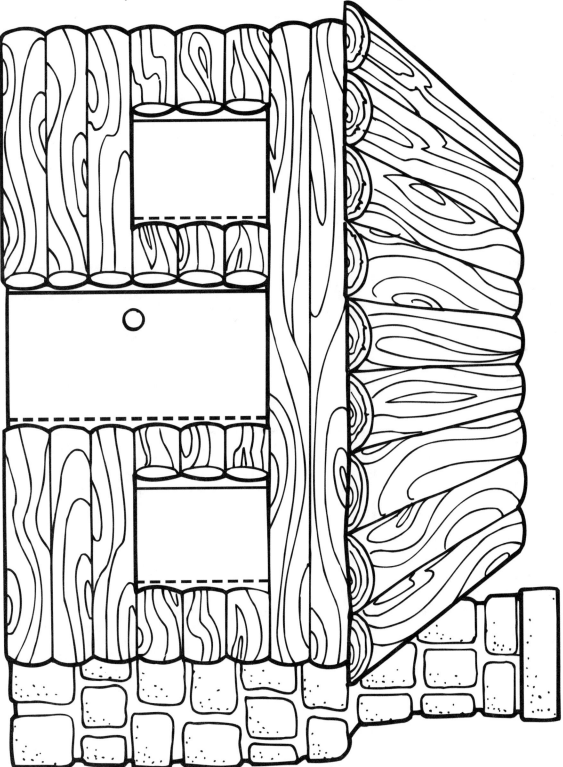

Lincoln's Log Cabin

Color the cabin. **Cut** the door and windows along the solid lines. **Fold** along the dotted line so that the door and windows can be opened. **Glue** the picture to another sheet of paper.

	Reading	**Language**	**Math**
Monday	**L, l and X, x** Form upper- and lower-case letter *l*'s with your body. Lie straight for the lower-case *l* and bend at the waist for the upper-case *L*. Allow your child to trace you with his/her fingers. Then, have him/her form the letter *l*'s with his/her body. Have your child complete **Letter L, l** (p. 254).	Teach your child the poem "Seven Kites in March." *See* Language, Week 25, number 1. This poem is great for reviewing the days of the week. As you say each day, have your child point to the appropriate day on a calendar.	**Basic Concepts** Set out two groups of blocks, one clearly containing more than the other. Point out that this pile has *fewer*. Point out that the other pile has *more*. Ask your child how he/she could tell which has more without counting the blocks. Rearrange the blocks and ask again. Repeat this activity several times. *See* Math, Week 25, number 1.
Tuesday	Draw a ladder on a large sheet of construction paper. Have your child cut out letter *l* pictures to glue along each of the rungs. *See* Reading, Week 25, numbers 1–8 for additional activities.	Teach your child the poem "This March Wind." *See* Language, Week 25, number 2. Brainstorm other words and phrases to describe the wind. Then, encourage your child to compose an additional verse for the poem, imitating the style of the poet.	Review the number words from one to ten by writing them on cards and having your child put them in order from one to ten.
Wednesday	Teach your child the sound that letter *l* makes. Describe the following *l* words and challenge your child to guess as many as he/she can in 5 minutes: *lion, ladder, lake, lamb, lamp, land, lap, large, leaf, leg, letter, lettuce, lid, lick, lemon, love, lunch, listen, laugh, lip.* Have your child complete **Light It Up!** (p. 255).	On a sheet of lined paper, write every fourth letter of the alphabet. Draw three lines before each of those letters. Have your child fill in the blanks with the missing alphabet letters.	Set out ten objects in a row. Pointing to each object, describe its order using ordinal numbers. **Example:** *This is first, second, third, fourth, fifth, sixth, seventh, eighth, ninth, tenth.* Have your child repeat each word after you. Focus on the ordinal numbers *first* through *fifth* today. Ask your child to lift up specific objects to reinforce the concept. For example, *Lift the fourth block.*
Thursday	Teach your child how to form upper- and lower-case *x*'s and teach him/her the sound it makes. Explain that the *x* sounds like the *k* and *s* sounds together. Tell your child that this sound is often heard at the end of words. Say several words. Have your child form an *x* with his/her hands when he/she hears the sound of *x* in a word. Have your child complete **Letter X, x** (p. 256).	Explain that many baby animals are born in the spring. You've already talked about rabbits and chicks—now talk about lambs. Teach your child the following poem about a little lamb. *Little lamb, fuzzy lamb,* *Prancing on the hilltop.* *You look so merry that I think* *You'll never, ever stop.*	Set out a sheet of paper on which you have drawn each of the following shapes: circle, triangle, square, rectangle and star. Give your child directions such as *Color the star blue* or *Make a smiley face in the circle.* *See* Math, Week 25, number 2.
Friday	Have your child go through the house and find as many objects with the sound of *x* as possible. Each time he/she finds one, he/she should use yarn to make an *x* on the object and say *X marks the spot!* Have your child complete **Ending Sounds** (p. 257).	Watch the movie *The Lion King* in honor of *L* Week. Have lemonade and licorice for a snack.	Return to your work with ordinal numbers today, focusing on the numbers *sixth* through *tenth*. Have your child complete **Roller Coaster Ride** (p. 258).

250

Science	**Social Studies**	**Gross/Fine Motor**
Spring/Weather Read *When Spring Comes* by Robert Maas. After reading, have your child flip through the book and use the pictures to retell the story in his/her own words. *See* Science, Week 25, numbers 1 and 2.	**Staying Safe** Talk to your child about ways to stay safe. Have him/her list as many ways as possible to keep safe. When he/she is finished, add any others you feel are important. Be sure to cover home, outside, bicycle, traffic and emergency safety procedures. Have your child complete **Be Safe!** (p. 259).	Cut out kite shapes from pieces of poster board. Tape a long piece of jute to the bottom of each one. Have your child decorate the kites by putting a different number of large stickers on each one. (You may prefer to cut out different colors of construction paper shapes to be glued on.) Have your child count the number of stickers on each kite and clip that many clothespins onto the kite's jute tail.
Take a walk in the warmer, yet crisp air. Have your child tell you how he/she can tell spring is near. Ask what spring smells like, feels like, sounds like, etc. Take your child near a rushing stream so he/she can hear it. Have him/her spread his/her hands in dirt or through the grass to feel it. Provide as many different sensory experiences of spring as you can. *See* Science, Week 25, number 3.	Read *The Berenstain Bears Learn About Strangers* by Stan and Jan Berenstain. Talk with your child about strangers. Discuss what to do and what not to do with a stranger. *See* Social Studies, Week 25, number 1. Have your child complete **Stranger Safety, Week 25, number 1.** (p. 260).	Have your child pretend that he/she is a kite in the spring wind. Have him/her gradually "take off." Then, have your child "flutter" and "flap" in the breeze, making noises as he/she goes. Have your child "dip" and "dive" in the wind gusts and "soar" and "fly" in the updrafts. Then, gradually have him/her "land" again. Work with your child to create a poem or song to go along with the movements he/she made.
Look through *Get Set…Go! Spring* by Ruth Thomson. Let your child choose an activity or craft for you to do together.	Read *Home Safety* by Nancy Loewen. As you read this book, point out the different areas in your own house that are mentioned. Reinforce the rules stated in the book. *See* Social Studies, Week 25, numbers 2 and 3.	Play "Teacher Says," using *l* words, such as *laugh, leap, lean, leg, listen, look, lick, lap, land* and *love*. Afterwards, ask your child if he/she noticed anything special about your commands. If he/she doesn't, repeat the *l* words you used. *See* Gross/Fine Motor Skills, Week 25, number 1.
Read *In Spring* by Jane Belk Moncure. Read several poems about spring to your child. Ask your child to tell which one is his/her favorite and why. *See* Science, Week 25, number 4.	Talk to your child about poisonous substances. Explain that medicines and vitamins should only be taken with an adult's help. Too much can make a person very sick. Show your child where you store household cleaners (up high or in a locked cupboard). Explain to your child that they are poisonous to drink and will make him/her very ill. Show your child ipecac syrup and explain that it is used when someone has swallowed something poisonous.	Teach your child the saying *March comes in like a lion and goes out like a lamb.* Help him/her make a lion mask from a paper plate. Show him/her how to glue strips of curled yellow construction paper to the plate to form a curly mane. Cut out the eyeholes and have your child draw a face. Punch a hole in each side of the mask and attach a piece of yarn to each side. Tie the mask around your child's head and have him/her prowl around like a lion.
Spring is a time for new growth. To celebrate growth, have your child plant grass seeds in a foam cup. Have your child draw a face on the cup with markers. As the grass grows, it will look like hair. Water the seeds gently and place the cup in a sunny window. Have your child check his/her plant every day and water it as needed.	Read *Traffic Safety* by Nancy Loewen. Discuss the general rules presented in the book. *See* Social Studies, Week 25, numbers 4.	Make a lamb mask. Cut out two "hanging" ears for your child to glue onto a paper plate. Use cotton balls for the rest of the lamb's head. Cut out eyeholes, then let your child add eyes, a nose and a mouth. Punch a hole in each side of the mask and attach a piece of yarn to each side. Tie the mask on your child's head and have him/her prance around like a little lamb. Have your child complete **Lost Little Lamb** (p. 261).

Learn at Home, Grade K

TEACHING SUGGESTIONS AND ACTIVITIES

READING (L, l and X, x)

▶ 1. Have your child draw a picture, incorporating several letter *l* objects.

▶ 2. Write the lower-case letters of the alphabet on plastic lids. Have your child put the lids in order and put an object that begins with each letter on top of the correct lid. Time your child to see how quickly he/she can do this.

▶ 3. Make a special lunch in honor of *L* Week. With your child, brainstorm some favorite letter *l* foods to make.

LANGUAGE

▶ 1. "Seven Kites in March" (poem)

> *Here's a kite for Monday,*
> *And one for Tuesday, too.*
> *Here's a kite for Wednesday,*
> *All day I think of you.*
> *Here's a kite for Thursday,*
> *And Friday—see me throw it!*
> *Here's a kite for Saturday,*
> *I like you and you know it.*
> *Here's a kite for Sunday,*
> *I like to hear you speak.*
> *I flew all seven kites today,*
> *For each day in the week.*

▶ 2. "This March Wind" (poem)

> *This March wind rattles the windows and doors.*
> *This March wind whistles and blusters and roars!*
> *This March wind seems angry and bends giant trees.*
> *This March wind will scatter whatever it sees.*
> *This March wind blows softly, a kind, gentle breeze.*
> *Then I go to sleep nicely, as ever you please.*

MATH (Basic Concepts)

▶ 1. Reinforce the concepts of *more* and *fewer* throughout the week. When taking books back to the library, ask your child who has more and who has fewer. When spooning out food on your plate and your child's, ask who has more and who has less. The more opportunities you take to use these terms, the better your child will understand them and the better he/she will become at estimating.

▶ 2. On a warmer day, take your child out for a walk. Ask him/her to find objects that are shaped like a circle, triangle, square or rectangle.

SCIENCE (Spring/Weather)

▶ 1. Read *Spring* by David Webster for a number of spring activities and projects.

▶ 2. Make or find a puddle. Let your child have fun playing in it with dump trucks, kitchen funnels or colanders. Let your child enjoy the earthy feel and smell of spring.

▶ 3. Lie on a grassy hill with your child and look up at the clouds. Encourage your child to use his/her imagination to look for animal shapes in the clouds. Talk together about what you see. Have your child tell you a story based on the movement of the clouds.

▶ 4. Have your child write a poem about spring and what it feels like or make a short book in which he/she completes the following sentences, one per page. Have your child add illustrations as a final touch.

> *I like spring because . . .*
>
> *Spring looks like . . .*
> *Spring feels like . . .*
>
> *Spring sounds like . . .*
> *Spring smells like . . .*
> *Spring tastes like . . .*
> *I love spring!*

SOCIAL STUDIES (Staying Safe)

▶ 1. Have your child act out what he/she would do if a stranger approached him/her.

▶ 2. Go through your house with your child and make sure that everything is safe. Look for loose or dangling cords, poisonous cleaners within reach and other safety hazards.

▶ 3. Help your child label the poisonous substances in your house. Draw frowning faces on brightly colored round stickers. Put these stickers on all cleaners and other harmful substances.

▶ 4. Take your child on a walk during which you cross several streets. Observe your child to see if he/she is using safety skills, such as looking both ways before crossing and crossing only at a crosswalk. Praise him/her if he/she is. If he/she needs improvement, talk about how he/she could do better.

GROSS/FINE MOTOR SKILLS

▶ 1. Make a special lunch in honor of *L* Week. With your child, brainstorm some favorite letter *l* foods to make.

Letter L, l

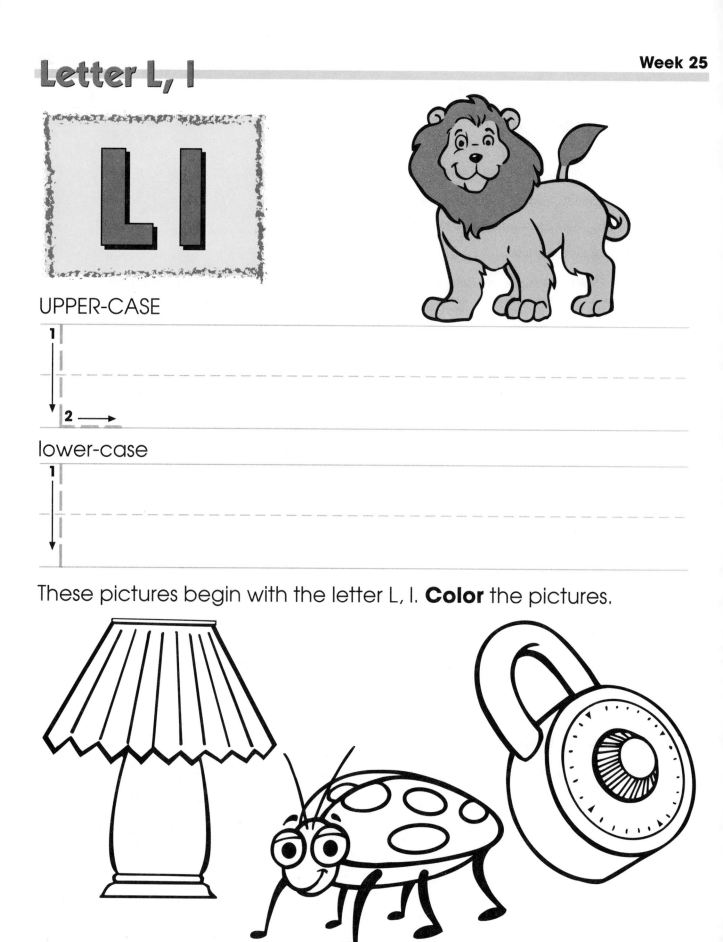

UPPER-CASE

lower-case

These pictures begin with the letter L, l. **Color** the pictures.

Light It Up!

Draw a line from the light to each picture which begins with the sound of L, l. Then, **color** the L, l pictures.

Learn at Home, Grade K

Letter X, x

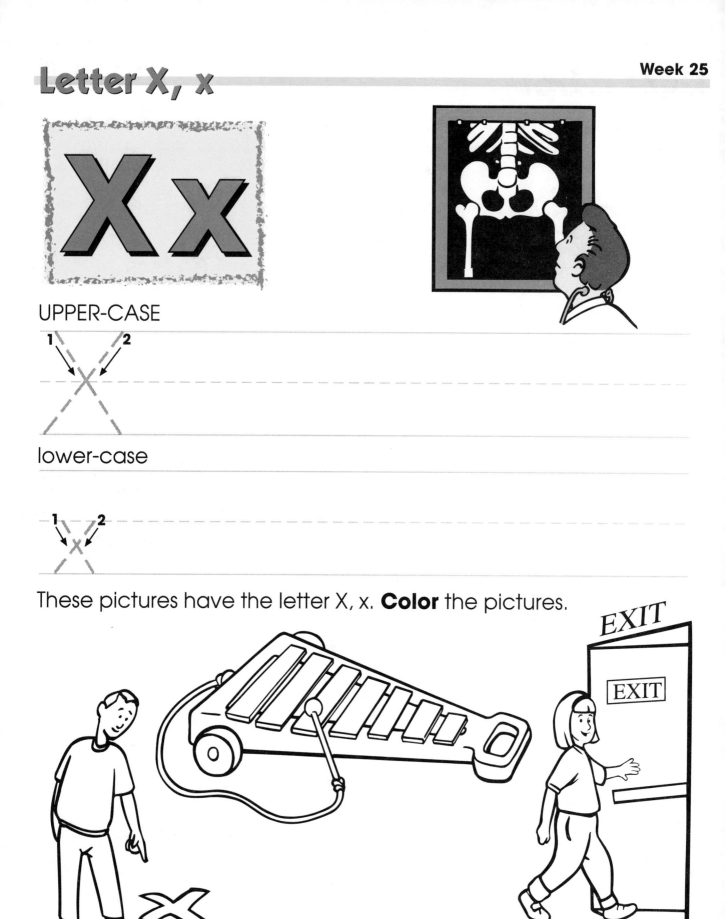

UPPER-CASE

lower-case

These pictures have the letter X, x. **Color** the pictures.

EXIT

EXIT

Ending Sounds

Circle the ending sound for each picture.

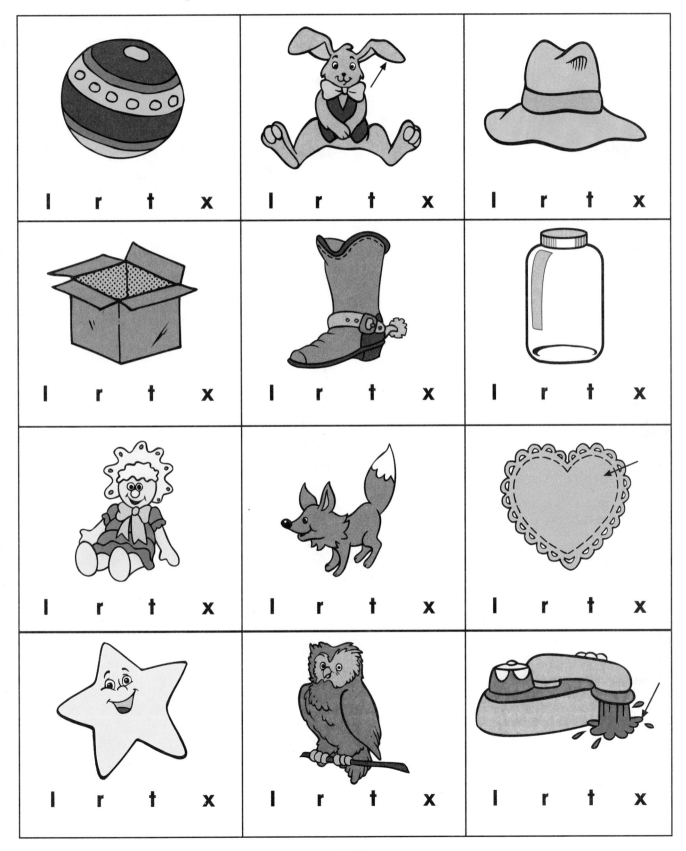

l r t x	l r t x	l r t x
l r t x	l r t x	l r t x
l r t x	l r t x	l r t x
l r t x	l r t x	l r t x

257

Roller Coaster Ride

Write the word that tells each animal's place in line.

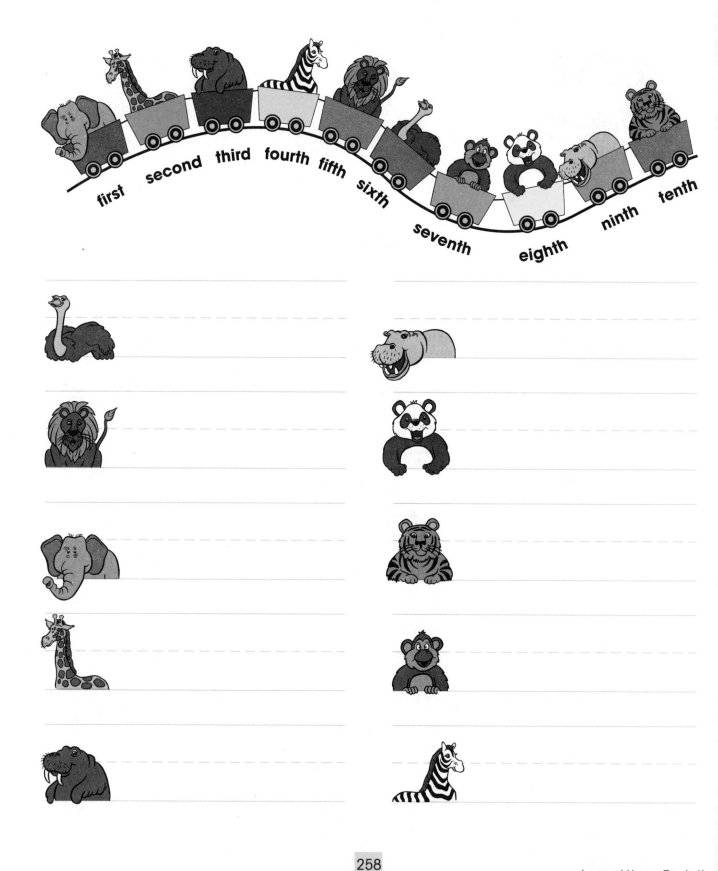

Be Safe!

Color each **X** red. **Cut out** the **X**'s. **Glue** them on the things that are **not safe**. **Color** the pictures.

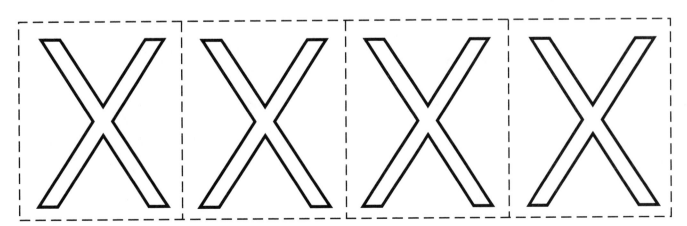

Learn at Home, Grade K

Stranger Safety

Draw an **X** on the pictures that are **not safe**. **Color** the pictures that are **safe**.

Lost Little Lamb

Draw a line to help the lamb get home to the barn.

Learn at Home, Grade K

	Reading	**Language**	**Math**
Monday	**Q, q** Get out a quart of paint. Paint upper- and lower-case q's on a sheet of paper. Explain to your child that a quart is an amount of liquid. Have your child hold the quart, then paint an upper- and lower-case letter q. Have your child complete **Letter Q, q** (p. 266).	Read *Nosing for Numbers* by M.C. Leeka. Have your child find the numbers mentioned in the book.	**16 — Sixteen** Introduce the number 16 by having your child count out sixteen pretzel sticks. Show him/her the numeral and the number word. Help your child see the word *six* in sixteen. Then, have him/her shape the sixteen pretzels into the number 16. Have your child complete **Number 16** (p. 268).
Tuesday	Have your child make the center square of a quilt. Using pinking shears, cut squares from a variety of materials. Have your child lay out the squares in a pattern. Remove the center square and have your child use fabric paint to paint upper- and lower-case q's on it. Let your child continue working on the quilt over the next few days. *See* Reading, Week 26, number 1 and 2.	**Field Trip:** Visit a fire station. Have a firefighter explain fire safety tips to your child. Fire stations often have brochures and coloring books for children. When you get home, review these with your child.	Write the numbers 1–16 on colorful construction paper circles. Shuffle them and have your child place them in numerical order. Have your child color a page from a coloring book. Glue the page onto a piece of poster board, then cut it into sixteen pieces. Then, ask your child to put it back together like a jigsaw puzzle. *See* Math, Week 26, number 1 and 2.
Wednesday	Tell your child the sound letter q makes. Have him/her repeat it with you. Then, have your child use fabric paint to paint letter q objects on half of the remaining quilt squares.	Read the poem "Puddles." *See* Language, Week 26, number 1.	Set out groups of marbles. Form groups containing the following number of marbles: two, six, eleven, sixteen and twenty-five. Ask your child which has the most, which has the fewest, which looks most like ten, which looks about like five, etc. Then, after your child has made his/her estimate, let him/her count the marbles in each group. Provide your child with many opportunities such as this for estimating numbers of objects.
Thursday	Assemble the quilt by gluing the squares together (overlapping them slightly) onto a large sheet of bulletin board paper found at a teacher or office supply store. Alternately place the painted and unpainted squares to form a quilt pattern. After the glue dries, cut a 1-inch slit in the paper behind the center of each fabric square. Fill the quilt with stuffing or cotton balls and tape the slits shut.	Read and discuss *Big Sarah's Little Boots* by Paulette Bourgeois.	Have your child count to 100 by ones, then by tens. Then, have him/her make ten sets of ten. Slide over one set of ten. Have your child figure out how many singles he/she needs to slide over to equal the number 16. Have your child complete **Bonkers Over Balls!** (p. 269).
Friday	Say various words and ask your child to listen for a beginning q sound. When he/she hears it, he/she is to whisper *Q, Q, quiet Q. Q, Q, I love you.* Have your child complete **A Q Quilt** (p. 267).	Read the poem, "The Wind and the Kite," for a review of ordinal numbers. *See* Language, Week 26, number 2. When saying *first*, have your child hold up one finger; when saying *second*, hold up two fingers; and so on.	Show your child a penny, nickel, dime and quarter and put them in order according to their value. Then, shuffle them and see if your child can remember the correct order. Have your child order them next by size and group them by color. Ask questions comparing the coins by their size, color, value and appearance.

Learn at Home, Grade K

Science	Social Studies	Gross/Fine Motor
Spring/Weather Talk with your child about different types of weather. Make a large calendar for this month on a piece of poster board. Each morning for the rest of the month, have your child check the weather, find the date and tape on the correct weather pattern for the day. Have your child use **Weather Patterns** (p. 270) with the calendar.	**Staying Safe** Discuss fire safety with your child. Practice the "stop, drop and roll" technique of putting out a fire on your clothing. Explain the importance of getting out of the house in case of a fire. Explain that the best place to be when in a smoke-filled room is on the floor, because smoke rises. Discuss the hazards of playing with matches, cigarette lighters or anything hot that could burn.	Have your child chant the following rhyme and act it out every time you say *Stop, drop and roll:* *Stop, drop and roll,* *Stop, drop and roll.* *If a fire catches you,* *You stop, drop and roll.*
Have your child complete the weather chart for today. Then read *Crow Moon, Worm Moon* by James Skofield. *See* Science, Week 26, number 1–2 for additional activities.	Help your child draw a fire escape route map. Draw several routes to show the different ways to escape, depending on the location of a fire. Establish a meeting place that is a safe distance from the house where the family should gather after getting out of the house.	Have your child jump rope to this rhyme: *Little kite, little kite,* *Little kite, little kite,* *Turn around.* *Toward heaven's prayer.* *Little kite, little kite,* *Little kite, little kite,* *Dip toward the ground.* *Soaring in flight.* *Little kite, little kite,* *Little kite, little kite,* *Soar in the air.* *What a sight!*
Talk with your child about why we need rain and write his/her responses on a chart.	Read *Outdoor Safety* by Nancy Loewen. Discuss the tips. *See* Social Studies, Week 26, number 1 and 2. Have your child complete **Safe and Sound** (p. 271).	Make a cardboard pattern of an umbrella top. Have your child trace it 26 times on a piece of poster board. After he/she traces the umbrellas, cut them out for him/her. Then, have your child tape a pipe cleaner to the back of each one, curling up the end for a handle. Use these umbrellas for Thursday and Friday's Gross/Fine Motor Skills lessons.
Discuss the importance of dressing correctly for the weather. Propose different weather scenarios and have your child draw the correct clothing to wear in each type of weather.	Read *Bicycle Safety* by Nancy Loewen. Discuss the tips with your child.	On each of the 26 umbrellas, have your child write one letter of the alphabet, both upper- and lower-case. Then, have him/her decorate each umbrella with stickers or markers. Next, cut out 26 raindrops from blue construction paper. Punch a hole in each one. Save them for tomorrow's lesson. *See* Gross/Fine Motor, Week 26, number 1.
Go outside with your child and talk about wind. How can we tell if there is wind? Can we see it? Can we smell or taste it? How can we tell which direction the wind is blowing? Have your child face the wind. Explain that the way his/her hair is blowing is the way the wind is blowing. Release a helium balloon into the air. This will confirm which way the wind is blowing. Also let your child experiment with a wind sock. Discuss your child's observations with him/her.	Read *Emergencies* by Nancy Loewen. Be sure your child can dial 911 on the phone in case of an emergency. Talk with your child about what constitutes a true emergency and what information needs to be relayed to the dispatcher when you call 911. Use an unplugged telephone to allow your child to practice dialing 911 and giving this information to the "dispatcher."	With your child, cut out pictures to represent each letter of the alphabet and glue them onto the raindrops. Or, have your child draw pictures directly on the raindrops. Then, have your child match each raindrop to the correct umbrella, sliding the raindrop onto the pipe cleaner handle. Play this game frequently with your child.

Learn at Home, Grade K

TEACHING SUGGESTIONS AND ACTIVITIES

READING (Q, q)

1. Make a queen's crown to put on your child. Have him/her write a *q* on it. Before stapling it to fit your child's head, have him/her cut out or draw pictures of letter *q* objects to glue on the crown. Let your child decorate it up by gluing on sequins, glitter or beads.

2. Have your child shape the entire alphabet out of pipe cleaners, then put the letters in order.

LANGUAGE

1. "Puddles" (poem)

> *One puddle, two puddles,*
> *Made by the rain.*
> *Three puddles, four puddles,*
> *Down in a lane.*
> *Five puddles, six puddles,*
> *We can wade through.*
> *Seven puddles, eight puddles,*
> *Quite muddy, too!*
> *Nine puddles, ten puddles,*
> *Covering tiny roots.*
> *Eleven puddles, twelve puddles,*
> *We all need our boots.*

2. "The Wind and the Kite" (poem)

> *The first wind said, "I'll sail a kite."*
> *The second wind said, "But not at night."*
> *The third wind said, "When it is light."*
> *The fourth wind said, "Just do it right."*
> *The fifth wind said, "With all your might."*
> *The first wind blew. The kite took flight,*
> *And soon the kite was out of sight.*
> *The first wind said, "I'll sail a kite,*
> *But not at night.*
> *When it is light*
> *I'll do it right,*
> *With all my might!*
> *If it takes flight,*
> *I hope it won't*
> *Go out of sight."*

MATH (16 — Sixteen)

1. Set out several jars filled with numbers of jelly beans no greater than 16. Ask your child to guess how many jelly beans are in each jar. Have him/her write down each guess on a sheet of paper and place it next to the jar. Have your child count the jelly beans in each of the jars to see how close his/her guess was.

2. Cut 34 squares from poster board. On half of the squares, draw zero through sixteen dots; on the rest of the squares, write out the numerals 0 through 16. Have your child match the dots to the correct number by putting the squares end-to-end to form a domino. For a variation, make a third set of cards with the number words *zero* through *sixteen*. Have your child match these to the numerals or to the dots.

SCIENCE (Spring/Weather)

1. Make a weather mobile using a hanger. Tie pieces of yarn to the hanger. Have your child draw or cut out pictures of the different types of weather and attach them to the pieces of yarn.

2. Help your child learn about tornadoes. Go to the library and check out books on tornadoes. Then, discuss tornado safety and conduct your own tornado drill.

3. Watch the weather forecast with your child on your favorite news station. Ask your child how he/she will dress for the following day. The next day, ask your child whether the forecast was accurate or not.

SOCIAL STUDIES (Staying Safe)

1. When you notice your child acting foolishly, ask him/her to think about why his/her behavior is dangerous. Simply lecturing or reprimanding won't usually help your child to think about his/her actions. Ask your child to consider the consequences of his/her behavior.

2. Discuss the importance of putting safety first, even before friends. Describe scenarios to your child in which a friend is doing something dangerous and tries to entice your child to do the same. Have your child role-play what he/she would say.

GROSS/FINE MOTOR SKILLS

1. "Umbrella" (action rhyme)

   *I put on my raincoat,
   I put on my hat.
   I put up my umbrella,
   Just like that!
   Umbrellas go up,
   Umbrellas go down,
   When the rain clouds are dark
   All over town.
   One raindrop and two,
   Two raindrops and three,
   My up and down umbrella
   Is up over me.
   Four raindrops and five,
   Six raindrops and seven,
   Raindrops are tumbling
   Down from the heavens.
   Drip, drip, drip, drip!
   I am dry as can be.
   My up and down umbrella
   Is up over me.*

Letter Q, q

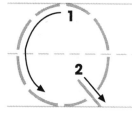

UPPER-CASE

lower-case

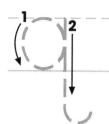

These pictures begin with the letter Q, q. **Color** the pictures.

266

A Q Quilt

Color and **cut out** each picture which begins with the sound of Q, q. **Glue** each Q, q picture on the quilt. **Trace** the letters.

Learn at Home, Grade K

Number 16

This is the number 16. **Color** the pictures.

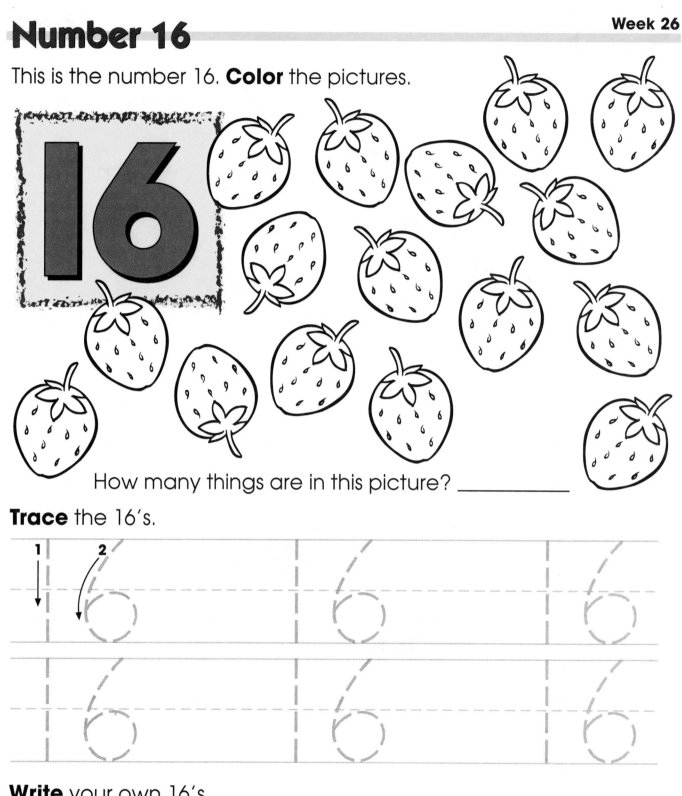

How many things are in this picture? _____

Trace the 16's.

Write your own 16's.

Bonkers Over Balls!

Estimate how many balls. **Circle** the best estimate. **Count** to check.

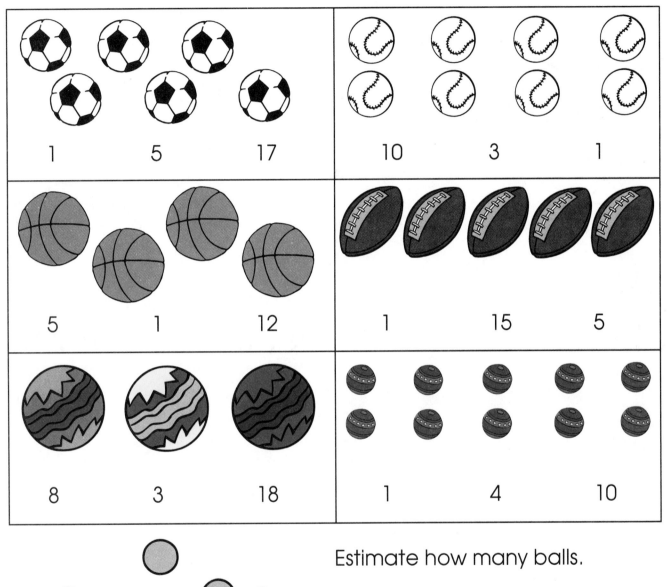

1	5	17
10	3	1
5	1	12
1	15	5
8	3	18
1	4	10

Estimate how many balls.

Write your guess. _____

Count the balls.

Write the number. _____

Did your estimate match the number?

_____

Learn at Home, Grade K

Weather Patterns

Safe and Sound

Look at the first picture in each row. **Color** the picture that shows what should happen next.

Learn at Home, Grade K

	Reading	Language	Math
Monday	**Consonant Review** Have your child work on his/her review letter booklet, adding the letters *l* and *q*. Cut a sheet of construction paper in half and have your child write the upper- and lower-case letter *l* at the top of one page and letter *q* at the top of the other. Have him/her glue on pictures that begin with each of those letters. *See* Reading, Week 27, number 1–4 for additional activities.	Teach your child the finger play "My Pets." *See* Language, Week 27, number 1.	**17 — Seventeen** String a clothesline or a piece of rope between two kitchen chairs. Give your child instructions such as *Place seventeen clothespins on the line. Take off two. How many are left?* Write 17 and *seventeen* on a sheet of paper. Have your child read the number with you. Have your child complete **Number 17** (p. 277).
Tuesday	Read *My First ABC* by Jane Bunting. Have your child name the different pictures that begin with each letter. If he/she names a word that doesn't begin with that letter, have him/her tell you the first letter of that word. Have your child complete **How Do I Begin?** (p. 276).	Have your child write a tongue twister about a reptile. Then, have him/her practice saying it.	Have your child create a tower or a house using seventeen building blocks. While he/she works, you create one also. Then, have your child compare the two. Which is taller? Which is longer? *See* Math, Week 27, number 1–3 for additional activities.
Wednesday	Play the umbrella alphabet game you and your child made last week.	Teach your child the finger play "Five Black Kittens." *See* Language, Week 27, number 2.	Organize a "number scavenger hunt" for your child. Write your child a note using a number in the directions and have the first note lead your child to the second note, and so on until he/she comes to a prize. Be sure to use the number 17 in at least one of the notes. Have your child complete **What Do I See in the Tree?** (p. 278).
Thursday	Give your child a sheet of lined paper. Have him/her number down the left side of the paper from 1 to 18. Say *number 1*, then a word that begins with a review letter. Have your child write the first letter of that word, both upper- and lower-case, next to number 1 on his/her paper. Repeat until you have gone through all the review letters.	Have your child put on the cat costume as described in today's Gross/Fine Motor lesson. Have him/her memorize the poem "Frolicky Kitten" and act it out, while you videotape or audiotape him/her. *See* Language, Week 27, number 3.	Play the following game with your child: *Seventeen,* *Seventeen's the number to find.* *Seventeen, seventeen* *[Girls' names]...now try!* After you say the rhyme, your child must try to list seventeen girls' names (or some other category). Vary the category in brackets and play this game several times.
Friday	Have your child write the lower-case alphabet in order, using chocolate pudding as finger paint. Encourage your child to sing the alphabet song over and over to remember the correct order.	Read *Petcetera: The Pet Riddle Book* by Meyer Seltzer. Work with your child to make up some of his/her own pet riddles.	Play "Bowling for Numbers." Write the numbers 11–17 on cards and place them facedown. Let your child choose one and read the number aloud. Meanwhile, set up twenty-one pins or blocks in bowling pin fashion. Your child must roll a ball and try to knock down the designated number of blocks. He/she can roll as many times as necessary but loses it he/she knocks down too many blocks.

Learn at Home, Grade K

Science	Social Studies	Gross/Fine Motor
Water Animals Play "I'm thinking of a water animal that _____." Go on to explain the sound it makes, where it lives, what it eats, etc., until your child guesses the animal. Then, switch roles and have your child think of an animal. Play this game several times. *See* Science, Week 27, number 1–3 for additional activities.	**Caring for Pets** Have your child name some common pets while you make a list. Then, talk about why people have pets. Using your list as a reference, discuss the pros and cons of each type of pet. Have your child complete **Pet Trading Cards** (p. 279). Your child may color the cards and trade them with a friend or use them in a "Memory" game.	Read "A Little Green Frog," an action rhyme. *See* Gross/Fine Motor Skills, Week 27, numbers 1 and 2.
Read *The Magic School Bus Gets Cold Feet* by Joanna Cole. Discuss these terms: *reptile, cold-blooded, sweat glands* and *hibernation.*	Read *Let's Get a Pet* by Harriet Ziefert. Discuss the considerations that must be made before choosing a pet. *See* Social Studies, Week 27, number 1–3 for additional activities.	Take turns with your child pantomiming the movement of a variety of pets while the other has to guess.
Field Trip: Go to a zoo and visit the reptile house. On the way there, have your child make a list of the reptiles from the Magic School Bus book you read yesterday. *See* today's Gross/Fine Motor Skills lesson.	Read *Kitten Care and Critters, Too!* by Judy Petersen-Fleming and Bill Fleming. Discuss if a kitten would be a good pet for your family. Why or why not?	Have your child choose three of his/her favorite reptiles. Have him/her sketch them while you are in the reptile house at the zoo.
Read *Pond Life* by Barbara Taylor. Read pages 8 and 9 and the pages on water animals (Newts: 14 and 15, Fish: 18 and 19, Frogs: 20–23).	Visit a friend who has a kitten. Allow your child to pet and play with it. Have your child ask the owner any questions he/she may have.	Using face paint, have your child draw on a kitten face. Have him/her put on a black, grey or white sweatsuit, then act like a cat. *See* today's Language lesson.
Take your child to a pond. Bring along a net for scooping. Quietly walk along the edge looking for the animals you have read about. Allow your child to dip the net in the water and see if he/she can scoop up some of them. Can he/she identify what he/she has found? Continue searching until your child loses interest. If you find something neither of you can identify, stop at the library and check out an animal identification book for reference.	Go to a discount store and look at the water pets which are available. Have your child price a fish tank, food, stones and different types of fish. Talk about the cost of fish and other water pets. Allow your child to look through the selection available. Which are his/her favorites? Why? Have your child ask a salesperson any questions he/she may have.	Cut a pond shape from blue poster board. Have your child draw pictures on construction paper of the creatures he/she saw on your trip to the pond. *See* today's Science lesson. Have him/her cut out and glue them onto the poster board.

TEACHING SUGGESTIONS AND ACTIVITIES

READING (Consonant Review)

▶ 1. Have your child write the upper-case letters of the alphabet in shaving cream in the bathtub.

▶ 2. Play "I spy a word that begins with the letter ___."

▶ 3. Read the following poem. Have your child shout out a word that begins with the letter you name. Play this game a number of times until you have called out each review letter.

> *I'm thinking of a letter.*
> *It happens to be (b).*
> *I'm thinking of a letter.*
> *Name a word, won't you please?*

▶ 4. Make play dough. Have your child shape each of the upper-case letters of the alphabet. Then, have him/her put them in order.

LANGUAGE

▶ 1. "My Pets" (finger play)

> *There are a lot of pets in my house.*
> *I have one gerbil and one white mouse.* **(Hold up 1 finger on each hand.)**
> *I have two kittens and two green frogs.* **(Hold up 2 fingers on each hand.)**
> *I have three goldfish and three big dogs.* **(Hold up 3 fingers on each hand.)**
> *Some folks say that is a lot!*
> *Tell how many pets I've got.* **(Your child should respond with the correct number: 12)**

▶ 2. "Five Black Kittens" (finger play)

> *Five black kittens stayed up late,* **(Hold up five fingers.)**
> *Sitting on top of the garden gate.*
> *The stars came out and the moon did, too.* **(Wiggle fingers. Make circle for moon.)**
> *The five little kittens began to mew.* **(Show five fingers.)**
> *Along came the mother with a lovely purr,* **(Move thumb of opposite hand toward "kittens.")**
> *And she took the kittens home with her.*

▶ 3. "Frolicky Kitten" (poem)

> *A frolicky kitten,*
> *All pouncy and gay,*
> *Dove on a red ball.*
> *Oops! It ran away.*

Learn at Home, Grade K

MATH (17 — Seventeen)

▷ 1. Write the numerals 1–17 and the number words *one* through *seventeen*, each on a separate card. Shuffle the cards, then turn them over. Play a memory game. The person with the most matches wins.

▷ 2. Have your child name a toy he/she has at least seventeen of, such as toy cars, dolls or stuffed animals. Have him/her line up the toys and put them in order from smallest to largest.

▷ 3. Draw a number line on a sheet of paper. Explain to your child how it works. Then, give him/her instructions such as *Put your pencil on the number 10 and hop up 7 spaces. What number are you on now?*

SCIENCE (Water Animals)

▷ 1. Fill your child's wading pool with water and see if you and your child can create an environment in which frogs, tadpoles, insects and other animals can live. You may want to cover the pool with a fine mesh screen to prevent the animals from escaping. Be sure to provide enough food for them to survive. Release the creatures after observing them.

▷ 2. If you live near an ocean, the book *Seashore Surprises* by Rose Wyler is a great source for seashore activities.

▷ 3. Read *Fish* by Donna Bailey.

SOCIAL STUDIES (Caring for Pets)

▷ 1. Visit horse stables towards the end of the day. See if you can arrange for your child to go on a horseback ride. Then, see if your child can watch as the stable workers care for the horses.

▷ 2. Check with your zoo to see what children's classes they offer. Many zoos offer classes on caring for pets.

▷ 3. Offer to pet-sit for a friend while he/she is away on vacation. This will give your child the opportunity to see what is involved in caring for an animal.

GROSS/FINE MOTOR SKILLS

▷ 1. "A Little Green Frog" (action rhyme)

A little green frog in a pond am I.
Hoppity, hoppity, hop!
I sit on a leaf that is high and dry.
Hoppity, hoppity, hop!

I watch all the fish as they swim by.
Hoppity, hoppity, hop!
SPLASH! How I make the water fly!
Hoppity, hoppity, SPLASH!

Ask your child to leap like a frog whenever you say, *hoppity, hoppity, hop!*

▷ 2. Play leapfrog with your child.

How Do I Begin?

Write the beginning sound for each picture. **Color** the pictures.

Number 17

This is the number 17. **Color** the pictures.

How many things are in this picture? _____

Trace the 17's.

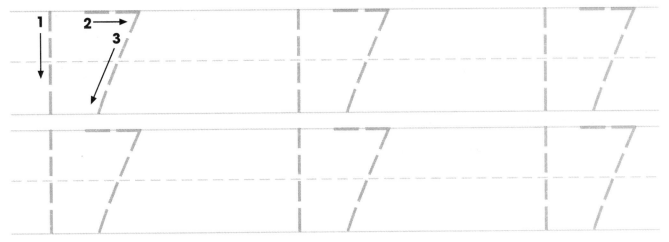

Write your own 17's.

Draw 17 birds in the tree. **Color** the picture.

Learn at Home, Grade K

Pet Trading Cards

dog

cat

fish

hamster

bird

rabbit

Learn at Home, Grade K

	Reading	**Language**	**Math**
Monday	**Y, y** Trace your footprints onto yellow paper. Make enough footprints to create upper- and lower-case letter *y*'s that are each 1 yard long. Then, lay out your footprints to form the *y*'s. Have your child walk over each of the *y*'s. Collect the footprints and have your child recreate the shapes of the upper- and lower-case *y*'s. Have your child complete **Letter Y, y** (p. 284).	Read the poem "Goldfish Pets." *See* Language, Week 28, number 1. Use the fish from today's Gross/Fine Motor lesson to act out the poem on a flannel board.	**Basic Concepts** Set out dolls or stuffed animals in a line. Review the ordinal numbers *first* through *tenth* with your child. Ask your child to point to the sixth doll, the second doll, etc., until you are confident that he/she knows all ten ordinal numbers. *See* Math, Week 28, numbers 1 and 2. Have your child complete **Riders in a Row** (p. 286).
Tuesday	Have your child glue yellow yarn onto a sheet of paper in the shape of upper- and lower-case *y*'s. Then, have him/her use other colors of yarn to make "yo-yo" designs by gluing a circle of yarn in a swirling pattern. *See* Reading, Week 28, number 1.	Read *Swimmy* by Leo Lionni. *See* today's Gross/Fine Motor lesson for an art activity to accompany the book.	Set out blocks and begin a pattern. Have your child continue the pattern and repeat it three times. Repeat this procedure with several different patterns.
Wednesday	Teach your child the *y* sound and have him/her repeat it with you. Then, say various words and ask your child to yell "*Y!*" if it starts with a *y*. *See* Reading, Week 28, number 2. Have your child complete **Y Yo-Yo's** (p. 285).	Teach your child the finger play, "Here Is a Starfish." *See* Language, Week 28, number 2.	Introduce the concepts of *before* and *after*, using a number line. Have your child complete **Hop-Along Numbers** (p. 287).
Thursday	Staple two sheets of yellow construction paper together along the sides and bottom, forming a pocket. Do the same with two sheets of white construction paper. On the yellow pocket, write upper- and lower-case *y*'s; on the white pocket, write upper- and lower-case *w*'s. Cut out a variety of *y* and *w* pictures from magazines. Then, have your child put each picture in the correct pocket.	Read *Clifford, the Big Red Dog* by Norman Bridwell. Ask your child if Clifford is real or pretend. Ask how he/she knows. Then, discuss the ways in which Clifford is different from a real dog.	Continue working on the number line with your child. Review the terms *before* and *after*. *See* Math, Week 28, number 3. Have your child complete **Look Before You Leap!** (p. 288).
Friday	Read *Sleepy ABC* by Margaret Wise Brown. Then, look back through the book at the ABC's. Have your child look at each consonant and tell you its name and the sound it makes.	Celebrate *Y* Week by watching the movie *Yankee Doodle Cricket*.	Set up the penny store again; attach a price to each object in the store. *See* the Math lesson from Week 24 on Wednesday. Have your child "purchase" several objects in the store using real pennies.

Learn at Home, Grade K

Science	Social Studies	Gross/Fine Motor
Water Animals Read pages 34 and 35 of *Seashore* by Steve Parker. Have your child choose a favorite fish. Why is it his/her favorite? *See Science, Week 28, numbers 1 and 2.*	**Caring for Pets** Read the *Berenstain Bears* and the *Trouble With Pets* by Stan and Jan Berenstain. Discuss some of the difficulties of owning pets. *See Social Studies, Week 28, numbers 1–4.*	Make a goldfish pattern on a piece of poster board. Have your child trace the pattern onto orange construction paper five times, then cut out the fish. Glue a small square of felt onto each fish. As you and your child read the poem "Goldfish Pets," have your child place each fish on a flannel board as the poem counts higher.
Read pages 36 and 37 of *Seashore*. If you have any real sponges, show them to your child. If not, go to the store and show him/her what a real sponge looks like. *See Science, Week 28, number 3.*	Read *Puppy Care and Critters, Too!* by Judy Petersen-Fleming and Bill Fleming. After reading the book, have your child tell you how he/she would take care of a puppy.	Cut fish shapes out of man-made sponges. Have your child make an ocean scene by dipping his/her fish sponges into finger paint and pressing the sponges onto paper. Encourage your child to complete his/her scene by painting blue swirls and sea plants, just like the illustrator of *Swimmy*.
Read pages 38–41 of *Seashore*. Have your child order the starfish from smallest to largest. Help your child make a windsock using pictures of sea animals. Staple a 2" x 18" tagboard strip to form a circle. Then, help your child to glue blue and green crepe paper strips in varying lengths to the inside of the circle to represent the ocean's waves. Have your child color copies of the **Sea Animal Patterns** on pages 289–291. He/she will complete the windsock tomorrow.	Read *Arthur's New Puppy* by Marc Brown. Discuss some of the difficulties that Arthur faced. Ask your child what Arthur could or should have done to prevent each problem.	Read and perform "Wiggling Puppies," an action poem. See Gross/Fine Motor, Week 28, number 1. Have your child act out the words of the poem.
Read pages 44 and 45 of *Seashore*. Take your child to a store that has hermit crabs and let him/her observe them. Have your child continue work on his/her sea animal windsock by stapling or gluing the animals to the strips of crepe paper at different heights. Finally, punch two holes opposite each other on the tagboard circle and tie a length of yarn from one hole to the other. The yarn can then be tied together to hang up the windsock.	Visit a friend who has a puppy. Allow your child to play with the puppy and ask the owner questions. Ask the owner's permission to let you and your child take the dog for a walk.	Have your child make a starfish by drawing a star shape on a sheet of blue paper. Have him/her trace the outline and fill in the center with glue. Then, help your child pour sand onto the glue, shaking off the excess. *See Gross/Fine Motor Skills, Week 28, number 2.*
Read pages 48 and 49 of *Seashore*. Discuss animal relationships in which each animal benefits from the other. *See Science, Week 28, number 4.*	Read *Goodbye, Mitch* by Ruth Wallace-Brodeur. Discuss what it is like when a pet dies. If your child has ever lost a pet, encourage allow him/her to tell you how he/she felt. If he/she has never had a pet that died, discuss how painful it is, but stress that having the chance to love a pet makes the hurt worthwhile.	Have your child bang on a drum or clash cymbals made from pan lids while marching around the house singing "Yankee Doodle." See Gary Chalk's *Yankee Doodle* for lyrics and music. *See Gross/Fine Motor Skills, Week 28, number 3.*

TEACHING SUGGESTIONS AND ACTIVITIES

READING (Y, y)

▶ 1. Hide a variety of objects in your yard. Ask your child to collect only those objects that begin with the letter *y*.

▶ 2. Have your child draw a picture of *y*'s and *y* objects.

LANGUAGE

▶ 1. "Goldfish Pets" (poem)

One little goldfish
Lives in a bowl.
Two little goldfish
Eat their food whole.
Three little goldfish
Swim all around.

Although they move,
They don't make a sound.
Four little goldfish
Have swishy tails.
Five little goldfish
Have pretty scales.

▶ 2. "Here Is a Starfish" (finger play)

Here is an octopus	**(Place two palms together, interlace fingers, wiggle fingers.)**
Here is a shell.	**(Show palm, hand slightly cupped.)**
Here is a fish,	**(Cup two palms together.)**
Who swims very well.	**(Make swimming motions.)**
Here is the ocean.	**(Make waving motions.)**
Here is a starfish.	**(Place one hand on table, fingers spread apart.)**
Here is a chance	
To make your heart's wish.	**(Place one hand over heart.)**

MATH (Basic Concepts)

▶ 1. When standing in line at the grocery store, ask your child to point out the first person in line, the second, the third, etc.

▶ 2. Show your child pictures of his/her siblings and talk about the age of each child. Then, using ordinal numbers, have your child tell you who was born first, second, third, etc.

▶ 3. Make a large number line by laying a long line of masking tape across your floor. Write the numbers on cards and tape them to the floor along the line. Give your child various directions in which he/she must move up three jumps or back four jumps, etc.

SCIENCE (Water Animals)

▶ 1. Have your child cut sponges into the shapes of various water animals. He/she can then play with these floatables while taking a bath.

▶ 2. Watch the movie *Freddie the Frog*.

▶ 3. Work together with your child to name a water animal that starts with each letter of the alphabet.

▶ 4. Read *Discover My World: Ocean* by Ron Hirschi. See if your child can answer the water animal riddles correctly.

SOCIAL STUDIES (Caring for Pets)

▶ 1. Watch the movie *101 Dalmatians*.

▶ 2. Read *Only One Woof* by James Herriot.

▶ 3. Read *Pet Bugs: A Kid's Guide to Catching & Keeping Touchable Insects* by Sally Kneidel.

▶ 4. Read *Gipper the Guinea Pig* by Jane Burton.

GROSS/FINE MOTOR SKILLS

▶ 1. "Wiggling Puppies" (action poem)

> *One little puppy, one,*
> *Wiggled his tail and had wiggling fun.*
> *Two little puppies, two,*
> *Wiggled their bodies as puppies do.*
> *Three little puppies, three,*
> *Wiggled their noses happily.*
> *Four little puppies, four,*
> *Wiggled their shoulders and wiggled some more.*
> *Five little puppies, fat and round,*
> *Wiggled their ears when they heard a sound.*

▶ 2. Make water animals by bending wire into animal shapes. Pour glue on the wire outline and attach a piece of tissue paper to the wire figure. When the glue dries, cut away the excess tissue paper outside the wire figure.

▶ 3. Listen to the soundtrack from the movie, *The Little Mermaid*. Dance to the music.

Letter Y, y

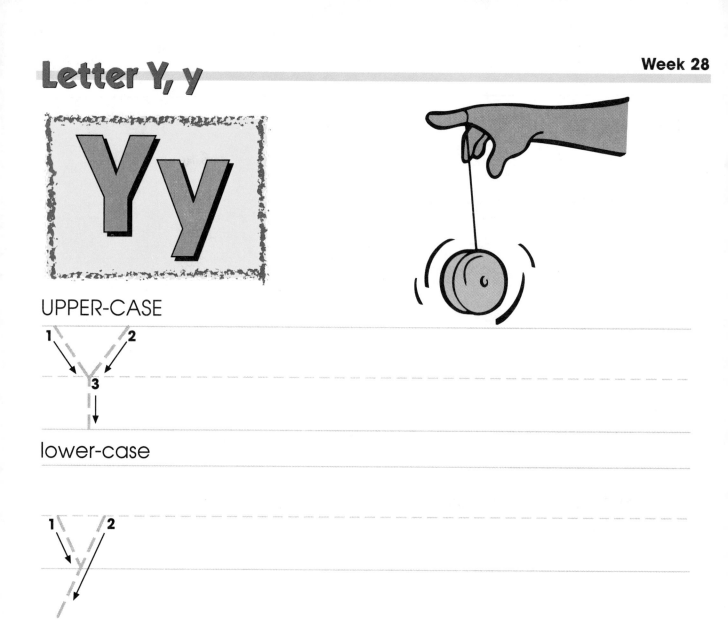

UPPER-CASE

lower-case

These pictures begin with the letter Y, y. **Color** the pictures.

Yogurt

Y Yo-Yo's

Draw a line from the girl to each picture which begins with the sound of Y, y. **Color** the Y, y pictures.

Yogurt

Learn at Home, Grade K

Riders in a Row

1. **Draw** a box around the **second** person in line.

2. **Draw** a line above the **fourth** person in line.

3. **Draw** an **X** on the **first** person in line.

4. **Draw** a line under the **fifth** person in line.

5. **Circle** the **third** person in line.

Hop Along Numbers

This is a number line.

Number lines show numbers in order. The frog is sitting on 4. If it jumps ahead 1 space, it will land on 5. If it jumps back 1 space, it will land on 3.

Use the number line. **Write** the number that comes **after**.

2, _____   7, _____

0, _____   9, _____

Write the number that comes **before**.

_____ ,5   _____ ,9

_____ ,2   _____ ,7

Write the number that is **between**.

7, _____ ,9   5, _____ ,7

0, _____ ,2   8, _____ ,10

Look Before You Leap!

Write the missing numbers on the number line.

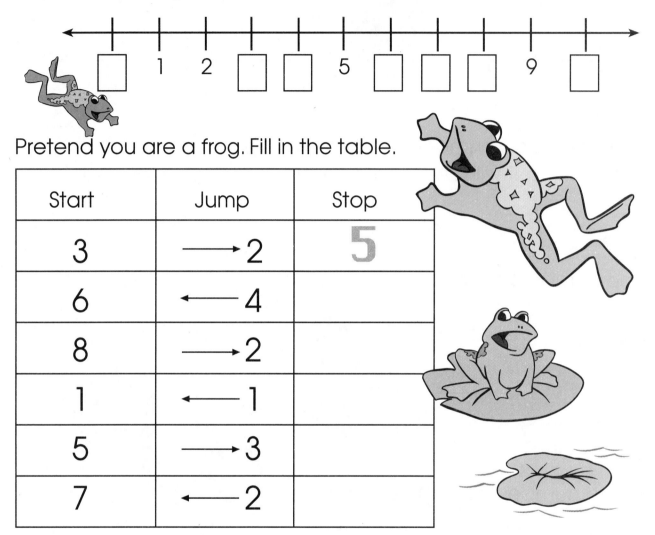

| ☐ | 1 | 2 | ☐ | ☐ | 5 | ☐ | ☐ | ☐ | 9 | ☐ |

Pretend you are a frog. Fill in the table.

Start	Jump	Stop
3	⟶ 2	5
6	⟵ 4	
8	⟶ 2	
1	⟵ 1	
5	⟶ 3	
7	⟵ 2	

Write a number on each lily pad. **Match** each frog to its place on the number line.

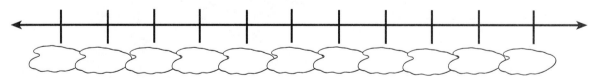

Learn at Home, Grade K

Sea Animal Patterns

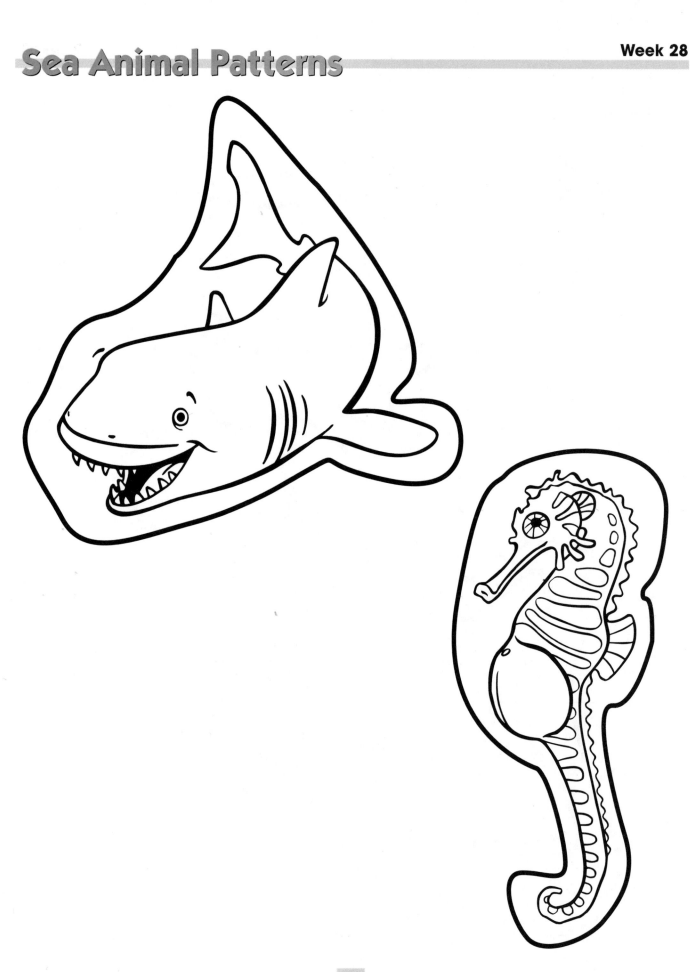

Learn at Home, Grade K

Sea Animal Patterns

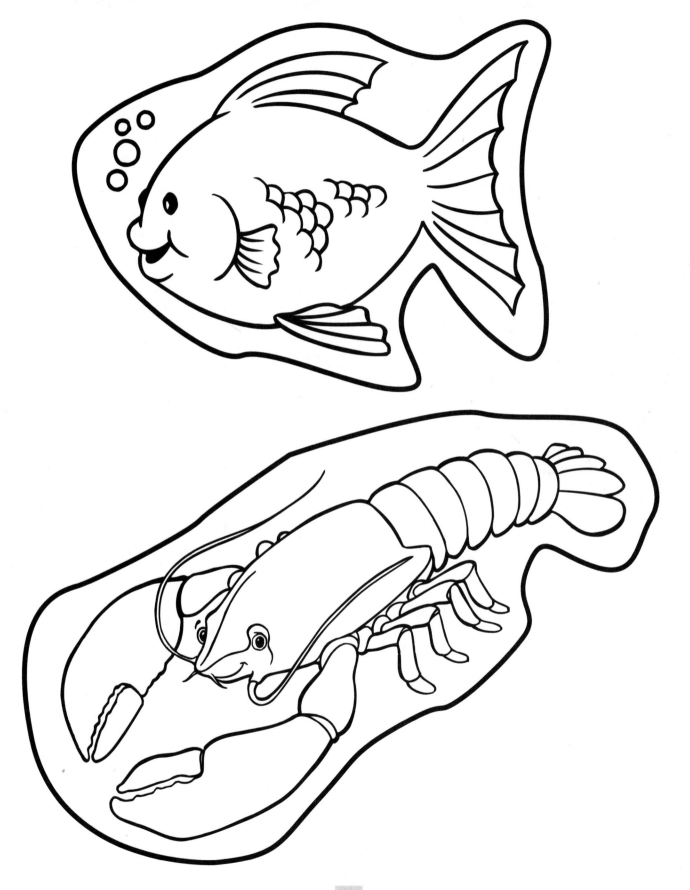

Learn at Home, Grade K

	Reading	**Language**	**Math**
Monday	**Z, z** Arrange your child's toy zoo animals to form the letter z. Then, rearrange the animals and have your child form the letter z, both upper- and lower-case. Have your child complete **Letter Z, z** (p. 296).	Read *Ira Sleeps Over* by Bernard Waber. Discuss the importance of being yourself.	**18 — Eighteen** Go outside and use sidewalk chalk to draw a large number line. Have your child write the numbers 1–20 along the top. Then, give your child directions such as *Hop up eighteen steps, then hop back two jumps. What number are you on?* Later, write out the word *eighteen* in chalk and help your child sound it out.
Tuesday	Cut a sponge into the shape of the numeral 0. Have your child dip the sponge in finger paint and make upper- and lower-case letter z's with the sponges. *See* Reading, Week 29, number 1.	Read the poem "I Am a Sunflower." *See* Language, Week 29, number 1.	Have your child write the number 18 on a sheet of construction paper. Have him/her line the numbers with glue. His/her goal is to find 18 of a food or object that he/she can lay in the glue to form the number. *See* Math, Week 29, number 1. Have your child complete **Number 18** (p. 298).
Wednesday	Make the letter z sound for your child. Have him/her repeat it with you. Then, say a variety of words, some of which begin with the letter z. When your child hears the letter z at the beginning of a word, have him/her call out *Zap! See* Reading, Week 29, number 2. Have your child complete **Zep Zebra's Zoo** (p. 297).	Show your child pictures of you and your friends as children. Talk about situations in which you did what your friends wanted to do, even though you would rather have done something else. Then, talk about times they did special things for you. Discuss the sharing and compromising that good friendships require. *See* Language, Week 29, number 2.	Set out groups of marbles, each containing various quantities from 1 to 18. Have your child count each group out loud for you. Next, have him/her count to 100 by ones, then by tens. *See* Math, Week 29, number 2. Have your child complete **Domino Dots** (p. 299).
Thursday	Read *The A to Z Beastly Jamboree* by Robert Bender. Randomly open the book to a page, cover up the words at the bottom and have your child tell you what letter that page represents. Going through the book in random order will make it more challenging for your child. Then, on a sheet of lined paper, have your child write the upper-case letters of the alphabet.	Teach your child this zoo rhyme: *Here we go off to the zoo,* *Off to the zoo, the zoo,* *On this beautiful day!* *Look at the elephant's nose.* *She has a long nose, and it works like* * a hose.* *On this beautiful day!* *Look at the big baboon.* *He makes faces at you from inside the* *zoo On this beautiful day!*	Ask your child to create his/her own dot-to-dot picture, using exactly eighteen dots. Have him/her number the dots in the order they should be connected, then give the picture to you to complete. After you have connected the dots, return the page to your child. Ask him/her if you connected the dots correctly. Then, have your child color the picture and write the number 18 eighteen times around the border.
Friday	Chant the following rhyme with your child to practice the sound of the letter z: *Z, z, letter z,* *Zipper, zebra,* *Zero, zoo.* *I like z's, I like z's* *How about you?* *See* Reading, Week 29, numbers 3 and 4.	Help your child write a poem about his/her favorite zoo animal.	Play a board game with your child that involves two dice. *See* Math, Week 29, numbers 3 and 4.

Science	Social Studies	Gross/Fine Motor
Growing Time Have your child name as many kinds of plants he/she can, including fruits and vegetables. Ask your child what a plant needs to grow. Tell your child that he/she will learn how to grow carrots and string beans over the next 2 weeks. *See* Science, Week 29, number 1.	**Caring for Friends** Introduce the theme of friendship with a discussion about your child's friends. Ask who his/her best friend is and why. What does he/she like to play or do with that friend? Does the friend ever make him/her angry? When? Then, discuss your own best friend as a child. Let your child ask you questions about that friendship. *See* Social Studies, Week 29, numbers 1 and 2.	Help your child make a friendship bracelet for one of his/her good friends. Buy inexpensive beads for your child to string together. Be sure to include the letters in the friend's name. Or you may wish to teach your child how to make a braided bracelet. Use embroidery string or yarn. Tie the strands in a knot at each end of the bracelet and cut, leaving enough string for your child's friend to tie around his/her wrist.
Read *The Magic School Bus Plants Seeds* by Joanna Cole. Discuss these terms: *nectar, pollen, stigma* and *anther*.	Read chapter 1 of *Emily and Alice* by Joyce Champion. Discuss what Emily and Alice did and said that helped them like each other and become friends. *See* Social Studies, Week 29, number 3.	Make poster board patterns for several sizes of flowers. Have your child trace them onto different colors of construction paper and cut them out. Have him/her glue cotton balls in the center of each flower and arrange the flowers on a background of green construction paper. Read and have your child act out the rhyme "Things That Grow." *See* Gross/Fine Motor Skills, Week 29, number 1.
Read *The Berenstain Bears Grow It: Mother Nature Has Such a Green Thumb* by Stan and Jan Berenstain. *See* Science, Week 29, number 2. Have your child color the **Plant Sequencing Cards** (p. 300). Cut them apart, mix them up and have your child lay the cards down in the correct order.	Read chapter 2 of *Emily and Alice*. Ask your child what Emily did for Alice. Did she really want to? If not, why did she do it?	Allow your child to invite several friends over to play their favorite game(s). *See* Gross/Fine Motor Skills, Week 29, number 2.
Complete the carrot experiment found in the back of *The Berenstain Bears Grow It*. Have your child monitor the plant's growth each day and record his/her observations on a simple chart. *See* Science, Week 29, number 3.	Read chapter 3 of *Emily and Alice*. Discuss why togetherness is important to friendship.	Make shredded wheat compound and have your child shape carrots out of it. *See* Social Studies, Week 6, number 1.
Read *The Tiny Seed* by Eric Carle. Have your child complete **Flower Fun** (p. 301).	Read *The Berenstain Bears and Too Much Teasing* by Stan and Jan Berenstain. Ask your child who was being a good friend in the story and who was not. Discuss the proper way to treat others. *See* Social Studies, Week 29, number 4.	Visit the zoo with your child and one of his/her friends to celebrate friendship during *Z* Week.

Learn at Home, Grade K

▬▬▬▬▬▬ **TEACHING SUGGESTIONS AND ACTIVITIES** ▬▬▬▬▬

READING (Z, z)

▶ 1. Have your child sponge paint zeros on a sheet of bulletin board paper. After the zeros dry, have him/her draw a letter z object inside each zero.

▶ 2. Have your child make a magic wand using a dowel rod with a foam ball pushed on the end. Have your child decorate the ball with glitter, beads, paint, etc. Have him/her "zap" letter z objects by making a letter z motion with the wand and tapping the object while saying *Zap!*

▶ 3. Buy a zipper at a fabric store and glue it across the top of a manila folder. Have your child write upper- and lower-case z's on the front of the folder. Ask him/her to cut out letter z pictures from magazines and zip them into the pouch.

▶ 4. Draw these z words for your child to guess: *zipper, zebra, zero, zoo, zig-zag.*

LANGUAGE

▶ 1. "I Am a Sunflower" (poem)

> I am a sunflower,
> Growing by the hour.   **(Stand up slowly.)**
> Now I am grown,
> And my petals full-blown.   **(Stand tall with arms outstretched.)**
> I turn to the right,   **(Turn head to right.)**
> And I face the light.   **(Make a circle for sun.)**
> The sun sets in the west,   **(Turn head to left.)**
> And I have my rest.   **(Clasp hands beside face.)**
> I awake with the sun,   **(Make circle for sun.)**
> A new day has begun.

▶ 2. Have your child create a song about the growing process using a familiar tune.

MATH (18 — Eighteen)

▶ 1. Play a game of number flash cards with your child, using both numerals and number words.

▶ 2. Have your child write the numerals 1–18 as many different ways as he/she can. **Examples:** marker, finger paint, sidewalk chalk, shaving cream, etc.

▶ 3. Watch the movie *Clifford's Fun With Numbers.*

▶ 4. Check your local public library for games on numbers and counting which can be checked out.

SCIENCE (Growing Time)

▶ 1. Choose experiments from *Science Fun With Peanuts and Popcorn* by Rose Wyler. There are many simple experiments for you and your child to do together.

▶ 2. Visit a local nursery. Show your child the large variety of plants, and choose a new one to bring home.

▶ 3. Visit a friend or acquaintance who gardens. Allow your child to talk to him/her and ask questions.

SOCIAL STUDIES (Caring for Friends)

▶ 1. Have your child discuss a time he/she was treated unkindly by another child. Talk about how
▶   he/she felt. Talk about the importance of treating friends with kindness and respect.

▶ 2. Read *Isabelle's New Friend* by Laurent de Brunhoff.

▶ 3. Help your child set up a tea party with stuffed animal "friends." Have your child practice good manners and show kindness to his/her guests.

▶ 4. Read *Franklin Plays the Game* by Paulette Bourgeois.

GROSS/FINE MOTOR SKILLS

▶ 1. "Things That Grow" (action rhyme)

> *Here is my little garden bed.*
> *Here is one tomato, ripe and red.*
> *Here are two great, long string beans.*
> *Here are three bunches of spinach greens.*
> *Here are four cucumbers on a vine.*
> *This little garden is all mine!*

Have your child imitate the subject in each line.

▶ 2. Have your child jump rope to the following poem:

> *Esmerelda dressed in yella'*
> *Went upstairs to see Drucella.*
> *Made a mistake and greeted a snake.*
> *How many doctors did it take?*
>
> *1, 2, 3, 4, 5, 6, 7, 8 . . .*

Have your child keep counting until he/she misses a jump or a number.

Learn at Home, Grade K

Letter Z, z

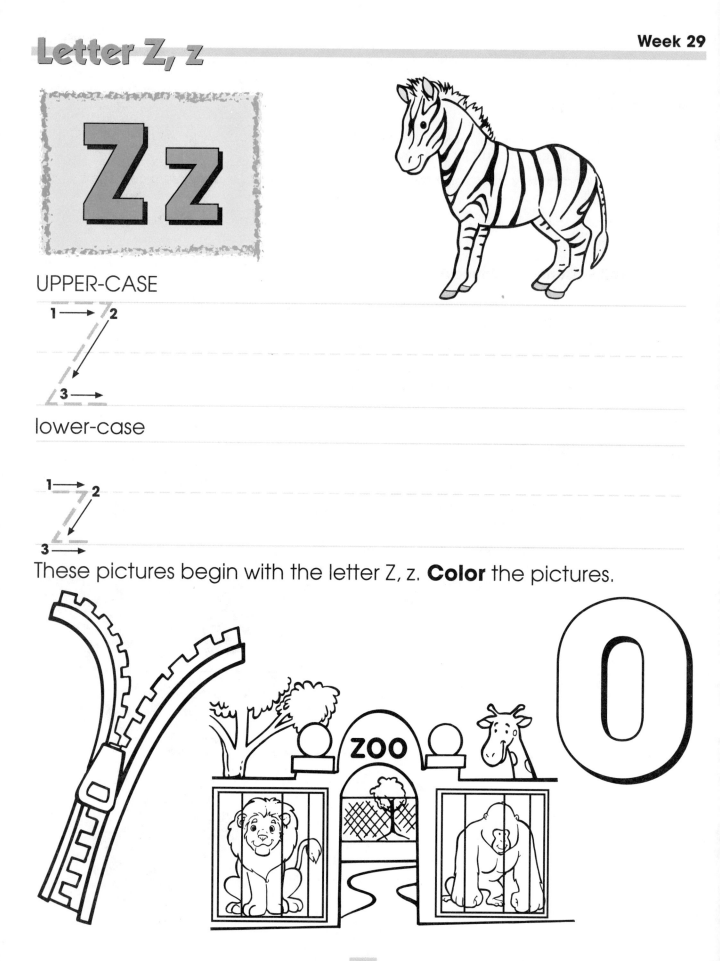

Z z

UPPER-CASE

1 → 2
3 →

lower-case

1 → 2
3 →

These pictures begin with the letter Z, z. **Color** the pictures.

ZOO

296

Zep Zebra's Zoo

Zep Zebra likes living in the zoo. **Color** each picture that begins with the sound of Z, z.

Learn at Home, Grade K

Number 18

This is the number 18. **Color** the pictures.

How many things are in this picture? _____

Trace the 18's.

Write your own 18's.

Domino Dots

Write the correct number on each domino.

Learn at Home, Grade K

Flower Fun

Flowers have petals, stems and leaves. **Draw** all the missing stems.
Draw leaves on the stems. **Color** the flowers.

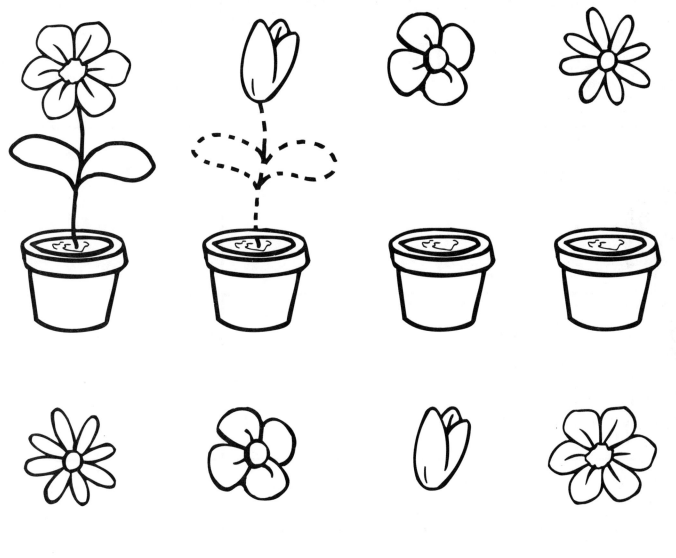

Learn at Home, Grade K

	Reading	**Language**	**Math**
Monday	**Consonant Review** Have your child add the letter *z* to his/her alphabet review booklet. Explain that letters are either consonants or vowels. Tell your child that all the letters he/she has learned so far are consonants. There are only six vowels: *a, e, i, o, u* and sometimes *y. Y* is usually a consonant when another vowel is in the word. Tell your child that, in English, a word cannot be made without a vowel.	Role-play a variety of situations in which you play the part of a friend who tries to convince your child to do something he/she shouldn't do. Use this exercise to help your child see how easily people can be influenced by others and to role-play ways to say no to friends.	**19 — Nineteen** Have your child count out nineteen dry beans. Then, have him/her line up the beans in the shape of the number 19. Write out the number word *nineteen* so your child can see it and sound it out with you. *See* Math, Week 30, numbers 1 and 2. Have your child complete **Number 19** (p. 309).
Tuesday	Set out various objects that begin with consonants. Have your child write the beginning letter of each object on a slip of paper and place it next to the appropriate object. *See* Reading, Week 30, number 1. Have your child complete **Consonant Review** (p. 306).	Have your child write a brief letter to a friend who has moved away. If he/she doesn't have any friends that have moved away, encourage your child to write an "I'm glad you're my friend" note to one who still lives nearby.	Draw a hopscotch grid outside with sidewalk chalk. Have your child fill in the squares with the numbers from 1 to 19. As your child hops on each number, have him/her call it out. *See* Math, Week 30, number 3. Have your child complete **A Jar Full of Cookies** (p. 310).
Wednesday	Have your child roll play dough into long tubes, then use it to shape each upper-case letter of the alphabet. *See* Reading, Week 30, number 2. Have your child complete **Alphabet Review** (p. 307).	Have your child write a tongue twister about his/her best friend.	Using number flash cards, see how quickly your child can recognize and name the numbers from 1 to 19. *See* Math, Week 30, number 4. Have your child complete **Lots To Share** (p. 311).
Thursday	Have your child match each of his/her upper-case note cards with the corresponding lower-case ones. *See* Reading, Week 30, number 3. Have your child complete **Letter Match** (p. 308).	Review the rules of proper phone etiquette, then let your child call a friend. Be available to help your child if he/she has any questions or problems placing the call. Praise your child for a job well done once the call has been completed.	Read *Starting To Subtract* by Karen Bryant-Mole and Jenny Tyler. Let your child choose several activities from the book.
Friday	Play "I Spy a Word That Begins With the Letter…" Take turns with your child giving clues and guessing. *See* Reading, Week 30, number 4.	Read the poem "My Spring Garden." *See* Language, Week 30, number 1.	Set up several simple, real-life story problems for your child to solve. **Example:** *If I give you five apples, and you put two back in the refrigerator, how many are left?*

Learn at Home, Grade K

Science	Social Studies	Gross/Fine Motor
Growing Time Have your child grow string beans. Begin by soaking a few beans in water overnight. Roll up paper towels and place them in a jar. Put a bean between the paper towels and the jar. Add enough water to the jar to moisten the paper towels. Put the jar in a warm place. Have your child observe what happens over the next few days.	**Caring for Friends** Read the *True Francine* by Marc Brown. Discuss what to do when a best friend wants you to do something you know is wrong. Ask your child to compare his/her own experiences with the events in the story.	Have your child perform the action rhyme "Small and Round" *Small and round, small and round.* *A bulb is deep inside the ground.* *Stretch and grow, stretch and grow.* *Up the stalk comes, slowly—slow.* *Buds are seen, buds are seen.* *The petals grow and they are green.* *Straight and tall, straight and tall.* *Flowers grow beside the wall.*
Read *From Seed to Plant* by Gail Gibbons. *See* Science, Week 30, numbers 1–3 for other activities.	Read *Annie Bananie* by Leah Komaiko. Discuss what it was like for you when a good friend moved away.	Teach your child the action rhyme "Ten Brown Seeds." *See* Gross/Fine Motor Skills, Week 30, number 1.
Read *The Science Book of Things That Grow* by Neil Ardley. There are several simple plant experiments for your child to try.	Today and tomorrow, help your child create a small photo album of his/her special friends. Organize it chronologically, beginning with your child's earliest friends and continuing through his/her friends today. Enjoy looking through your child's photos in the photo album. Let your child choose the friends and pictures he/she wants to include.	Help your child make his/her best friend's favorite cookies today. Bring them over to him/her while they are still warm, if possible.
Have your child plan his/her own mini-garden. It could be as simple as vegetable experiments in the kitchen or as big as a small garden outside. To help you decide what to plant, you may need to go to a gardening store or nursery and look at the back of the seed packets. Find out what plants would work in your area. *See* Science, Week 30, number 4.	Have your child complete his/her *Friends* photo album. Encourage your child to display the album in his/her room. *See* Social Studies, Week 30, number 1.	Have your child shape flowers out of shredded wheat compound. *See* Social Studies, Week 6, number 1. Coat each flower with cookie sprinkles or small candies. When they are dry, place the flowers in a small basket for display.
Visit a botanical garden and look at the different kinds of plants.	Help your child celebrate friendships by inviting a favorite friend over to watch a movie about friends. *See* Social Studies, Week 30, numbers 2 and 3 for other activities.	Buy several fresh-cut flowers and some greenery. Bring them home and allow your child to arrange the flowers in a vase.

TEACHING SUGGESTIONS AND ACTIVITIES

READING (Consonant Review)

▶ 1. Draw pictures of objects for your child to name. After he/she names each one correctly, have him/her write the first letter of the word on a sheet of paper. Set a timer to see how many objects your child can guess within a set amount of time.

▶ 2. Have your child finger paint a mural that represents every letter of the alphabet.

▶ 3. Make a hopscotch grid. Draw a picture of an object that begins with a consonant in each square. As your child jumps across the squares, he/she must name the beginning letter of each object pictured.

▶ 4. Give your child a sheet of lined paper and have him/her number down the left side from 1 to 21. Say *Number 1* and hold up an object that begins with a consonant. Your child must write the beginning letter of the object next to the number 1 on his/her paper. Continue through the number 21, using a different beginning consonant for each word.

LANGUAGE

▶ 1. "My Spring Garden" (poem)

Here is my garden.	**(Make a bowl shape with hands.)**
Some seeds I will sow.	**(Motion of scattering seeds.)**
To rake the ground,	**(Scratch with fingers.)**
Here is my hoe.	**(Arms straight in front of body, fingers bent downward.)**
Here is the big, round, yellow sun.	**(Make circle with arms.)**
The sun warms everything.	
Here are the rain clouds in the sky,	**(Point to sky.)**
The birds will start to sing.	**(Move forefinger and thumb several times.)**
Little plants will wake up soon,	**(Kneel, then slowly rise.)**
And lift their sleepy heads.	**(Raise arms.)**
Little plants will grow and grow	
From their warm earth beds.	

MATH (19 — Nineteen)

▶ 1. Have your child make a list of his/her nineteen favorite foods. Write them out so he/she can see the numbers. Use the ordinal numbers first, second, third, etc.

▶ 2. See how many sets of nineteen objects your child can make in 3 minutes.

▶ 3. Draw an outline of a butterfly on paper. Have your child draw nineteen circles on its wings.

▶ 4. Buy a dot-to-dot coloring book. This is great counting practice for your child.

SCIENCE (Growing Time)

▶ 1. Pick your own fresh fruit as it comes into season this summer.

▶ 2. Go to the library and learn about unusual plants to grow at home, such as cotton.

▶ 3. Talk to a local farmer about how he/she cares for so many crops.

▶ 4. Let your child pick out a plant for his/her bedroom. Explain that he/she will be responsible for caring for the plant. Choose a plant that is easy to care for, such as a cactus.

SOCIAL STUDIES (Caring for Friends)

▶ 1. Have your child make a collage of friends' pictures to hang on his/her bedroom wall.

▶ 2. Encourage your child to befriend a child who is new to your neighborhood, church or community.

▶ 3. Encourage your child to befriend an elderly neighbor or relative.

GROSS/FINE MOTOR SKILLS

▶ 1. "Ten Brown Seeds" (poem)

> Ten brown seeds lay in a straight row,
> Said, "Now it is time for us to grow."
> Up, up, the first one shoots,
> Up, up, from its little roots.
> Up, up, the second one is seen,
> Up, up, up, in its little coat of green.
> Up, up, up, the third one's head
> Comes up, up, up, from its little earth bed.
> Up, up, up, the fourth one goes,
> Up, up, up, we can see its little nose!
> Up, up, up, the fifth one pops,
> Up through the soil and then it stops.
>
> Up, up, up, the sixth we see,
> Up it comes and it looks at me.
> Up, up, up, the seventh one peeps!
> Up, up, through the soil it leaps.
> Up, up, up, the eighth we spy,
> Up, up, up, stretch to the sky.
> Up, up, up, the ninth one springs,
> Up, up, up, and everything sings.
> Up, up, up, the tenth grows fast,
> Up, up, up, and it is the last.
> Up, up, up, the seeds, every one,
> Become ten plants who smile at the sun.

Have your child curl up very small like a seed. As you recite the poem, have him/her stand up very gradually until he/she is fully grown by the last two lines.

Consonant Review

Say the name of each picture. **Write** the letter that makes the beginning sound.

1. _____

2. _____

3. _____

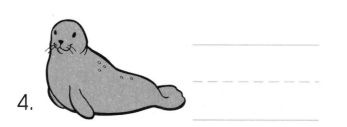

4. _____

5. _____

6. _____

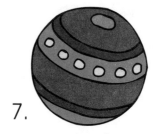

7. _____

8. _____

Alphabet Review

Trace the UPPER-CASE letters.
Write the missing UPPER-CASE letters.

A _____ _____ E _____

_____ H _____ _____ L _____

_____ N _____ P _____

_____ T _____ V _____

X _____ Z

Learn at Home, Grade K

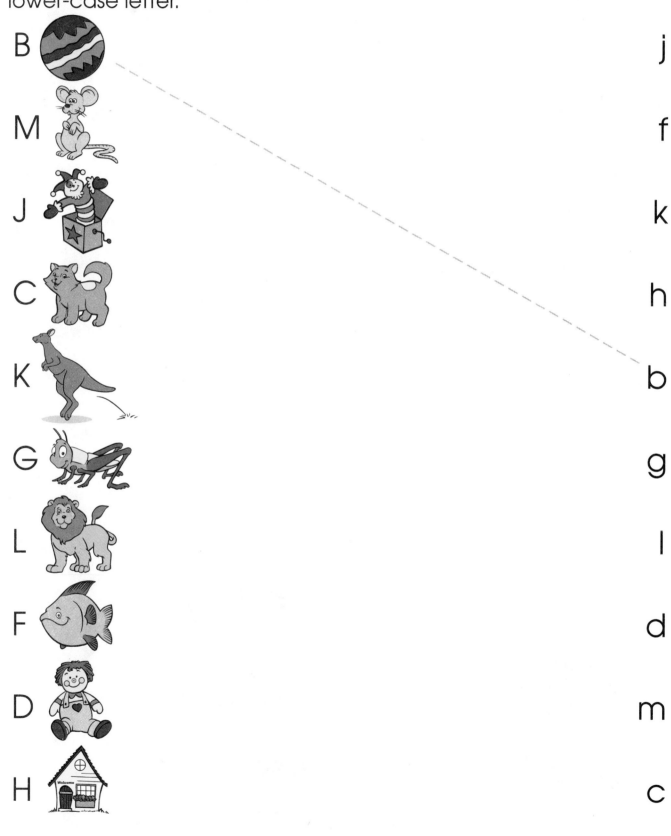

Letter Match

Draw a line to match each UPPER-CASE letter with the correct lower-case letter.

B   j

M   f

J   k

C   h

K   b

G   g

L   l

F   d

D   m

H   c

Learn at Home, Grade K

Number 19

This is the number 19. **Color** the pictures.

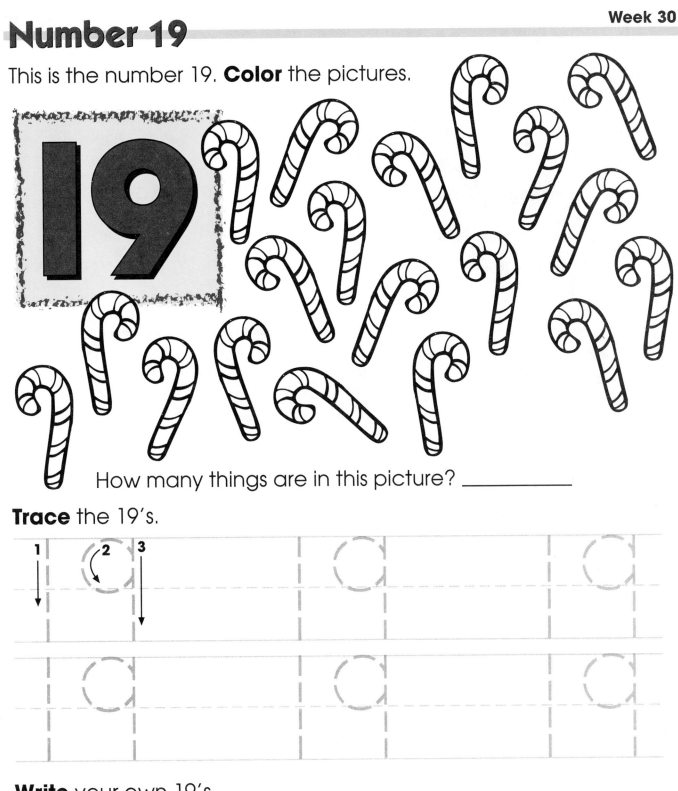

How many things are in this picture? _____

Trace the 19's.

Write your own 19's.

_____

_____

Learn at Home, Grade K

A Jar Full of Cookies

Draw 19 cookies in the cookie jar. **Color** the cookies. Number them from 1 to 19.

Lots To Share

Sharing is fun! **Count** the things that are being shared. **Write** the number in the boxes. **Color** the pictures.

Learn at Home, Grade K

	Reading	**Language**	**Math**
Monday	**A, a** Shape alphabet magnets to form upper- and lower-case letter *a*'s. Then, mix up the magnets and have your child do the same. *See* Reading, Week 31, number 1. Have your child complete **Letter A, a** (p. 316).	Explain that there are six vowels in the alphabet. Write out the word *vowel* and have your child say it with you. Sing the following song to the tune of "Twinkle, Twinkle, Little Star": *A, E, I, O, U and Y* *Are unique, I wonder why.* *Is it 'cause each word needs you?* *Look at that—I see it's true.* *A, E, I, O, U and Y* *Are unique and I know why!*	**Basic Concepts** Make shape flash cards. Hold up a card and have your child identify the shape. *See* Math, Week 31, number 1. Have your child complete **Get In Shape!** (p. 319).
Tuesday	Have your child drag a toy airplane through finger paint so that the wheels are coated. Then, have him/her roll the plane in the shape of upper- and lower-case letter *a*'s on a large sheet of newsprint or craft paper. Have your child complete **Amazing A's** (p. 317).	Sing the vowel song with your child. Then, open a book and have your child identify the vowel or vowels in each word.	Set out two groups of various objects. Ask your child which group has fewer objects and which has more. Change the number of objects in each group and repeat the questions. Repeat this activity several times. Have your child complete **Great Graphing!** (p. 320).
Wednesday	Teach your child the short *a* sound, as in the word *apple,* and practice saying this sound with your child. Then, cut out an apple pattern from poster board. Have your child trace and cut out two apples from red construction paper. Staple the apples together along the sides and bottom, forming a pocket. Have your child cut out pictures of letter *a* objects from magazines and place them inside the apple.	Have your child sing the vowel song again. Cut out six star shapes and ask your child to write a different vowel on each one. Have him/her glue the stars onto a sheet of blue construction paper with the caption *Vowels shine bright!*	Have your child tell you the order of steps in washing the dishes or another familiar activity. Have your child complete **Cool Countdown** (p. 321).
Thursday	Play "Grandma's Trunk" with your child. Begin with letter *a,* saying *I'm going to Alabama and I'm taking an apple.* Have your child repeat the line, *I'm going to ____ and I'm taking a ____,* adding a letter *b* object. For example, *I'm going to Alabama and I'm taking an apple and a box.* Try to go through the entire alphabet, alternating turns.	Reread *The Very Hungry Caterpillar* by Eric Carle and discuss the caterpillar's food choices. Teach your child the finger play "New Butterfly." *See* Language, Week 31, numbers 1 and 2.	Set out several groups of three objects. Have your child point out the first, middle and last object in each group. Ask whose age and/or whose height makes him/her the middle one in your family. Have your child complete **First, Middle, Last** (p. 322).
Friday	Set out a variety of objects on the kitchen table and have your child pick up only letter *a* objects.	Read *The Very Lonely Firefly* by Eric Carle. Review color words. Have your child complete **Clowning Around With Colors** (p. 318).	Give your child a package of candies in an assortment of flavors. Have him/her arrange the candies in order from most favorite to least favorite. Then, have your child use ordinal numbers to describe the additional in which he/she would eat the candies. *See* Math, Week 31, numbers 2–4 for additional activities. Have your child complete **Monkeying Around** (p. 323).

Learn at Home, Grade K

Science	Social Studies	Gross/Fine Motor
Creepy Crawlers Skim *Bugs* by Jinny Johnson. Look at each page and name the type of bug shown. If your child expresses an interest in a particular bug, stop and read some of the information. Ask your child what he/she thinks about creepy crawlers. Which one(s) does he/she like best? Which ones are scariest? Which ones look the most unusual?	**Caring for My Community** Ask your child what a *community* is. Take a walk, beginning in your own backyard. Explain that a community is where people live. It includes homes, neighbors, parks, schools, churches, grocery stores and more. Tell your child that his/her community is where he/she lives and plays. Complete your walk by asking your child to name his/her favorite parts of the community.	Help your child make insect antennae by attaching two black pipe cleaners to a headband. Paint two plastic golf balls black. When they are dry, have your child wind the top of each pipe cleaner through a hole in the ball. Have your child use the antennae to act like his/her favorite insect. *See* Gross/Fine Motor Skills, Week 31, numbers 1–3.
Read *Insects* by Joy Richardson. This easy-to-understand book will help your child learn the differences between an insect and other types of creepy crawlers. Once you have read the book, review the last page which defines an insect. *See* Science, Week 31, number 1.	Have your child look through magazines and cut out pictures of houses and apartment buildings. Have him/her glue all these homes to a large sheet of butcher paper to create a community mural. Then, have him/her cut out pictures of people from magazines and newspapers and glue them in the collage.	Have your child act out this poem about insects and spiders. *Insects or spiders,* *Which are which?* *Insects have six legs* *To scratch and itch.* *Spiders have more,* *For they have eight.* *Eight legs to run* *So they won't be late!*
Skim *Butterfly and Moth* by Paul Whalley. Focus on pages 20–25 which show a caterpillar becoming a butterfly, or undergoing *metamorphosis*. Have your child look at each of the stages and describe what is happening. Ask your child: *How does one stage differ from the next?*	Reinforce the idea that a community begins with each person's home. Have your child tell you how he/she can take care of his/her home. Then, have him/her choose a special job to do at home. It could be planting flowers, pulling weeds or watering plants.	Have your child make butterflies out of play dough. Bake them and let them cool. Then, have your child paint the butterflies.
Look at the butterflies on pages 26 through the end of *Butterfly and Moth*. Encourage your child to use his/her observation skills by identifying the shapes and colors he/she sees in the butterflies' wings, etc. Then, have him/her order the butterflies on a given page from smallest to largest.	Ask your child to think of ways he/she can help take care of his/her neighborhood. Have him/her identify specific neighbors. Is there an elderly neighbor who could use help taking out the garbage each week? With your child, brainstorm specific things he/she could do to help this neighbor. Then, have him/her choose one idea and do it.	Give your child a net to catch butterflies. What different types can your child find? Have your child observe the butterflies through the net and then release them.
Help your child catch a variety of creepy crawlers in a jar. Let him/her observe them through a magnifying lens. Ask your child questions to help him/her observe the insect carefully. Have your child release the insects when he/she has finished observing them. *See* Science, Week 31, numbers 2 and 3 for additional activities.	Have your child think of ways to care for the park in your community. Is there something special he/she could do, such as plant flowers? Check with your city and see what projects you and your child could do together. Explain to your child that each person has an important role in caring for the community.	Have your child draw what he/she saw when looking through the magnifying lens at the creepy crawlers he/she caught. *See* today's Science lesson. Help your child start an ant farm. *See* Gross/Fine Motor Skills, Week 31, number 4.

TEACHING SUGGESTIONS AND ACTIVITIES

READING (A, a)

▶ 1. Draw a target on a piece of poster board. Place a letter *a* picture in every other ring. In the empty rings, place any picture. Label each letter *a* ring with increasingly higher points, with the bull's-eye at the center worth the most. In the center of the bull's-eye, write the letter *a*. Put your target on the floor. Let your child toss beanbags at the target and try to hit an *a*.

LANGUAGE

▶ 1. "New Butterfly" (finger play)

On a milkweed leaf,	
Here is a cocoon.	**(Cup hands.)**
Something is happening.	
Will it be soon?	**(Peek inside cupped hands.)**
Oh, here it comes	
With wings folded so.	
Now they are spreading,	**(Spread arms.)**
Ready to go.	
Look at the green and gold	
Butterfly!	
Fly away! Fly away! And good-bye!	**(Child "flies" away.)**

▶ 2. Have your child use a familiar tune to write a song about the beauty of a butterfly.

MATH (Basic Concepts)

▶ 1. Have your child use his/her geoboard to create shapes as you name them.

▶ 2. Have your child count the number of times he/she can hop on one foot. Then, have him/her count by tens until he/she reaches one hundred.

▶ 3. Have your child do all the measuring and mixing to make a homemade apple pie.

▶ 4. See how many ants your child can find. If he/she sees a line of them, have him/her tell you which is first, second, third, etc.

SCIENCE (Creepy Crawlers)

▶ 1. Flip through the pictures in *Bugs* by Jinny Johnson. Have your child identify which bugs are insects and which are not.

▶ 2. Consult *Make It Work! Insects* by Liz Wyse for experiments designed to help your child learn about the lives of insects.

▶ 3. Read *Backyard Insects* by Millicent E. Selsam and Ronald Goor. This very simple, interactive text is great for kindergartners.

GROSS/FINE MOTOR SKILLS

▶ 1. Help your child apply face paint and dress to look like a bumblebee. Have him/her "fly" around to various pieces of classical music, including Nikolai Rimsky-Korsakov's *Flight of the Bumblebee*.

▶ 2. Have your child make "edible insects." First, spread peanut butter between two round crackers. Then, place three pretzel sticks in each side. Finally, put a dab of peanut butter on two raisins and stick them on top of the cracker for "eyes."

▶ 3. Have your child make "ants on a log" by spreading peanut butter on a celery stick, then adding raisins for ants.

▶ 4. Have your child start his/her own ant farm. Kits are available at many discount stores.

Learn at Home, Grade K

Letter A, a

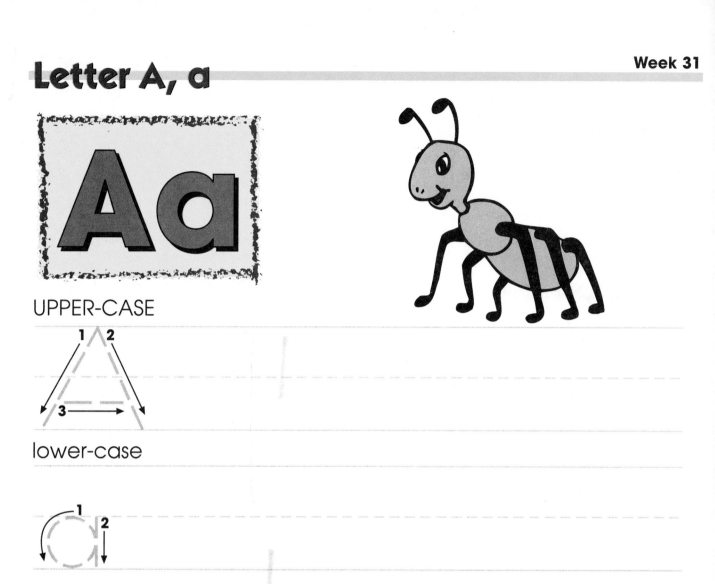

UPPER-CASE

lower-case

These pictures begin with the letter A, a. **Color** the pictures.

Amazing A's

Draw a line from each apple to a picture which begins with the sound of A, a. **Draw** an **X** on the picture which does not belong. **Color** the A, a pictures.

Clowning Around With Colors

Color each clown's hat. **Color** the balloons the correct colors.

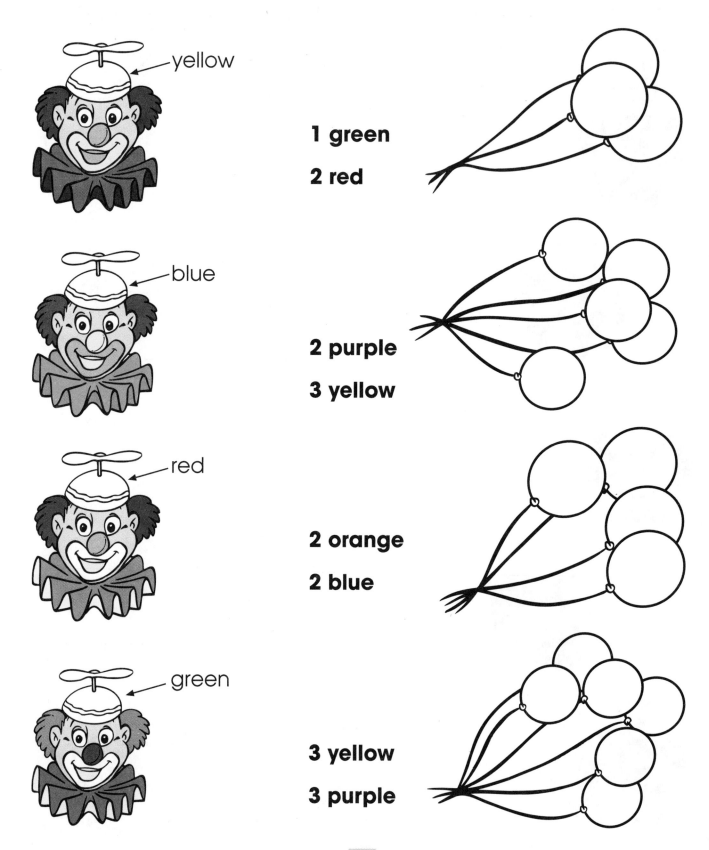

yellow

1 green

2 red

blue

2 purple

3 yellow

red

2 orange

2 blue

green

3 yellow

3 purple

Learn at Home, Grade K

Get In Shape!

Color the ☐'s **yellow**.
Color the ◯'s **blue**.
Color the ▲'s **red**.
Color the ▭'s **green**.

Learn at Home, Grade K

Great Graphing!

Count the animals. **Color** one picture on the graph for each animal.

1	2	3	4	5	6	7
🐷	🐷	🐷	🐷	🐷	🐷	🐷
🐄	🐄	🐄	🐄	🐄	🐄	🐄
🐑	🐑	🐑	🐑	🐑	🐑	🐑
🐥	🐥	🐥	🐥	🐥	🐥	🐥

Which are there more of? **Circle** the answer.

🐷 or 🐑 ?

🐥 or 🐄 ?

Cool Countdown

Write the numbers **1, 2, 3** and **4** to show the correct order. **Color** the pictures.

Learn at Home, Grade K

First, Middle, Last

Look at each group of three things. **Color** the **first** thing green.
Color the **middle** thing purple. **Color** the **last** thing orange.

322

Monkeying Around

Color to show the order.

second (green)

seventh (orange)

fifth (blue)

first (red)

Match.

sixth   ninth   third   second   fourth

	Reading	**Language**	**Math**
Monday	**E, e** Beat an egg. Use a pastry brush and the beaten egg to paint upper- and lower-case letter *e*'s on a sheet of black construction paper. Then, have your child do the same. *See* Reading, Week 32, number 1. Have your child complete **Letter E, e** (p. 328).	Ask your child what he/she wants to be when he/she grows up and why. Then, ask your child what that person does at his/her job. Be sure to record your conversation on video- or audiotape.	**20 — Twenty** Place two sets of ten on a table. Guide your child to count the objects by tens to arrive at twenty. Help if he/she has difficulty, counting 10, 20 as you point to each pile. Write *twenty* on a sheet of paper. Help your child sound it out. Add another set of ten. How many are there now? Continue until you have ten sets of ten. Have your child complete **Number 20** (p. 331).
Tuesday	Have your child form edible *e*'s using rope licorice. Have your child complete **"Egg-ceptional" E!** (p. 329).	Have your child fly his/her balloon bee (*see* today's Gross/Fine Motor lesson) while you read the "Five Busy Honey Bees" poem. *See* Language, Week 32, number 1.	Have your child measure out the ingredients for chocolate chip cookies. Have him/her place enough dough on a pan to make one giant cookie. Then, let him/her count out twenty chocolate chips to place on top in the shape of the number 20. Bake the cookie at 250° until it is thoroughly cooked in the middle.
Wednesday	The most common *e* sound is the short *e* as in *egg*. Have your child say it with you. Say the short letter *a* sound, then the *e* sound. Help your child hear the difference. Then, give your child clues to see if he/she can guess each of these letter *e* words: *elephant, egg, eat, envelope, eye, eagle, earth, eleven* and *elbow*. Have your child complete **Vowel Review** (p. 330).	Read *Fire Fighters* by Robert Maas. Compare the book to what you actually saw at the fire station. *See* today's Social Studies lesson. What was the same? What was different?	Play a board game with two dice or create your own game on a piece of poster board. Your child might enjoy adding pictures and ideas about how the game should be played. **Variation:** Instead of using dice, write the numbers 1–20 on slips of paper to be drawn at the beginning of each player's turn.
Thursday	Have your child use a large manila envelope to hold letter *e* pictures cut out from magazines.	Read the poem "Workers." *See* Language, Week 32, number 2. Have your child guess the community helper being described in each line.	Have your child write the numbers 1–20 on slips of paper and place them inside plastic eggs. Then, have your child count between one and twenty small candies to place in a second set of plastic eggs (one candy in one egg, fourteen in another, twenty in another, etc.). Take turns with your child trying to match the number eggs with the correct candy eggs.
Friday	Have your child make the letter *a* and *e* pages for his/her alphabet review booklet. *See* Reading, Week 32, numbers 2–4 for additional activities.	Have your child go to work with your spouse for the morning. Have your spouse explain each of the things he/she does at his/her job. Have him/her discuss with your child how he/she helps the community.	Plan an outdoor scavenger hunt in which each note directs your child to the next one. Be sure to include directional words, numerals and number words in the clues. *See* Math, Week 32, numbers 1 and 2 for additional activities.

Science	Social Studies	Gross/Fine Motor
Creepy Crawlers Read *The Magic School Bus Inside a Beehive* by Joanna Cole. Discuss the role of the queen bee, worker bee and drone. *See* Science, Week 32, number 1.	**Caring for My Community** Have your child name different jobs people in your community do. Write a list as your child dictates it. *See* Social Studies, Week 32, numbers 1–4.	Have your child act out the various community helpers in the poem "Different People." *See* Gross/Fine Motor, Week 32, number 1.
Review the types of bees you and your child discussed yesterday. Read *The Life Cycle of the Honeybee* by Paula Z. Hogan. Ask your child review questions as you go through the book a second time.	Discuss the jobs of doctors and nurses. If your child has a play doctor kit, have him/her explain the purpose of each piece of equipment in it. Then, talk about your child's own doctor and ask how he/she helps the community.	Have your child blow up a large yellow balloon and tie the balloon closed. Then, help your child turn it into a bee by adding stripes of black electrical tape. Have your child add black pipe cleaner antennae by taping them to a black stripe, then add eyes using a large black marker.
Teach your child about worms. Help your child find an earthworm and let him/her look at it under a magnifying lens. Have your child describe the parts of a worm he/she observes. Let your child discover if the worm floats or swims by placing one in a cup of water. Have your child put a stick inside the cup to see if the worm will crawl out. Help your child devise other experiments to help him/her learn about worms. *See* Science, Week 32, number 2.	**Field Trip:** Visit a fire station today and talk to a firefighter. Have your child ask him/her several questions. Then, walk around and observe the fire station and the fire engines.	Have your child act out the poem "Four Busy Firefighters." *See* Gross/Fine Motor, Week 32, number 2.
Read *Amazing Spiders* by Alexandra Parsons. Discuss which spiders are your child's favorites and why.	**Field Trip:** Go to the post office. Show your child the post office boxes, stamp machines, tellers at the windows and mail slots. Ask the postmaster if he/she will allow your child to observe the work done "behind the scenes." On the way home, discuss how mail carriers help the community.	Take a walk around your basement or outside and see if you and your child can find a spider web. If the web has no spider in it, allow your child to touch it. Discuss how spiders are born knowing how to make webs. Ask your child what the purpose of a web is. Talk about predators and prey.
Visit a pet store and look at some of the exotic spiders. Ask the store owner how he/she cares for these pets. *See* Science, Week 32, number 3.	**Field Trip:** Visit the police station with your child. Call ahead to see if someone can give your child a tour. Have your child prepare questions to ask the officers. On the way home, discuss how police officers help communities.	Have your child write a thank you letter to each community helper who gave him/her a tour and answered his/her questions.

Learn at Home, Grade K

TEACHING SUGGESTIONS AND ACTIVITIES

READING (E, e)

▶ 1. Play the game "E, e, e . . . What would you eat? Would you eat an (elephant with four feet?)" Have your child think of other letter *e* words and phrases to complete the question.

▶ 2. Play a matching game with plastic eggs. Put alphabet letters in one set of eggs and pictures of words that begin with those letters in another set of eggs. Have your child try to match each letter with the appropriate picture.

▶ 3. Have your child write the letter *e* on a sheet of paper. Have him/her turn that letter into a picture of a letter *e* word, such as *elephant* or *ear*.

▶ 4. Have your child write a short letter to a relative. Help him/her correctly address the envelope and show him/her where to place the stamp. Then, have your child drop the letter in a mailbox. Along with the letter, he/she could include a letter *e* picture from a coloring book.

LANGUAGE

▶ 1. "Five Busy Honey Bees" (finger play)

> *Five busy honey bees were resting in the sun.*
> *The first one said, "Let us have some fun!"*
> *The second one said, "Where shall it be?"*
> *The third one said, "Up in the honey tree!"*
> *The fourth one said, "Let's make some honey sweet."*
> *The fifth one said, "With pollen on our feet."*
> *The five little busy bees sang their buzzing tune,*
> *As they worked in the beehive all that afternoon.*

▶ 2. "Workers" (poem)

> *This worker feeds the lions at the zoo.*
> *This worker drives an engine to a fire.*
> *This worker makes a new sole for your shoe.*
> *This worker mends a high electric wire.*
> *This worker drives a sweeper through the streets.*
> *This worker bakes a cookie or a bun.*
> *This worker sells my parents food to eat.*
> *And I'm very glad we've got them, every one!*

MATH (20 — Twenty)

▶ 1. Using sidewalk chalk, have your child make a chart with the numbers 1–20 along the bottom. Ask him/her to draw stacks of objects above each number to represent the number. For example, he/she would draw one ball above 1, two balls (stacked) above 2, and so on.

▶ 2. Have your child write the numeral 20 on a sheet of wrapping paper. Let him/her pour glue on it, then cover it with glitter for a shimmery effect.

SCIENCE (Creepy Crawlers)

▶ 1. Buy honey still in the honeycomb and let your child taste it. Then, make a special recipe with the honey.

▶ 2. Make "dirt cups." Prepare chocolate pudding and pour it into separate cups. Crush your child's favorite cookies and sprinkle the crumbs over the top. Add candy worms and enjoy.

▶ 3. Let your child shape various creepy crawlers with sugar cookie dough. Bake the dough as directed and have your child frost the creatures in appropriate colors.

SOCIAL STUDIES (Caring for My Community)

▶ 1. Talk to the garbage collector. Find out how you and your child can make his/her job easier.

▶ 2. Have your child talk to a priest, pastor, rabbi or other church leader. What does he/she do? Is there a special job your child could do to help out at the church?

▶ 3. The next time your child has a dentist appointment, ask him/her to observe the office, the equipment and what the dentist does.

▶ 4. Have your child talk to a store clerk. Does he/she like the job? What does he/she like most and least?

GROSS/FINE MOTOR SKILLS

▶ 1. "Different People" (poem)

This person drives a taxi.
This person leads a band.
This person guides the traffic
By holding up a hand.

This person brings the letters.
This person rakes and hoes.
This person is a funny clown,
Who dances on tiptoes.

▶ 2. "Four Busy Firefighters" (poem)

Four busy firefighters could not retire,
Because they might have to put out a fire.
The first one rang a big brass bell.
The second one said, "It's the Grand Hotel!"
The third one said, "Down the pole we'll slide."
The fourth one said, "Get ready to ride."
The siren said, "Get out of the way!
We have to put out a fire today!"
The red fire truck sped on to the fire,
As the big yellow flames grew higher and higher.
Swish went the water from the firehose spout,
And in no time at all, the fire was out.

Letter E, e

E e

UPPER-CASE

1 2 →
3 →
4 →

lower-case

2
1 →

These pictures begin with the letter E, e. **Color** the pictures.

"Egg-ceptional" E!

Draw a line from each egg to a picture which begins with the sound of E, e.

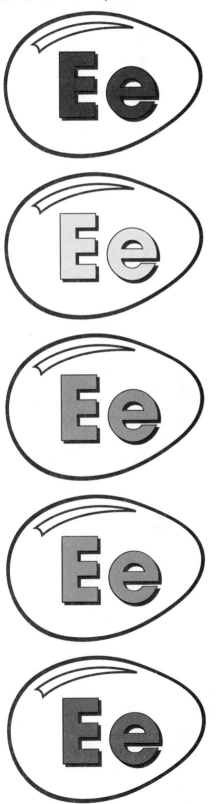

Learn at Home, Grade K

Vowel Review

Say the name of each picture. **Write** the letter that makes the beginning sound.

1.

2.

3.

4.

5.

6.

7.

8.

9.

10.

Learn at Home, Grade K

Number 20

This is the number 20. **Color** the pictures.

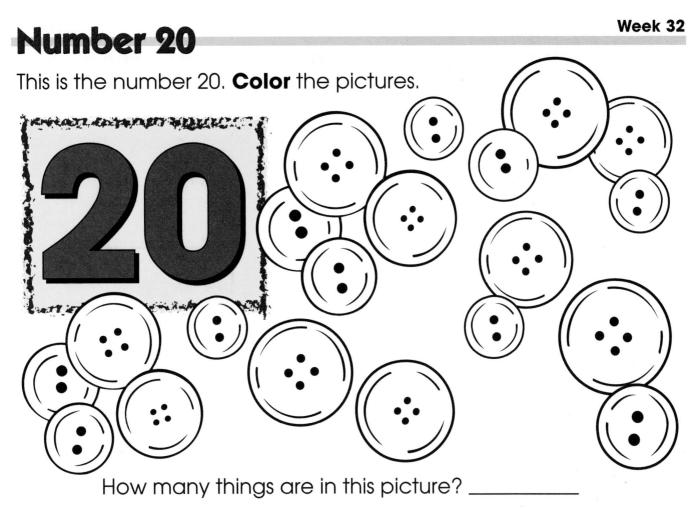

How many things are in this picture? _____

Trace the 20's.

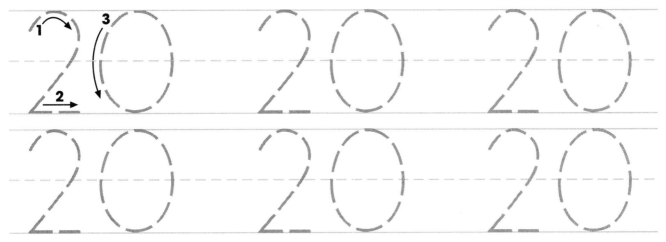

Write your own 20's.

_____

_____

	Reading	Language	Math
Monday	**I, i** Use pen and ink to write upper- and lower-case letter *i*'s on a sheet of paper. Have your child trace the letters with his/her finger. Then, have your child practice writing them him/herself. Have your child complete **Letter I, i** (p. 336).	Have your child make up a song about summer to the tune of a common nursery rhyme. Have your child complete **Summer Fun** (p. 338).	**Basic Concepts** Set out five pairs of something (socks, shoes, etc.) that belong to one member of your family. Have your child match each pair. Have your child complete **A Complete Picture** (p. 339).
Tuesday	Give your child a scoop of ice cream. Have him/her use sprinkles to "write" upper- and lower-case letter *i*'s on his/her ice cream. Have your child complete **An I, i Igloo** (p. 337).	Read *How I Spent My Summer Vacation* by Mark Teague. Have your child create his/her own make-believe story about summer vacation.	Cut a piece of yarn for both you and your child. Make a variety of shapes with your yarn. Have your child imitate your shapes. Have your child complete a copy of **Flying High** (p. 340).
Wednesday	Teach your child the short *i* sound and ask him/her to repeat the sound with you. Then, draw the following letter *i* words for him/her to guess: *inch, ice cream, ice, Indian, insect, iron, island, itch* and *idea*. Challenge your child to guess as many as he/she can in 3 minutes. *See* Reading, Week 33, number 1.	Read *Sunflakes* by Lilian Moore. Read as many summer poems as interest your child.	Set out two similar calendar scenes of the same month. Have your child compare the two scenes, naming similarities and differences. *See* Math, Week 33, number 1. Have your child complete **Same and Different** (p. 341).
Thursday	Have your child use finger paint to draw a large insect on a manila envelope. While the paint dries, have him/her find and cut out letter *i* pictures or objects to place inside the envelope.	Watch the video version of Dr. Seuss's *Hoober-Bloob Highway*.	Set out the penny store. *See* the Math lesson from Wednesday, Week 24. Give your child twenty pennies and allow him/her to purchase the various objects you have set out for "sale." *See* Math, Week 33, number 2.
Friday	Set out a variety of letter *a, e* and *i* objects or pictures of objects on the table. Review with your child the sound each vowel makes. Then, have him/her sort the objects into three categories: letter *a* words, *e* words and *i* words. Give your child as much time and practice as he/she needs to learn the vowel sounds. They are so similar in sound, it may take a great deal of practice for your child to master them. *See* Reading, Week 33, numbers 2–4.	Review the vowel song. *See* the Language lesson from Monday, Week 31. *See* Language, Week 33, numbers 1–4 for additional activities.	Have your child draw a number line (1–20) on a sheet of paper. Give him/her directions to use a variety of crayon colors. **Example:** *Using a brown crayon, start at number 10 and go up 3. What number are you on?* Then, give a different set of directions using another color. Explain to your child that when he/she "goes up," he/she is adding, and when he/she "goes down," he/she is subtracting. *See* Math, Week 33, number 3.

Learn at Home, Grade K

Science	Social Studies	Gross/Fine Motor
Oceans Help your child to locate the world's oceans on a map or globe. Explain to your child that raindrops come from oceans and lakes. Help him/her conduct an experiment in which he/she makes his/her own raindrops. *See* Science, Week 33, number 1.	**Caring for My World** Ask your child to tell you several ways he/she can take better care of the world. Write all your child's ideas on chart paper. Then, have him/her rank his/her best ideas from 1 to 5. Help your child implement one or more of them.	Have your child fold a sheet of paper in half, then in half again, forming four rectangles when the paper is opened. In each rectangle, have your child write a different season. While he/she is writing, cut out a sun, tree, snowman and flowers from construction paper. Have your child decide where to place each picture. Then, have him/her add additional details with crayons or markers.
Help your child explore the properties of water. Set out a variety of objects, such as wood, rocks, a sponge, paper, an apple, eraser, a nail, etc. Ask your child: *Which of these things will float and which will sink?* Have your child make a prediction about each object. Then, let him/her put the objects in water to test them. Discuss your child's results with him/her and let him/her compare the results with his/her predictions.	Introduce your child to the "Three R's" of recycling—*reduce, reuse* and *recycle*. Explain that the term *reduce* means that we try to throw away less trash. Talk about ways your family can reduce the amount of disposable items you throw away—diapers, paper plates, plastic or foam cups, paper towels, napkins and plastic garbage bags. Read *Love Earth, The Beauty Makeover* by Shelly Nielsen. *See* Social Studies, Week 33, number 1.	Take a walk with your child, bringing along a paper bag and gloves to collect trash.
Provide your child with balls of oil-based and plasticene clay and aluminum foil. Let him/her experiment to see which of the balls will float. If they float, can they be reshaped so they sink? If they sink, can they be reshaped so they will float? Let your child use a variety of objects in combination with the balls to see which sink and which float. For example, why does a rock, which sinks when it is put into water alone, "float" when it is placed in a toy boat?	Discuss the term *reuse*. Explain that reusing things instead of throwing them away is another way to help the Earth. Brainstorm with your child a list of ways to reuse more—coloring on both sides of a sheet of paper, using empty containers, such as shoe boxes and egg cartons, for storing things and using scraps of materials for art projects. Help your child collect "reusable" items and let him/her create an art project.	Have your child act out the action poem, "Summer Fun." *See* Gross/Fine Motor, Week 33, number 1.
Set out a variety of materials for your child to construct a simple sailboat. Let your child float the sailboat in a tub of water. Let him/her play the part of the wind so that he/she can observe how the moving air pushes the sailboat and moves it across the water. Let him/her experiment with different sizes, shapes and materials for his/her sail. Which one(s) work best? Why?	Introduce the term *recycle*. Explain that recycling is turning trash into new products. Set up a recycling center and teach your child how to sort materials such as glass, metal and paper. Read *Trash! Trash! Trash!* by Shelly Nielsen. *See* Social Studies, Week 33, numbers 2–4.	Collect a variety of trash (cardboard tubes, plastic bottles, cans, etc.) and have your child use it to make a picture or sculpture.
Explain to your child that waves are caused by wind—the stronger the wind, the bigger the waves. Let your child experiment with making "waves" with this experiment. Fill a clear plastic water bottle half-full of water tinted with blue food coloring. Fill the rest of the bottle with vegetable oil and twist the cap on tightly. Have your child hold the bottle on its side and gently shake it to create an "ocean" full of waves.	Teach your child that some trash is *biodegradable* which means that it will eventually go back into the Earth. Do an experiment to teach your child which materials will break down. Have him/her dig six holes and bury an apple core, leaves, grass clippings, a plastic bag, a foam cup and a glass jar. Have your child make signs to mark what is buried in each spot. Have your child wait 4 weeks and dig up the "trash." Discuss what he/she discovered.	Have your child act out the action poem "Ten Summer Seagulls." *See* Gross/Fine Motor Skills, Week 33, number 2.

TEACHING SUGGESTIONS AND ACTIVITIES

READING (I, i)

1. Have your child buzz like an insect whenever you say a word beginning with the letter *i*. Include words beginning with the letters *a* and *e*, since these will be difficult for your child to distinguish. *I* words: *itself, invite, into, interested, it, if, ill, in, important, inch, ice, ink.*

2. Let your child use various colors of ink to create a picture full of letter *i* objects.

3. Have your child write out the upper-case letters of the alphabet on him/herself in face paint.

4. Celebrate letter *I* Week by talking about a variety of instruments. Go to the library and look for a tape or CD to help you teach your child about the sounds of different instruments.

LANGUAGE

1. Make homemade ice cream with your child.

2. Help your child make homemade ice pops. Have your child pour his/her favorite juice into an ice cube tray. As it begins to harden, have him/her poke a craft stick or toothpick inside each cube. Then, let the ice pops continue to freeze.

3. Read *One Summer Night* by Eleanor Schick.

4. Have your child write the word *summer* down the left side of a sheet of paper. Have him/her think of a word or phrase beginning with each letter to describe summer.

MATH (Basic Concepts)

1. Play "Teacher Says" using directional words. Words to use: *between, above, below, beside, far, near, up, down, in, out, go, stop, high, low, off* and *on.*

2. Give your child a pocketful of pennies and take him/her to a store that sells penny candies. Allow your child to use his/her pennies to pick out a candy for each penny he/she has.

3. Have your child use finger paint to number his/her fingers and toes from 1 to 20.

SCIENCE (Oceans)

1. Have your child fill a glass jar half-full of water to represent the ocean. Have him/her set the lid of the jar upside down on top of the jar, completely covering the opening. Have your child pretend this is a cloud. Then, let the jar sit for 1 hour. The water in the jar (the "ocean") will evaporate and change into water vapor. The vapor will travel up to the lid (a "cloud"). Water vapor will gather on the bottom of the lid, form drops and fall back into the jar, creating "rain."

2. Look through *Get Set . . . Go! Summer* by Ruth Thomson for simple craft ideas.

3. Read *Summer* by David Webster. This book includes many summer science experiments.

4. Help your child make a summer mobile using outdoor nature objects strung from a hanger.

SOCIAL STUDIES (Caring for My World)

▷ 1. Visit a landfill. Talk to the operator about how much garbage comes in each day. Allow your child to ask any other questions he/she may have.

▷ 2. Visit a recycling center. See if you can arrange a tour before you go.

▷ 3. Start a compost pile to help recycle vegetable peels and other discarded food. Then, plant a garden there.

▷ 4. Let your child adopt several of your summer plants to care for during the season.

GROSS/FINE MOTOR SKILLS

▷ 1. "Summer Fun" (action poem)

> Summer, summer, swim, swim, swim,
> Summer, summer, jungle gym.
> Summer, summer, swing, swing, swing,
> Summer, summer, dance and sing.
> Summer, summer, fireflies in flight,
> Catch them, watch them light, light, light.
> Summer, summer, juicy fruit
> Running down my bathing suit.

▷ 2. "Ten Summer Seagulls" (action poem)

> Ten white seagulls,
> Just see them fly
> Over the mountain,
> And up to the sky.
> Ten white seagulls,
> Crying aloud,
> Spread out their wings,
> And fly over a cloud.
> Ten white seagulls,
> On a bright summer day,
> Pretty white seagulls,
> Fly, fly away!

Learn at Home, Grade K

Letter I, i

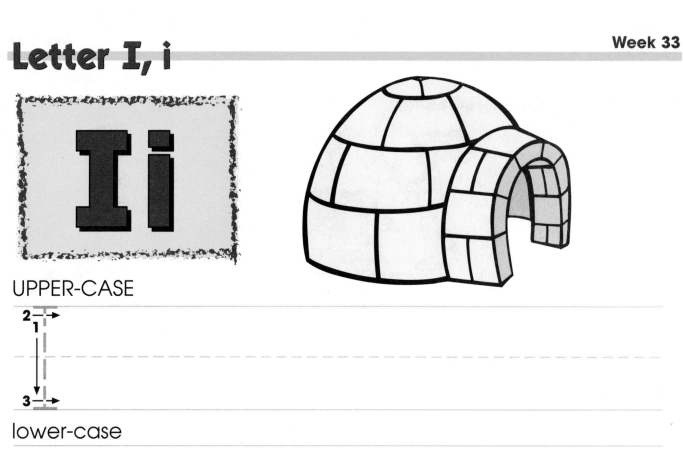

UPPER-CASE

lower-case

These pictures begin with the letter I, i. **Color** the pictures.

Learn at Home, Grade K

An I, i Igloo

Help build the igloo with I, i pictures. **Color** and **cut out** each picture which begins with the sound of I, i. **Glue** each I, i picture on the igloo.

Learn at Home, Grade K

Summer Fun

Color the umbrella yellow and purple. **Color** the big ball red and blue. **Draw** a green X on the boat. **Color** 2 blue fish in the water. **Draw** a yellow sun in the sky.

Learn at Home, Grade K

A Complete Picture

Draw the missing parts to make the pictures look the same. **Color** the pictures with the same colors.

Learn at Home, Grade K

Flying High

Cut out and **glue** the matching kite halves together. **Color** the kites.

Same and Different

Color the first picture. **Circle** the things which are different in the second picture.

Learn at Home, Grade K

	Reading	Language	Math
Monday	**O, o** Cut an onion in half. Cut a thin ring from the center, representing the upper-case letter O. Cut a second ring from the end, representing a lower-case letter o. Lay them side by side and have your child trace them with his/her fingers. See Reading, Week 34, number 1. Have your child complete **Letter O, o** (p. 346).	Read and discuss The Lorax by Dr. Seuss.	**Review: Numbers 1 — 20** Help your child make homemade play dough. Have him/her form thirty-two long tubes, then shape them into the numbers from 0 through 20. Have your child complete **Number Review** (p. 350).
Tuesday	Have your child write upper- and lower-case o's on a sheet of paper. Have him/her trace the letters with glue, then sprinkle them with oat cereal. See Reading, Week 34, number 2. Have your child complete **O, o Animal Search** (p. 347).	Read and discuss Miss Rhumphius by Barbara Cooney. Talk together about Miss Rhumphius' life and the way she chose to make the world more beautiful. Ask your child to think of a way, like Miss Rhumphius, he/she can make the world more beautiful. Help your child to act on his/her plan.	Use sidewalk chalk to write a number between 0 and 20. Then, have your child draw an equal number of objects. Repeat this activity several times. Then, vary the game by drawing pictures of objects for your child to count. Have him/her write the correct number with the chalk.
Wednesday	Teach your child the short o sound, as in the word ox. Have your child say it with you several times. Then, review each of the vowel sounds your child has learned so far. Give your child clues to help him/her guess several letter o words. Have your child complete **Letter Match** (p. 348).	Consider allowing your child to join a group which helps care for the Earth. For lists of organizations, consult Earth Kids by Jill Wheeler (pages 27–30). Help your child write a letter requesting information about the group of his/her choice.	Review the numbers from 0 to 20 using flash cards. Hold up each card and have your child say the number. Go through the stack of cards at least twice. Then, have your child place them in order from 0 to 20. Have your child complete **A Face Full of Freckles** (p. 351).
Thursday	Have your child staple together two sheets of orange construction paper to form a pouch. Have him/her cut out or draw letter o pictures and store them in the pouch. Have your child complete **Alphabet Review** (p. 349).	Read "Five Little Seeds," a poem about plants. See Language, Week 34, number 1.	Give your child a stack of crackers. Ask him/her to divide them evenly, one for him/her, one for you, until the stack is gone. Have him/her count each stack to see if they are equal.
Friday	Have your child use his/her alphabet cards to match upper- and lower-case letters. Then, have your child arrange the letter pairs in alphabetical order.	Have your child make homemade lemonade. Mix 1 1/2 quarts of water, the juice of two lemons and 2/3 cup of sugar. Share this delicious summer treat together.	Have your child count to 100, first by ones, then by tens. See Math, Week 34, numbers 1–3 for additional activities.

Learn at Home, Grade K

Science	Social Studies	Gross/Fine Motor
Explain to your child that many ocean animals have shells—a hard outer covering to protect them from predators, extreme temperatures, the wind, the sun and the ocean. Collect a variety of seashells and let your child observe them with a magnifying glass. Ask him/her to describe the shells, using size, shape and color words. Then, let him/her sort the shells in a variety of ways, including by size, shape, color, design, etc.	**Caring for My World** Read selections from *Earth Kids* by Jill Wheeler. Choose a few stories about children who have made a difference caring for their world. Discuss the stories with your child. Ask him/her if he/she could do any of the things the children in the stories did to help care for the Earth. *See* Social Studies, Week 34, number 1.	Help your child make a sand castle. *See* Gross/Fine Motor Skills, Week 34, number 1.
Have your child choose several shells from yesterday's lesson. Have him/her order them in a variety of ways—from smallest to largest, lightest to heaviest, etc.	Teach your child this song sung to the tune of "Row, Row, Row Your Boat": *Save, save, save our Earth.* *Keep it nice and green.* *Reduce, reuse, recycle.* *That will keep it clean!* Take a walk with your child, picking up litter that people have left behind. *See* Social Studies, Week 34, number 2.	Have your child make a sand painting. Use food coloring to dye sand a variety of colors. Then, have your child make a design with glue in an aluminum pie pan. Let him/her choose a color of sand, sprinkle it on the pie pan, then shake off the excess. Continue until the design is complete.
Read *Ocean* by Ron Hirschi. This book provides a great deal of information about a variety of ocean animals in a simple guessing-game format. To help your child gain a better understanding of the size of some of these animals, use a measuring tape to measure the size of several animals and mark them with tape. Have your child compare and discuss the lengths of the ocean animals measured.	Role-play situations with your child in which he/she sees someone who is not taking care of the Earth. **Examples:** Someone litters on the street. Dad leaves the water running in the sink. A friend uses only half of her paper and then throws it away.	Bake a round cake in honor of the Earth. Help your child frost it blue and green and decorate it to make it look like the Earth. *See* Gross/Fine Motor Skills, Week 34, number 2.
Teach your child the poem, "Going to the Seashore": *I go to the seashore* *In the warm sand.* *I go walking with ten toes,* *And oh, it feels grand!* *I build a large castle* *In the warm sand.* *I shape it higher than my head* *With my own two hands.*	Read *Eco-Games* by Stuart A. Kallen. Let your child choose a game to play. Then, have your child make a poster that shows the importance of taking care of the Earth. *See* Social Studies, Week 34, number 3.	Have your child make an Earth-friendly mural on a large sheet of butcher paper. Provide your child with crayons, chalk and paints to complete his/her mural.
Reread the poem "Going to the Seashore." Take your child to the seashore, if possible. If you do not live near the seashore, take a walk outside with him/her and enjoy the summer sun. Ask your child to describe summer—what it looks, feels, smells, sounds and tastes like.	Have your child make a list of ways to tell his/her friends and neighbors about the importance of taking care of the Earth. Then, help him/her choose one of the ways and implement it. *See* Social Studies, Week 34, number 4.	Have your child draw a four-square court using sidewalk chalk. In three of the squares, have him/her draw ways to take care of the Earth; in the fourth square, a picture of the Earth itself. Tell your child that the goal is to reach the Earth square. Then, play a game of four-square with your child.

TEACHING SUGGESTIONS AND ACTIVITIES

READING (O, o)

▶ 1. Have your child name as many foods or objects as he/she can that are shaped like the letter *o*.

▶ 2. Help your child make a letter *o* centerpiece for the kitchen table.

LANGUAGE

▶ 1. "Five Little Seeds" (poem)

Five little seeds, five little seeds.	**(Hold up 5 fingers.)**
Three will make flowers	**(Hold up 3 fingers.)**
And two will make weeds.	**(Hold up 2 fingers.)**
Under the leaves and under the snow,	
Five little seeds are waiting to grow.	**(Hold up 5 fingers.)**
Out comes the sun,	**(Make a circle with arms.)**
Down comes a shower,	**(Raise arms, then lower them, wiggling fingers.)**
And up come the three pretty little	**(Hold up 3 fingers.)**
pink flowers.	
Out comes the sun	**(Circle with arms.)**
That every plant needs,	
And up come two funny little old weeds.	**(Hold up 2 fingers.)**

MATH (Review: Numbers 1 — 20)

▶ 1. Give your child several sets of objects. Have him/her count the number of objects in each set, write the number on a slip of paper and place it by the set. When he/she is finished, have your child arrange the sets in order from the fewest number of objects to the greatest.

▶ 2. Have your child stack as many blocks as he/she can and count them.

▶ 3. Have your child make a pyramid of different objects. For example, have him/her use five blocks for the base, then four coasters, then three crackers, then two pieces of pepperoni and, finally, one olive on top. Then, have your child count the total number of objects which make up the pyramid.

SOCIAL STUDIES (Caring for My World)

▶ 1. Skim *50 Simple Things Kids Can Do To Save the Earth* by John Havna.

▶ 2. Help your child act on what he/she has learned during the past few weeks. For example, encourage him/her to pick up litter, to recycle materials in your home, etc.

▶ 3. Read *My First Green Book* by Angela Wilkes. This book is full of simple experiments to test the health or pollution of the area in which you live.

▶ 4. Help your child form a neighborhood Earth Club. The club could meet once a week throughout the summer and plan activities to help take care of the Earth.

GROSS/FINE MOTOR SKILLS

▶ 1. Go to a beach and collect seashells. Have your child sort them by size, shape and color.

▶ 2. Videotape your child acting as a newscaster. Ask him/her to report on the condition of the Earth and what people can do to help.

Letter O, o

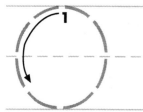

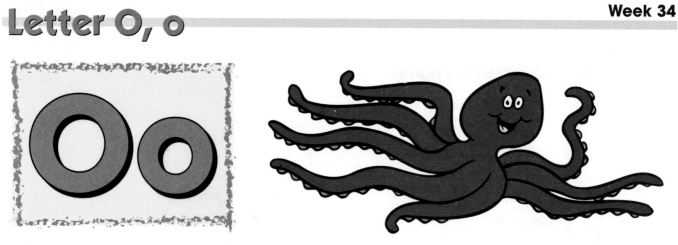

UPPER-CASE

lower-case

These pictures begin with the letter O, o. **Color** the pictures.

Learn at Home, Grade K

O, o Animal Search

Can you find the O, o animals? **Trace** each O, o. **Color** the animals which begin with the sound of O, o.

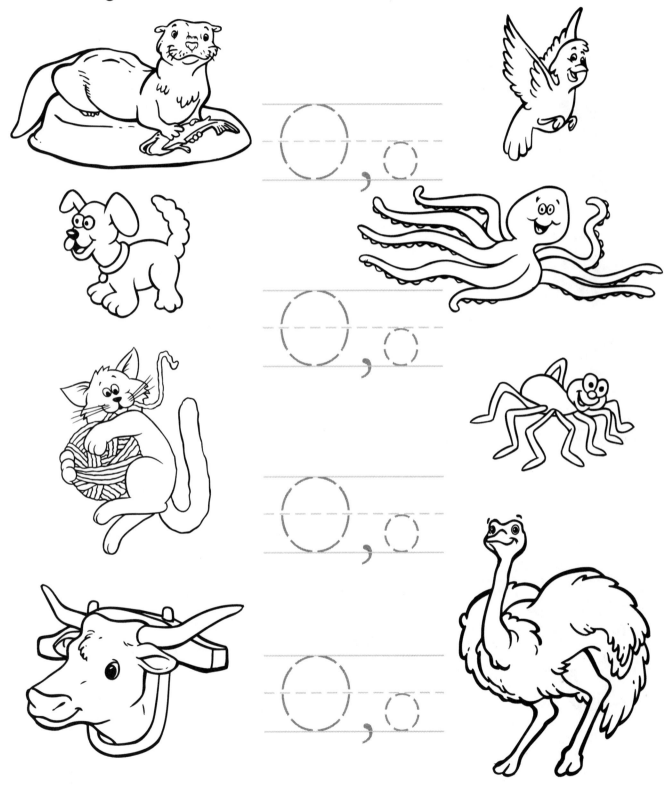

Learn at Home, Grade K

Letter Match

Draw a line to match each UPPER-CASE letter with the correct lower-case letter.

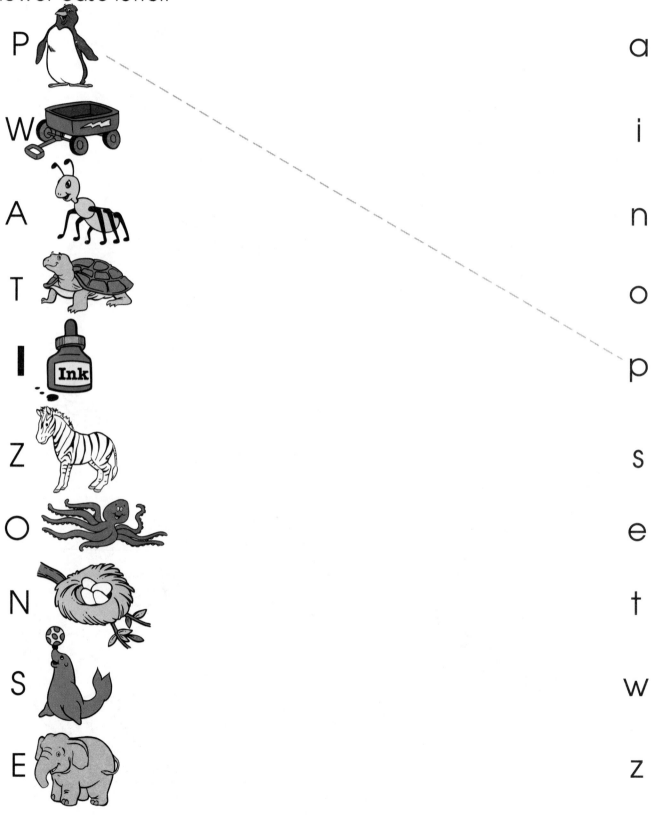

P   a

W   i

A   n

T   o

I   p

Z   s

O   e

N   t

S   w

E   z

Alphabet Review

Trace the lower-case letters. **Write** the missing lower-case letters.

a ___ c d ___ ___

g ___ i ___ ___ ___

___ ___ ___ ___ r s ___

___ v ___ x ___ z

Number Review

Write the missing numbers.

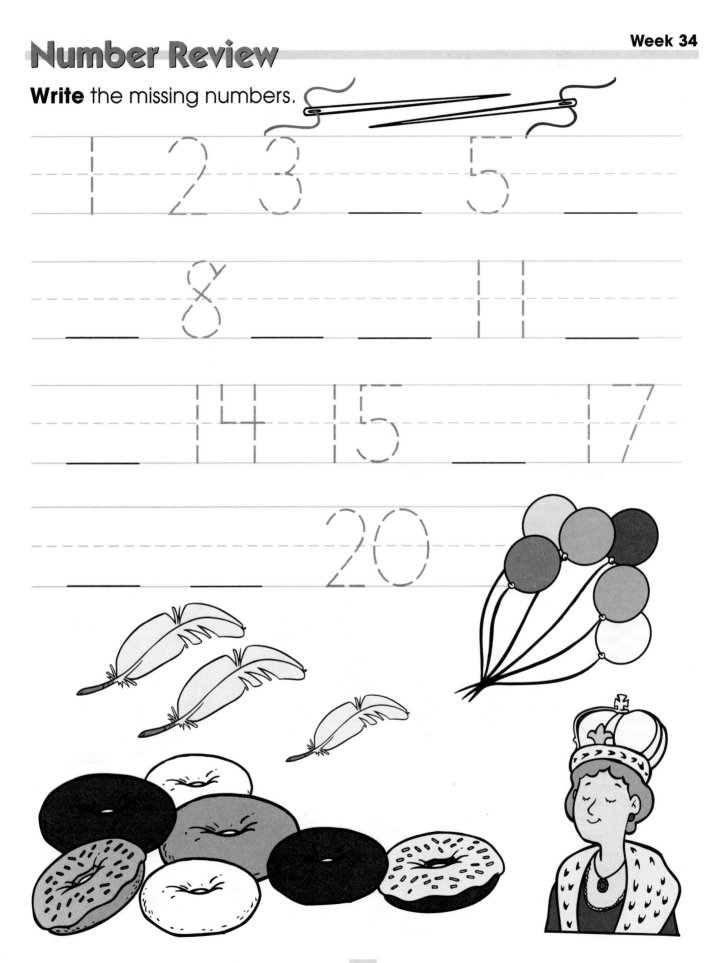

1 2 3 __ 5 __

__ __ 8 __ __ 11 __

__ __ 14 15 __ 17

__ __ __ 20

A Face Full of Freckles

Draw 20 freckles on the boy's face. **Color** the boy.

Learn at Home, Grade K

	Reading	**Language**	**Math**
Monday	**U, u** Use your finger to form the shape of upper- and lower-case *u*'s in shaving cream. Have your child do the same. *See* Reading, Week 35, number 1. Have your child complete **Letter U, u** (p. 356).	Skim *Festivals of the World: Italy* by Elizabeth Berg. Be sure to read the first page about the country and its location. Show your child where Italy is located on a globe. Look through the pages and read about the festivals that interest your child.	**Review: Shapes** Review shapes with a game of shape bingo.
Tuesday	Teach your child the short *u* sound as in the word *umbrella* and have him/her say it with you. Then, review the other short vowel sounds *a, e, i* and *o*. Draw two construction paper umbrellas for your child to color and cut out. Staple the umbrellas together along the top curve. Have your child cut out or draw letter *u* pictures and place them into the pocket formed by the upside-down umbrella.	Skim *Festivals of the World: Japan* by Susan McKay. Read the first page which contains information about the country. Find Japan on the globe for your child. Read the pages that most interest him/her.	Cook spaghetti noodles and rinse them in cold water. Have your child use the spaghetti to form a circle. Then, have him/her make a spaghetti square, triangle, rectangle and star. *See* Math, Week 35, number 1.
Wednesday	Set out a variety of objects, including several which have the sound of short *u*. Have your child say the name of each object and place the short *u* objects in an open upside-down umbrella. Have your child complete **Unusual Umbrellas** (p. 357).	Skim *Festivals of the World: Jamaica* by Bob Barlas. Read the first page which contains information about the country. Locate Jamaica for your child on a globe. Read the pages that he/she finds most interesting.	Read *Pa Grape's Shapes* by Phil Vischer. After you have read the book, go back through it and ask your child to name the various shapes. *See* Math, Week 35, number 2.
Thursday	Say a variety of words, having your child make an "unhappy" face when you say a word that begins with the sound of short *u*. Then, review all the letters of the alphabet using your child's alphabet cards as flash cards. Ask your child to shout out the letter as you hold up each card. *See* Reading, Week 35, number 2. Have your child complete **Reading Review** (p. 358).	Let your child read the color words on **Color Review** (p. 359) without help. If he/she has difficulty reading the words, encourage him/her to look at the beginning letter or letters of each word. Review color words if needed. Have your child color the puzzle.	Cut out various construction paper shapes in different sizes. Have your child divide them into piles according to shape. Have your child complete **Table Time** (p. 361).
Friday	Make alphabet review book pages for the letters *i, o* and *u*. Then, have your child put all the pages in order from *a* to *z* and staple them together inside the cover. *See* Reading, Week 35, numbers 3–5.	Skim *Festivals of the World: Mexico* by Elizabeth Berg. Read the first page which contains information about the country and its location. Find Mexico on a globe. Read the pages in the book that your child finds most interesting. *See* Language, Week 35, numbers 1–3 for additional activities. Have your child complete **Creature Feature** (p. 360).	Have your child use the construction paper shapes from yesterday's lesson to create a shape picture of his/her choice. *See* Math, Week 35, number 3.

Science	Social Studies	Gross/Fine Motor
Bubbles/Water Fun Read *Soap Bubble Magic* by Seymour Simon to your child. Do the experiments and answer the questions on pages 12–22.	**Children of the World/Festivals** Make a homemade pizza using french bread, spaghetti sauce, mozzarella cheese and your child's favorite toppings. For a real Italian pizza, try the recipe on page 30 of *Festivals of the World: Italy* by Elizabeth Berg. *See* Social Studies, Week 35, numbers 1–7 for additional activities to use throughout the week.	Have your child make a carnival mask from poster board, sequins and feathers. See page 29 of *Festivals of the World: Italy* for reference. *See* Gross/Fine Motor Skills, Week 35, numbers 1 and 2 for additional activities to use throughout this week.
Buy a large bubble wand or make one from a coat hanger bent into a circle and attached to a broom handle or long stick. Make your own bubble solution using equal parts of dish detergent and corn syrup mixed in a large basin of water. Have your child dip the wand in the solution and wave it through the air. If your child has difficulty forming bubbles, add more detergent and corn syrup.	Make stir-fried rice with your child. Obtain chopsticks from a local Chinese restaurant or a grocery store. Teach your child to eat his/her rice with the chopsticks.	Help your child make a Japanese hat. Have your child tape together two sheets of construction paper, side by side. Have him/her trace a large circle on the paper and cut it out. Then, cut a straight line from the outside edge to the center of the circle. Form a wide cone and tape the pieces together. Staple a piece of elastic string at the bottom of the cone for a strap.
Have your child see how many different objects he/she can use as a bubble wand. Have him/her try wands that are square or triangular instead of round. Does the shape of the wand affect the shape of the bubble? Does the size of the wand affect the size of the bubble? Which is his/her favorite wand and why? *See* Science, Week 35, number 1.	Cut open a fresh pineapple and mango and make a Jamaican fruit salad for your child. As you work, have your child describe the way each fruit looks, feels, smells and tastes.	Go to the library and check out a tape or CD of reggae or calypso music. Play the music for your child and encourage him/her to dance to it. Then, help your child make a drum from an oatmeal container and play along with the music.
Skim *Soap Science* by J. L. Bell. Have your child make the Zubroski on pages 34 and 35, using two straws and string. Challenge him/her to bounce a bubble as described on page 35.	Skim *Festivals of the World: Kenya* by Falaq Kagda. Read the first page about the country and its location. Show your child where Kenya is located on a globe. Read through any pages that interest him/her.	Use an egg carton to make the game *kigogo* described on pages 26 and 27 of *Festivals of the World: Kenya*. Then, play the game with your child.
Continue to look through *Soap Science*. Have your child test the electricity in a soap bubble with the experiment on pages 36 and 37. *See* Science, Week 35, number 2.	Help your child make a piñata. Have him/her tape streamers to a brown paper bag. Place wrapped candy inside and tie the bag closed with a string. Invite neighborhood children over to help celebrate the traditions of Mexico by breaking the piñata and eating the candy.	Have your child make edible "shape creatures." Have him/her start with an apple or orange, then add toothpicks with squares of pepperoni, cheese wedges or olives stuck on the ends of the toothpicks. After the "creature" is complete, ask your child to name all of the shapes he/she used to create it.

Learn at Home, Grade K

TEACHING SUGGESTIONS AND ACTIVITIES

READING (U, u)

▶ 1. Have your child climb a stair each time you say a *u* word. The goal is to climb *up* to reach the top of the stairs. If your child misses a word, he/she must take a step down.

▶ 2. Have your child draw a picture in which each letter of the alphabet is represented.

▶ 3. Buy coloring books that have alphabet dot-to-dot pictures. These provide great practice in arranging the alphabet in order.

▶ 4. Have your child make a long hopscotch grid in which he/she writes a letter of the alphabet and draws a picture of a word that begins with that letter in each square.

▶ 5. Have your child complete alphabet puzzles frequently. These will help develop letter recognition.

LANGUAGE

▶ 1. Have your child tell you what he/she would most like about living in a specific country. Ask the same question about several different countries.

▶ 2. Find library books about children who live in each of the countries discussed and what their everyday lives are like.

▶ 3. Check out other Festivals of the World books. There are many other volumes.

MATH (Review: Shapes)

▶ 1. Have your child make a variety of shapes on the geoboard. After your child makes a shape, he/she must tell you what shape it is.

▶ 2. Have your child find two of each shape from the above activity.

▶ 3. Plan a shape scavenger hunt for your child.

SCIENCE (Bubbles/Water Fun)

▷ 1. Look through *Bubblemania* by Penny Raife Durant. This book is filled with great bubble experiments.

▷ 2. Have your child make a bubble painting by mixing dish detergent with paint. Have him/her blow through a straw into the mixture, creating bubbles. He/she must capture the bubbles quickly by laying a sheet of white construction paper on the bubbles, causing them to pop on the paper.

SOCIAL STUDIES (Children of the World/Festivals)

▷ 1. For each of the countries represented this week, find tapes or CD's of traditional and popular music. Listen to the music while making crafts or while cooking, to create an atmosphere of the country being studied.

▷ 2. Visit some authentic restaurants that serve the foods from some of the countries being studied.

▷ 3. If your family knows people of different ethnic backgrounds, invite them over. Ask them to bring any photographs they have of their families or native country. Let your child enjoy learning more about the country from someone who knows it well.

▷ 4. Most libraries have movies about different countries. See if yours has any on the countries studied this week.

▷ 5. Buy a book of paper dolls that represent a variety of countries. Your child will enjoy seeing their traditional costumes and changing their clothes.

▷ 6. Teach your child about the money of other countries.

▷ 7. Ask your child to choose a country he/she would like to learn more about. Try to arrange a pen pal for your child from that country. Your child can exchange letters and pictures with the pen pal and learn all about his/her country. If you have access to a computer and modem, the children could exchange letters via e-mail or "talk" online.

GROSS/FINE MOTOR SKILLS

▷ 1. Help your child make paper dolls out of construction paper. Have him/her color each one to represent a different country.

▷ 2. Have your child make some of the crafts described in the Festivals of the World books.

Letter U, u

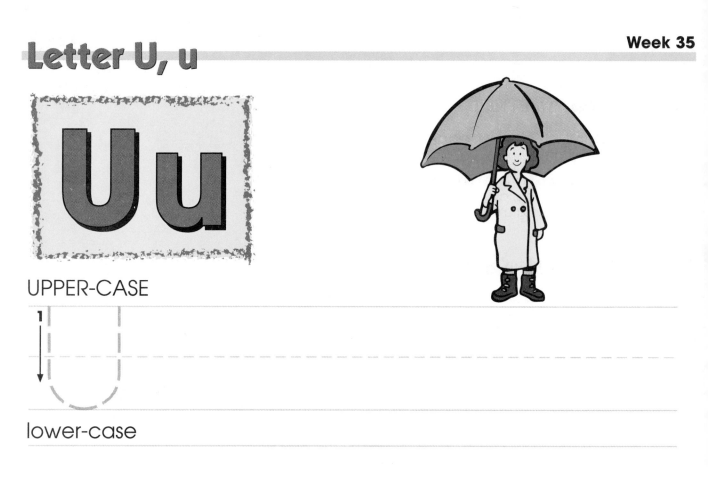

UPPER-CASE

lower-case

These pictures begin with the letter U, u. **Color** the pictures.

Unusual Umbrellas

Draw a line from each child to a picture which begins with the sound of U, u.

Learn at Home, Grade K

Reading Review

Say the name of each picture. **Write** the letter that makes the beginning sound.

1. _____

2. _____

3. _____

4. _____

5. _____

6. _____

7. _____

8. _____

9. _____

10. _____

Color Review

Use the correct colors to color the picture.

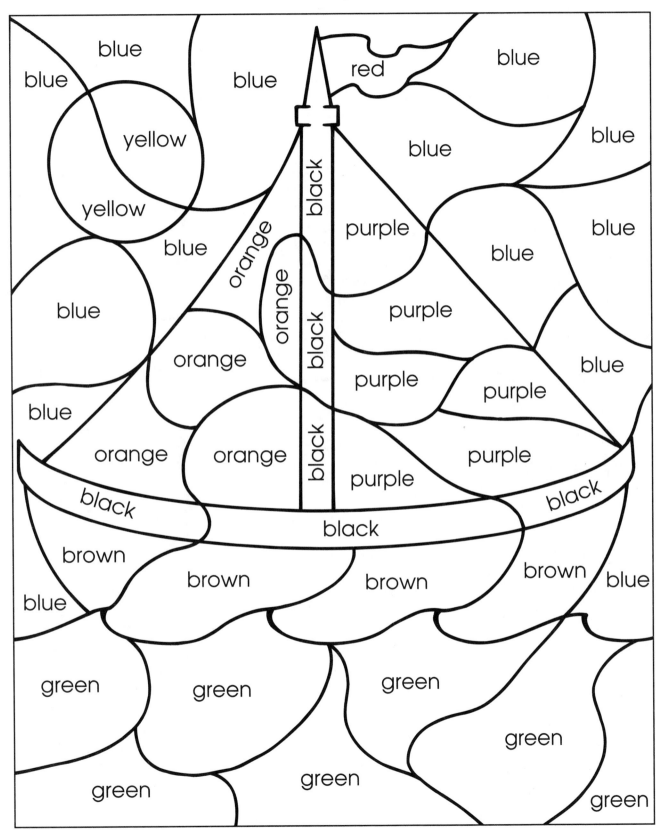

Learn at Home, Grade K

Creature Feature

Color each creature the color shown. **Color** and **cut out** each box.
Glue the boxes on the crayons to match each creature of the
same color.

1	**2**	**3**	**4**	**5**	**6**
red	**blue**	**yellow**	**purple**	**orange**	**green**

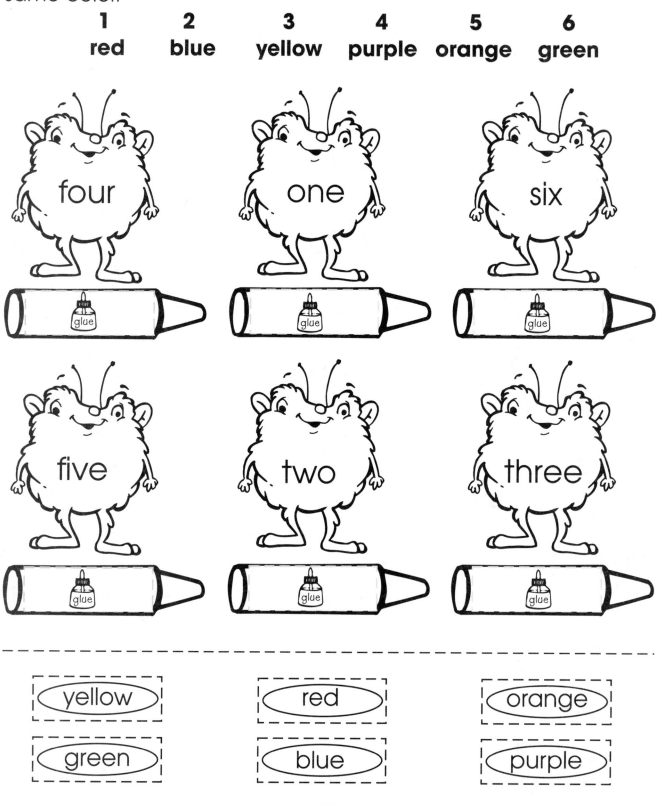

Learn at Home, Grade K

Table Time

How many shapes are there? Show the answer on the table below.

Shape	Number
◯	3
▢	
△	

Circle the shape that has more.

or

or

or

Learn at Home, Grade K

	Reading	Language	Math
Monday	**Review** Hold up alphabet flash cards one at a time and have your child shout out each letter. Go through each stack of cards—upper-case and lower-case letters—twice. Make copies and have your child make the **Alphabet Flash Cards** (pgs. 366–368).	**Review** Have your child sing you the vowel song below. Then, ask him/her why vowels are so important. *A, E, I, O, U and Y* *Are unique, I wonder why.* *Is it 'cause each word needs you?* *Look at that—I see it's true.* *A, E, I, O, U and Y* *Are unique and I know why!*	**Review** Hold up number flash cards and have your child identify the number. Then, hold up flash cards with the number words on them and have your child hold up the corresponding number flash card. Have your child complete **Number Train** (p. 377).
Tuesday	Have your child put the alphabet flash cards in alphabetical order. Have your child complete **Alphabet Antics** (p. 369).	Have your child design a menu for a new restaurant called the A to Z Café. Help him/her come up with a food or beverage beginning with each letter of the alphabet. Invent creative names for dishes that begin with difficult letters like *x*.	Have your child put the number flash cards in order. Then, have him/her put the flash cards with the number words in order. Lay out the flash cards again and have your child stack an equal number of blocks next to each number flash card. Have your child complete **Number Countdown** (p. 378).
Wednesday	Have your child match the upper- and lower-case alphabet flash cards. Have your child complete **Dinosaur Doings** (p. 370).	Give your child a taste test, touch test, scent test and hearing test. See how sharp your child's senses are.	Play shape bingo with your child. Have your child complete **Missing Number Roundup** (p. 379).
Thursday	Hold up the alphabet flash cards one at a time and have your child shout out the sound each letter makes. Have your child complete **Alphabet Review I** (p. 371) and **Alphabet Review II** (p. 372).	Make color flash cards. Then, hold up one color word at a time and have your child shout out the color word. Have your child complete **Color Balloons** (p. 376).	Have your child make a variety of shapes on his/her geoboard. Have your child complete **Ship Shape!** (p. 380).
Friday	Have your child lay out each of the alphabet flash cards. Then, have him/her find an object that begins with the sound of each letter and lay it next to the flash card. For some of the more difficult letters, your child may need to draw an object instead. *See* Reading, Week 36, numbers 1 and 2. Have your child complete **Consonant Review I** (p. 373), **Consonant Review II** (p. 374) and **Great Gumballs!** (p. 375).	Play "I Spy a Word That Begins With. . . ." *See* Language, Week 36, numbers 1 and 2.	Have your child count by ones, then by tens, up to one hundred. *See* Math, Week 36, numbers 1 and 2. Have your child complete **Holiday Match** (p. 381).

Learn at Home, Grade K

Science	Social Studies	Gross/Fine Motor
Review Have your child mix the primary colors using food coloring to form secondary colors. Have him/her identify the names of all the colors.	**Review** Review your child's address and phone number with him/her. Have your child dial his/her phone number on a phone that has been unplugged. Have your child complete **Mail for You!** (p. 382).	**Review** Take your child outside to draw a picture with sidewalk chalk. Write the beginning sound for the picture your child drew. Then, trade places with your child, drawing a picture for him/her and having him/her write the beginning sound. Check each other's work. Repeat this activity several times.
Set out various foods/snacks on the table. Have your child separate them into two groups: nutritious and non-nutritious foods. *See* Science, Week 36, number 1.	Read *Today Is Monday* by Eric Carle. Review the days of the week.	Design an obstacle course for your child. Use the location words he/she has learned, such as *over, under, between,* etc. Time your child as he/she completes the "course."
Have your child draw a picture of him/herself. Then, have him/her identify the different parts of his/her body.	Review the months of the year with the poem "Twelve Months." *See* Social Studies, Week 36, number 1.	Provide your child with recyclables from your home and let him/her create a sculpture.
Ask your child to name the four seasons. If your child does not remember the seasons, review the "Seasons" poem with him/her: *Summer sizzle, hot, hot, hot.* *Fall so breezy, leaves that drop.* *Winter snowing, brr...brr...brr....* *Springtime growing, green a blur.*	Have your child name the five senses. Take your child on a "five senses walk" in which he/she identifies each of the senses he/she uses.	Have your child play the umbrella game in which he/she pins the appropriate raindrop on each umbrella. *See* Friday's Gross/Fine Motor lesson from Week 26.
Have your child observe the leaves on trees. Have him/her compare and contrast the leaves on at least two different types of trees and write or draw his/her observations. *See* Science, Week 36, numbers 2 and 3.	Have your child name some important safety rules. Ask him/her what number he/she would dial in an emergency. Have him/her dial it on an unplugged phone. *See* Social Studies, Week 36, numbers 2–7 for additional activities.	Do something extra-special together to celebrate the last day of school! Go on a picnic with food that you and your child have prepared together. *See* Gross/Fine Motor Skills, Week 36, number 1.

TEACHING SUGGESTIONS AND ACTIVITIES

READING

▶ 1. Give your child a newspaper and have him/her follow the directions you give for different letters of the alphabet. **Example:** *Put a red circle around all of the lower-case a's.*

▶ 2. Select a special chapter book to read to your child each night. Some good choices would be the Little House on the Prairie books by Laura Ingalls Wilder or the Stuart Little books by E. B. White.

LANGUAGE

▶ 1. Have your child use his/her farm set to sing "Down on Grandpa's Farm" with you. Encourage your child to use the name of each animal in his/her farm set in the song.

▶ 2. Have your child write a tongue twister about his/her favorite food.

MATH

▶ 1. Have your child make a large number line outside. Have him/her practice moving up and down the number line according to your instructions.

▶ 2. Have your child put together puzzles.

SCIENCE

▶ 1. Have your child name five fruits and five vegetables. Ask him/her how he/she can tell the difference between a fruit and a vegetable.

▶ 2. Have your child design simple experiments to gather information. **Example:** *What will happen if I put sugar in water?*

▶ 3. Have your child draw a picture of the solar system.

SOCIAL STUDIES

▶ 1. "Twelve Months" (poem)

January brings the snow.
Cold wind makes our faces glow.
February brings valentines
With written messages on lines.
March brings winds to fly a kite.
Up among the clouds of white.
April brings the pattering rain
So that seeds will grow again.
May is time to dance and sing.
We are so glad that it is Spring.
June brings flowers dainty sweet.
Skates go skimming down the street.

July, the fourth, we celebrate,
A very patriotic date.
August days we ride around
On the merry, merry-go-round.
September, school begins and then
We can see our friends again.
October brings us Halloween
When many ghostly sights are seen.
November days bring cloudy skies,
Cranberry sauce and pumpkin pies.
December brings the Christmas tree
And Santa Claus (Hanukkah) for you and me!

▶ 2. Have your child name several ways to take care of the Earth.

▶ 3. Invite one of your child's friends over to your house. Monitor their interaction to be sure your child uses good manners and is kind to his/her friends.

▶ 4. Have your child name five community helpers and tell what they do.

▶ 5. Have your child tell you about Martin Luther King, Jr.

▶ 6. Have your child name four countries of the world. Can he/she locate them on a globe? What else does he/she know about those four countries and their inhabitants?

▶ 7. Have your child draw pictures of different types of transportation, then name each one.

GROSS/FINE MOTOR

▶ 1. Have your child build a palace out of blocks. Have him/her tell you all about it.

Alphabet Flash Cards

Color and **cut out** the alphabet cards. Use them as flash cards or use them to put your **ABC**'s in order.

Alphabet Flash Cards

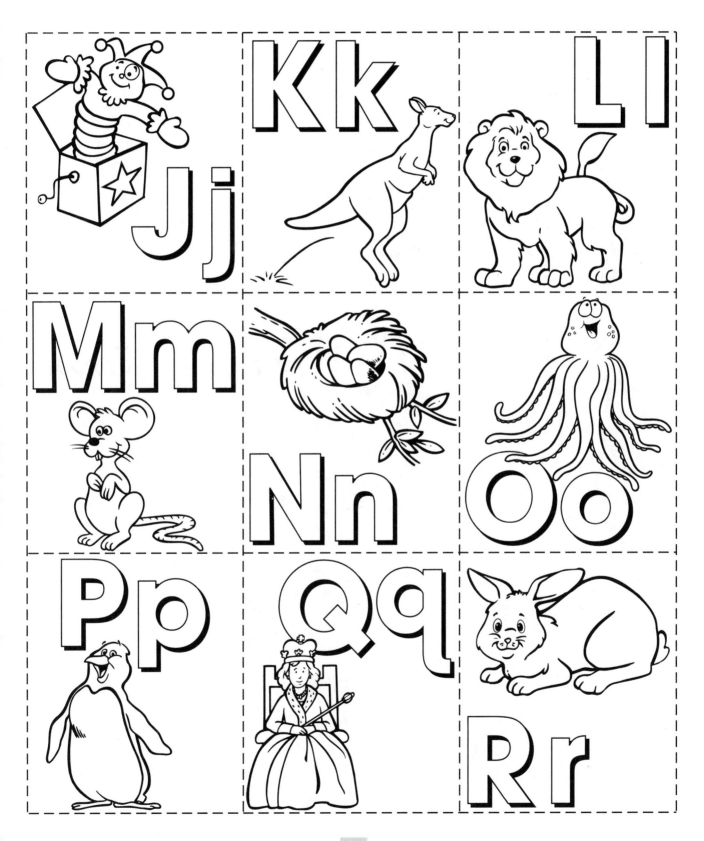

Learn at Home, Grade K

Alphabet Flash Cards

Alphabet Antics

Write the missing UPPER-CASE letters.

A ___ ___ D ___

___ G ___ ___

K ___ M ___ O

Q ___ S ___ U

___ W ___ Y ___

Learn at Home, Grade K

Dinosaur Doings

Write the missing lower-case letters.

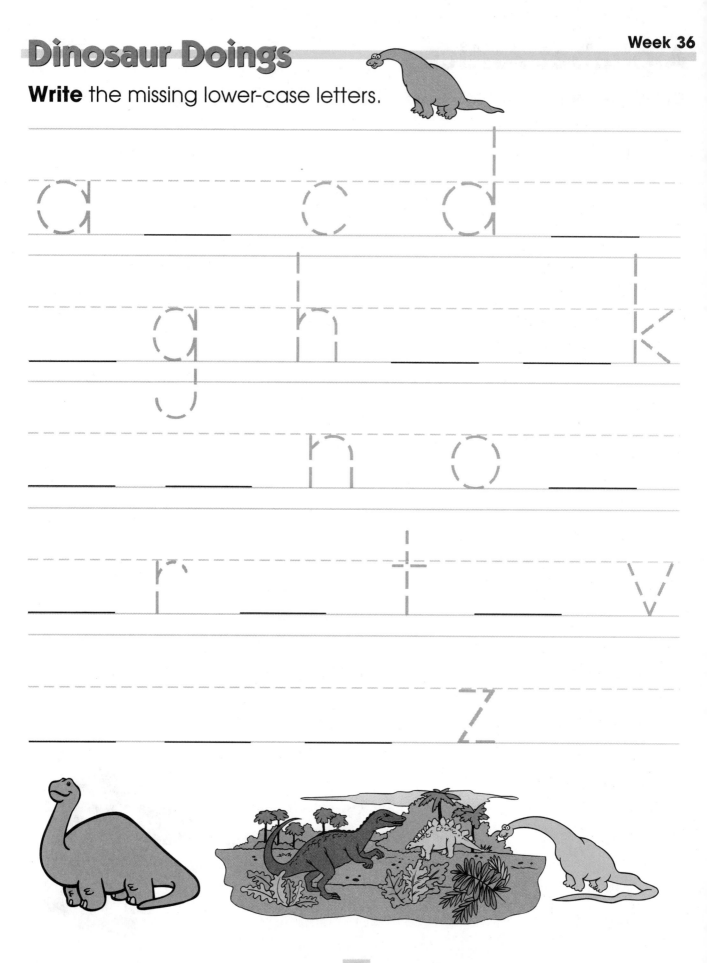

a ___ c ___ d ___

___ g h ___ ___ k

___ ___ n o ___

___ r ___ t ___ v

___ ___ ___ z

Learn at Home, Grade K

Alphabet Review I

Draw a line to match each UPPER-CASE letter with the correct lower-case letter.

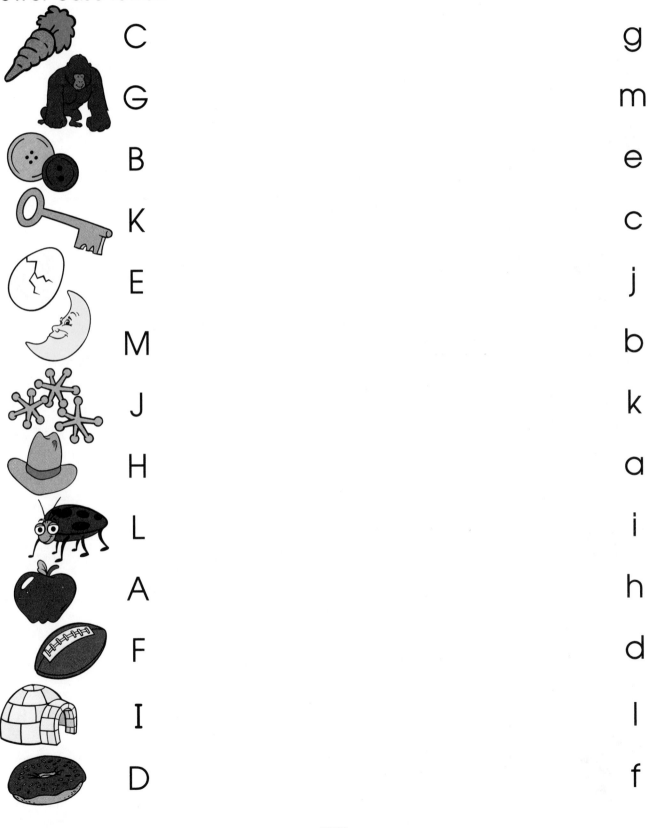

C   g

G   m

B   e

K   c

E   j

M   b

J   k

H   a

L   i

A   h

F   d

I   l

D   f

Learn at Home, Grade K

Alphabet Review II

Draw a line to match each UPPER-CASE letter with the correct lower-case letter.

R	v
N	r
Y	u
V	n
O	x
X	y
U	o
Z	w
S	z
P	t
W	p
Q	s
T	q

Learn at Home, Grade K

Consonant Review I

Say the name of each picture. **Write** the letter that makes the beginning sound.

1. _____

2. _____

3. _____

4. _____

5. _____

6. _____

7. _____

8. _____

9. _____

10. _____

Learn at Home, Grade K

Consonant Review II

Say the name of each picture. **Write** the letter that makes the beginning sound.

1.

2.

3.

4.

5.

6.

7.

8.

9.

10.

Great Gumballs!

Connect the dots from **A** to **Z**. **Color** the gumballs your favorite colors!

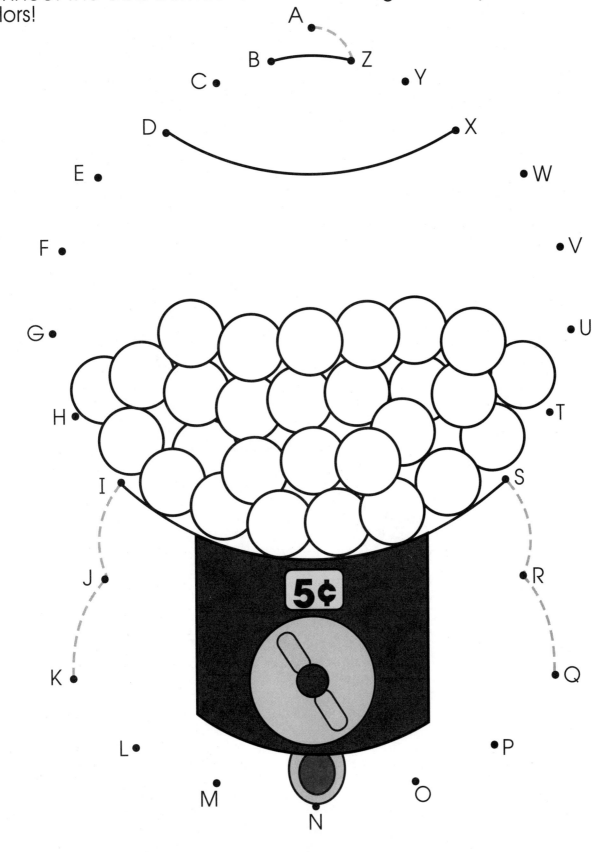

Learn at Home, Grade K

Color Balloons

Color the balloons.

1 purple	1 blue	1 orange
2 yellow	2 green	2 red

Learn at Home, Grade K

Number Train

Number the train from 1 to 5.

Draw a line from the number word to the correct number.

seven   1

two   8

five   3

nine   4

six   7

four   5

one   6

three   2

eight   9

Color the train cars: 1 – red   2 – blue   3 – green
                              4 – yellow   5 – orange

Learn at Home, Grade K

Number Countdown

Trace each number. **Cut out** and **glue** the numbers in the correct order. Say the numbers backward for the countdown!

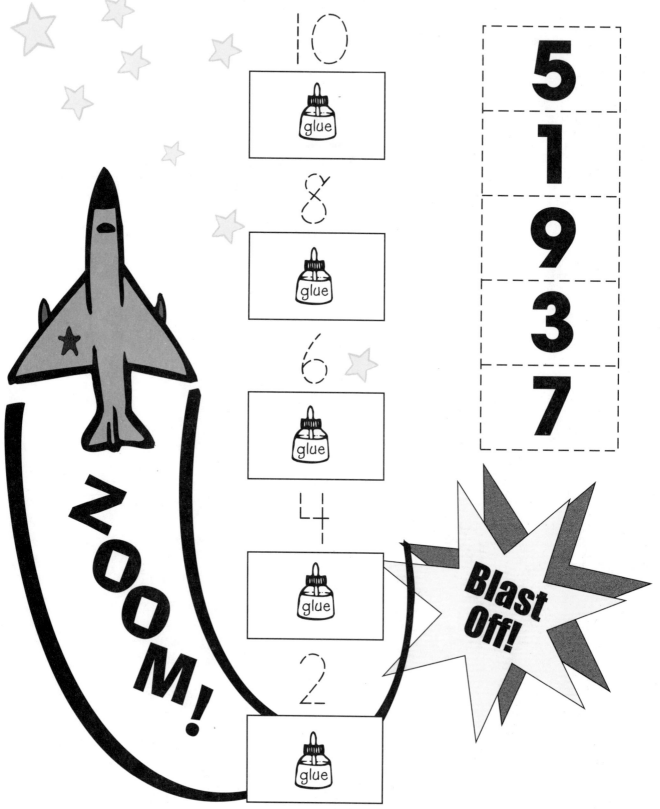

5
1
9
3
7

glue
glue
glue
glue
glue

ZOOM!

Blast Off!

378

Missing Number Roundup

Write the missing numbers in each row.

1 __ 3 __ 5

2 __ 4 __ 6

5 __ 7 __ 9

8 __ 10 __ 12

7 __ 9 __ 11

4 __ 6 __ 8

Learn at Home, Grade K

Ship Shape!

Match the shapes.

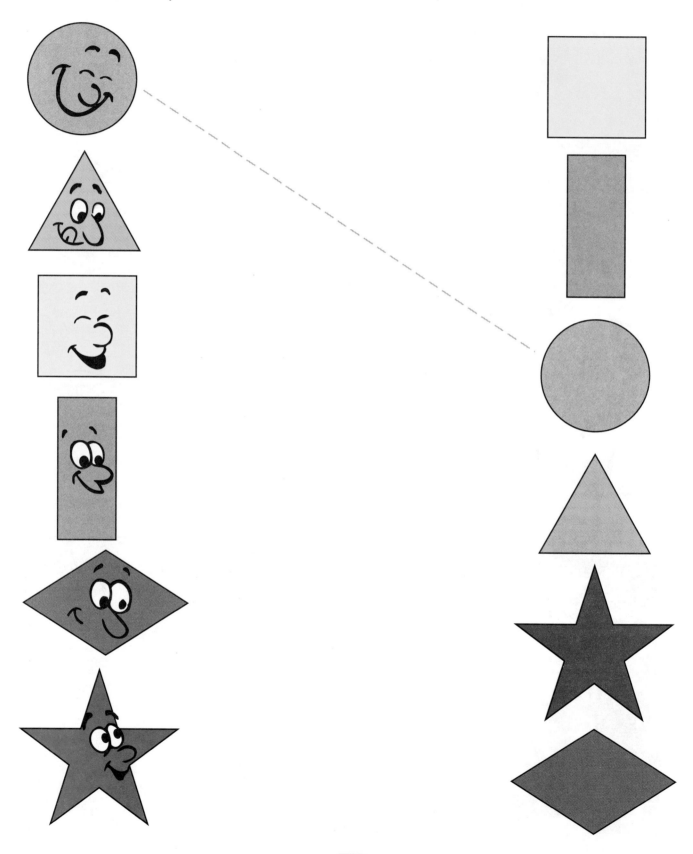

Learn at Home, Grade K

Holiday Match

Color the first picture. **Color** each picture that is the same as the first one.

Learn at Home, Grade K

Mail for You!

Write your name and address on the mailbox. **Color** the pictures.

Alphabet Badge

CONGRATULATIONS! You know your alphabet! Color and cut out this badge! You can wear it or hang it up for everyone to see!

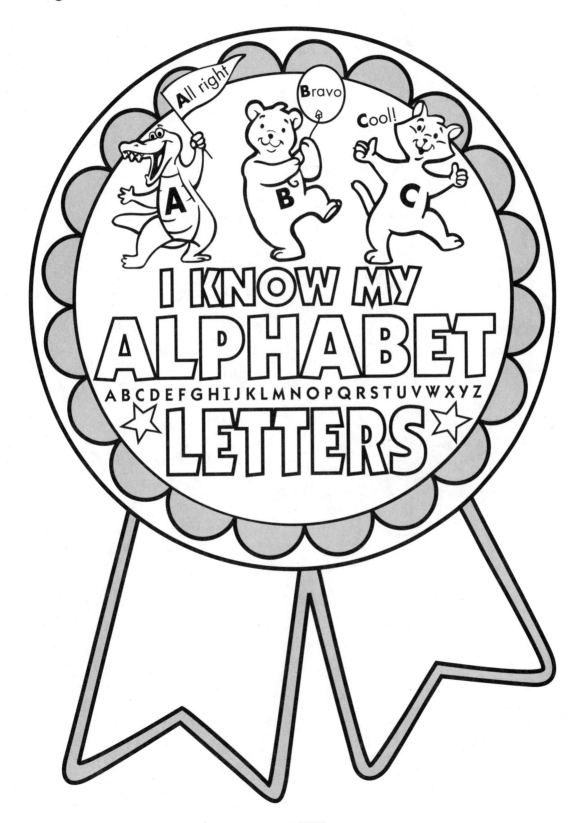

Learn at Home, Grade K

Number Badge

CONGRATULATIONS! You know the numbers from 1 to 20! Color and cut out this badge! You can wear it or hang it up for everyone to see!

Name

Date